FPC

STUDY TEXT

Paper 2

Protection, Savings and Investment Products

MAY 2000 EDITION

- **Exam focus points** and **Key terms** identified: see inside front cover.

- Full coverage of April 2000 tax changes, for **exams from July 2000 to April 2001.**

UPDATES ARE AVAILABLE ON OUR WEBSITE:
www.bpp.com
(see page (v) for more details)

BPP Publishing
May 2000

First edition 1995
Sixth edition May 2000

ISBN 0 7517 9936 X (previous edition 0 7517 9951 3)

British Library Cataloguing-in-Publication Data
A catalogue record for this book
is available from the British Library

Published by

BPP Publishing Limited
Aldine House, Aldine Place
London W12 8AW

www.bpp.com

Printed in Great Britain by W M Print
Frederick Street
Walsall
West Midlands WS2 9NE

We are grateful to the Chartered Insurance Institute for permission to reproduce in this text the syllabus of which the Institute holds the copyright.

We acknowledge the major contribution of Carole Nicholls FCII, ASFA to earlier editions of this Study Text.

Page

BPP PUBLISHING

INTRODUCTION TO THIS STUDY TEXT

This Study Text has been designed to help you get to grips as effectively as possible with the content and scope of FP2: *Protection, Savings and Investment Products.*

Each *chapter* of the Study Text is divided into *sections* and contains:

- A list of topics covered, cross-referenced to the syllabus
- An introduction to put the chapter in context
- Clear, concise topic-by-topic coverage
- Examples and questions to reinforce learning, confirm understanding and stimulate thought, with answers at the end of the chapter
- Exam focus points with hints on how to approach the exam
- A roundup of the key points in the chapter
- A quiz (with answers at the end of the Study Text)

Practice examinations

At the end of the Study Text, you will find two full practice examinations. You should attempt both of these before you sit the real examination.

A note on pronouns

On occasions in this Study Text, 'he' is used for 'he or she', 'him' for 'him or her' and so on. No prejudice or stereotyping according to gender is intended or assumed.

Updates to this Study Text

To cover changes occurring in the twelve months after the publication of this Study Text, we provide free **Updates**.

Possible changes to be covered in Updates are:

- Syllabus changes, which normally take effect from January. (Look out for an Update in November or December.)

- Changes in legislation, which for FPC may be examined 8 weeks after they become legally effective, or 3 months in the case of AFPC papers. The main legislative changes are likely to be those following the 2001 Budget. (Look out for an Update in April.)

To obtain and print out your free Updates, go to our website **www.bpp.com**. *You are advised to check the website when you begin your studies, and again during the run-up to your exam.*

Firms whose employees use BPP's Study Texts for FPC and AFPC can download the free Updates from our website for adding to their Intranet or other internal systems.

If you do not have Internet access and your firm does not make copies of our Updates available internally, please telephone our Customer Service Team on 020 8740 2211 to request a printed copy of Updates.

BPP PUBLISHING

CII SYLLABUS

Aims

The aims of the syllabus for Paper 2 are:

- to develop in the candidate generic product knowledge and understanding relevant to the work of a person who is not dealing with highly sophisticated cases;

- to develop in the candidate an ability to apply product knowledge and understanding required by a person who is offering unaccompanied but supervised advice on a variety of products and providers to satisfy client needs.

Structure

The subject content of this paper is dividend into four units:

Unit A	Protection
Unit B	Savings and investment
Unit C	Pensions
Unit D	Mortgages

Each **unit** is divided into **elements**, which are further broken down into a series of learning objectives.

The units follow a broadly similar structure.

Financial planning context

The **Protection** unit and the **Savings and investment** unit require the candidate to know the circumstances giving rise to protection needs and the factors influencing a client's individual needs. The **Pensions** unit requires the candidate to know how to evaluate a client's pensions needs and understand the factors which affect these needs. The **Mortgages** unit concentrates on arranging a mortgage and the use of mortgage-related products.

The product range

Candidates will be expected to demonstrate that they can provide advice on the range of products referred to in the syllabus.

Use of products

Paper 2 will test candidates' ability to apply the products which can be used to satisfy clients' needs. This may involve choosing appropriate products for given circumstances, and knowing which products are not suitable in those circumstances.

Comparing products and providers

Candidates will be expected to know what to take into account when comparing different types of products and the appropriate options offered by different providers, and to understand how to compare the providers themselves.

Detailed syllabus

Notes

1   Each learning objective should be read in conjunction with the description of the corresponding element.

2   The syllabus is examined on the basis of English law and practice.

**Covered in
Chapter**

Unit A Protection

Element A1

Protection in the financial planning context.

On completion of this element, the candidate should:

A1.1   know the circumstances in which protection needs arise;   1

A1.2   know the factors on which a client's protection requirements depend, eg
        age, dependants, income, financial liabilities.   1

Element A2

Knowledge of the range of protection products.

On completion of this element, the candidate should:

A2.1   know, in a generic sense, the providers, product features, policy benefits
        and their possible limits, tax treatment of   2

- term assurance: level, decreasing, convertible, family income benefit,
  renewable, increasing
- whole of life: with and without profit (non-profit), unit-linked,
  universal, low cost
- health insurance (individual and group): permanent health
  insurance, critical illness, medical expenses, long-term care
- general protection insurance: redundancy, personal accident and
  sickness
- business protection insurance: key person, partnership, shareholder
  protection.

Element A3

Use of protection products.

On completion of this element, the candidate should:

A3.1   be able to apply the products defined in A2 to satisfy clients' needs in
        particular circumstances.   3

Element A4

Knowledge of factors to be considered when comparing products and providers.

On completion of this element, the candidate should:

A4.1   know factors taken into account when comparing different types of
        products, eg surrender values, premium levels, charging and
        commission structure, tax treatment (including qualifying and non-
        qualifying rules);   4

A4.2   know factors to be taken into account when comparing the various
        options available from different providers of the same product type;   4

A4.3   know basic factors to be taken into account when comparing different
        providers of a particular product, eg financial strength of the provider,
        quality of service, underwriting factors, investment choice and
        performance.   4

Covered in
Chapter

Unit B Savings and investment

Element B1

Savings and investment in the financial planning context.

On completion of this element, the candidate should:

B1.1 know the circumstances in which there is a need for savings and
investment advice; 5

B1.2 know the factors on which a client's savings and investment
requirements depend, eg disposable income, assets, attitude to risk. 5

Element B2

Knowledge of the range of savings and investment products.

On completion of this element, the candidate should:

B2.1 know, in a generic sense, the providers, returns, contribution limits,
penalties, tax treatment, risk and accessibility of 6

- bank and building society accounts, including existing TESSAs
- national savings products: capital bonds, income bonds, children's
bonus bonds, first option bonds, premium bonds, ISAs, pensioners
bonds, certificates, investment and ordinary accounts;

B2.2 know, in a generic sense, the providers, income and capital growth
prospects, risk and accessibility, tax treatment, buying and selling
mechanisms and charges of 6

- shares: quoted, unquoted, ordinary, preference
- gilts
- corporate bonds
- employee share option schemes;

B2.3 know, in a generic sense, the providers, product structure and features,
benefits, risk and accessibility, tax treatment, penalties, charges of

6

- investment bonds
- investment trusts
- guaranteed growth bonds
- guaranteed equity bonds
- guaranteed income bonds
- existing PEPs
- maximum investment plans
- endowments (including traded endowments)
- unit trusts
- open-ended investment companies
- annuities: immediate, deferred, temporary, life, guaranteed, capital
protected, escalating, level, home income plans;

B.2.4 know, in a generic sense, the providers, product structure and features,
contribution limits, benefits, risk and accessibility, tax treatment, penalties,
CAT standards and charges of individual savings accounts (ISAs).

Element B3

Use of savings and investment products.

On completion of this element, the candidate should:

B3.1 be able to apply the products defined in B2 to satisfy clients' needs in
particular circumstances. 7

Element B4

Knowledge of factors to be considered when comparing products and providers.

On completion of this element, the candidate should:

B4.1   know factors taken into account when comparing different types of products, eg the investment objective of the product, surrender values, charging and commission structure, risk and accessibility, tax treatment (including qualifying and non-qualifying rules);   8

B4.2   know factors to be taken into account when comparing the various options available from different providers of the same product type;   8

B4.3   know basic factors to be taken into account when comparing different providers of a particular product, eg financial strength of the provider, quality of service, investment choice and performance.   8

Unit C Pensions

Element C1

Pensions in the financial planning context.

On completion of this element, the candidate should:

C1.1   know how to evaluate a client's pension requirements;   9

C1.2   understand the factors on which a client's pension requirements depend, eg age, income, dependants, previous and current pension arrangements, state provision.   9

Element C2

Knowledge of the range of pension products.

On completion of this element, the candidate should

C2.1   know, in a generic sense, the providers, eligibility, contributions, benefits and options, tax treatment, statutory and Pension Schemes Office rules relating to   10

- occupational pension schemes: contracted in or out of SERPS
- additional voluntary contributions
- executive pension schemes;

C2.2   know, in a generic sense, the providers, eligibility, contributions, benefits, options, tax treatment, statutory and Pension Schemes Office rules relating to   10

- personal pension schemes (including appropriate personal pension schemes), group personal pension schemes, pension term assurances
- free standing additional voluntary contributions
- retirement annuity contracts ('section 226')
- section 32 buy-out bonds;

and how the proposed introduction of stakeholder pensions affects personal pension plans and the advice an adviser gives on them;

C2.3   know the basic distinguishing features of small self-administered schemes, self-invested personal pensions, funded unapproved retirement benefit schemes; and   10

C2.4   know the options available on retiring from or on leaving early from a pension scheme.   10

D2.5   know the use in connection with mortgages of ancillary products – mortgage protection, redundancy protection, sickness and accident protection, life cover and critical illness.   14

Element D3

Use of mortgage products.

On completion of this element, the candidate should:

D3.1   be able to apply the products defined in D2 to satisfy clients' needs in particular circumstances.   15

Element D4

Knowledge of factors to be considered when comparing products and providers.

On completion of this element, the candidate should:

D4.1   know factors taken into account when comparing different types of mortgages, eg redemption penalties, flexibility of repayment term, arrangement fees, overall APR;   16

D4.2   know basic factors to be taken into account when comparing different providers of a particular mortgage, eg annual payment review, portability, quality of service, whether any ancillary products are compulsory, availability of further advances.   16

THE EXAMINATION PAPER

The assessment based on the content of the four units will test candidates on their knowledge and understanding of the syllabus, and also their ability to apply this knowledge and understanding to investment planning situations to satisfy clients' needs.

Assessment will be by means of an **objective test of 100 items**. The paper will contain 60 multiple-choice items and 40 multiple true/false items. The examination will be of two hours duration and the **pass mark** will be in the region of 65%. This may vary slightly from one session to another to ensure that the pass standard is the same.

Example of a multiple true/false item to be used in the paper

What options are available to a member leaving an exempt approved occupational pension scheme to effect a personal pension?

1 A transfer of the cash equivalent of accrued benefits from the occupational scheme to the personal pension.   *True/False*

2 Take a tax free refund to the value of accrued employee and employer contributions in the occupational scheme.   *True/False*

3 Leave the accrued benefits in the occupational scheme and effect a completely new personal pension.   *True/False*

4 A transfer of the cash equivalent of accrued benefits to a buy-out plan ('section 32') and continue to contribute to the buy-out plan.   *True/False*

In this case 1 and 3 are true; 2 and 4 are false. To get this item right, the candidate has to get all four responses correct.

Legislation

The general rule is that the FPC examinations are based on the English legislative position **eight weeks** before the date for the examination. This means that changes are tested eight weeks after they become legally effective. Tax changes announced in the Budget usually take legal effect from the start of the next tax year, 6 April, and so they would be tested eight weeks after that date even if the Finance Bill had not been passed by that date.

Where legislation for a change has already been enacted, but does not take effect until an already announced future date, knowledge of the change will be tested eight weeks after the enactment of the legislation.

So how up-to-date is your BPP study material?

This Study Text is up-to-date as at 1 May 2000. In particular, it has been updated for relevant changes announced in the 2000 Budget. Legislation which affects FPC from May 2000 up to the time of publication of the next (May 2001) edition of this Study Text will be covered by our free Updates, available on our website at **www.bpp.com** (see page (v) for further details). Provided that you obtain our free Updates, you will be able to use this Study Text for exams up to and including July 2001.

Part A
Protection

Chapter 1

PROTECTION IN THE FINANCIAL PLANNING CONTEXT

Chapter topic list	Syllabus reference
1 The circumstances in which protection needs arise	A 1.1
2 Factors on which a client's protection requirements depend	A 1.2

Introduction

In this chapter we will investigate the circumstances in which the need for financial protection arises. Pay particular attention to the information contained in this chapter as it is the foundation upon which to build the need for specific contracts.

1   THE CIRCUMSTANCES IN WHICH PROTECTION NEEDS ARISE

Protection of possessions

1.1   Most of us make sure that the contents of our house, our TV and video, our car and even our favourite dog or cat are **protected against loss** by theft, fire or flood. Obviously we protect ourselves against this financial loss by means of insurance. We pay a small premium into a pool with others. In the event of an unexpected happening such as our car being stolen or our carpet being burnt by a log from the fire, then a claim is paid.

1.2   We are happy to protect our possessions but we should also be **protecting our income** and that of our clients. What will happen to our families if our income ceases through **death, sickness or redundancy**? Let us look at these three situations separately.

Protecting a loss of income through death

1.3   This can be as a result of an accident or from natural causes. The question to ask is 'Who will suffer a financial loss in the event of a particular person's death?'

(a)   First remember that some clients have **nobody dependent** upon them. Therefore they do not need protection. However, this situation may change in the future so the situation will need to be reviewed.

(b)   The most likely person is the **spouse,** husband or wife. Remember that many people are in long term relationships with members of the same or opposite sex and these people may also suffer financial hardship if they can no longer share their partner's income, so they too need protection.

(c) Sometimes it is a **parent** who will suffer a financial loss. If an adult son or daughter still lives at home, the loss of the income he brings into the household may be a financial blow.

(d) **Aged parents** are often financially helped by their children either at home or in a residential or nursing home. If the financial carer dies in these circumstances it can have far reaching consequences.

(e) Although it is important to protect a husband or wife against the loss of their partner's income, it is even more vital to provide protection once there are **children**. The cost of bringing up children is high, often increasing as they get older when there may be need for private education, foreign trips, university courses etc. It should not be forgotten that in these times of high divorce rate there may be a need financially to protect children from a former marriage.

(f) In some circumstances there will be a **handicapped child** of a family. It will be necessary to ensure that there is financial protection for this child for the rest of his or her life.

(g) In most cases there will be an outstanding **loan or mortgage** which must be protected in the event of the borrower's death. In fact the lender will normally insist on this.

(h) For a rich client who appears to have effectively protected his family, there may be a further circumstance in which he will need protection and that is against a claim for inheritance tax. In this case the **estate** needs protecting so that as many assets as possible can pass to the family free of tax.

Question 1

(a) Look at your own personal circumstances and list those people who are dependent upon your income and need protection in the event of your death.

(b) Consider a person close to you, a sister, brother, parent or friend whose circumstances are different from your own. List the people they should be protecting in the event of their death.

Protecting a loss of income through sickness

1.4 Although many people are aware of the need to protect income in the event of death, as we have outlined above, few people realise the importance of protecting their income if they are unable to work for long periods due to an **accident or sickness**.

1.5 In deciding whether there is a need for sickness cover the client should consider the following.

(a) The **level of income he will receive from the State**. Recent changes in legislation have considerably reduced the long term State sickness benefits so it is inadvisable to rely too heavily on this source of income.

(b) The income he will receive from his **employer** and for how many months.

(c) The level of his **regular outgoings** in the event of sickness, for example the mortgage, heating costs, council tax, food etc.

(d) His **savings** and how long these will last in the event of a long term illness.

(e) If he is **self employed**, how long his income will continue in the event of inability to run the business through sickness.

(f) If, rather than a long term illness, he suffered a **critical or terminal illness**, such as a severe heart attack or a cancer, would his savings be sufficient to see his family through this trauma and pay for additional nursing and home alterations.

Protecting a loss of income through redundancy

1.6 The recession brought home to everyone the financial problems which result from **redundancy**. Many families lost their homes because they were unable to maintain the mortgage payments and the house was repossessed by the lender.

1.7 The level of protection in the event of redundancy is **limited**. Insurers will normally only cover the mortgage repayments for up to a maximum of two years. The Government are keen for insurance companies to expand this market. They wish to reduce the individual's reliance on the State to help meet mortgage payments.

1.8 However, for the long term unemployed, they have first to live on their redundancy payments, if any, then their savings and when these are sufficiently depleted, the State via the **job seekers' allowance**.

Business protection

1.9 In the previous pages we have looked at protecting a client's family and dependants. It is equally important to protect the financial viability of a **business** upon the death or incapacity of a partner or director. Let us look at a number of situations.

(a) **The sole proprietor**. The main needs are as follows.

(i) **Protection for the family**. On his death his income will cease and in many cases one man businesses are worth very little once the 'one man' is no longer available to do the work.

(ii) **Protection of income in the event of long term disability**. If the sole trader cannot work, the business ceases to operate and receive revenue. After an illness it is vital for him to get back to work as quickly as possible and permanent health insurance plays a vital role for income replacement.

(b) **The partnership**. The main needs are as follows.

(i) **Protecting the business in the event of one partner's death**. The surviving partner will need sufficient funds quickly to be able to buy out the deceased partner's share of the business. He does not want to have to resort to expensive borrowings which could seriously curtail the development of the business

(ii) **Protecting partnership income in the event of a partner's long term sickness or a critical illness**. If a partner is sick for a long period his ability to bring in income to the partnership ceases but at the same time the firm may need to hire someone to carry on some of the work. The sick partner may also, under the terms of the partnership agreement, have a continuing right to a share of the profits. The partnership must protect this loss of income.

(c) **The company**: The main needs are as follows.

(i) **Protecting the business in the event of a director's death**. In this instance the surviving directors will need sufficient capital to buy out the shares of the deceased director and repay his loan account, if any. The alternative could be a member of the deceased's family sitting on the board and influencing the future of the company.

    (ii)   **Protecting the company's income in the event of the long term sickness or critical illness of a director**. Again the directors must protect themselves against the loss of income to the company and provide funds to employ a replacement during the director's absence.

(d) **Key employees of any business (sole trader, partnership or company)**. In all businesses there are key employees, eg the marketing manager, the computer programmer or the product development manager. If any of these employees dies suddenly or has a long term sickness there will be an immediate loss of income to the firm and a need to bring in a replacement as quickly as possible. This potential financial loss needs to be protected.

Question 2

Peter Jackson is a chartered accountant. He is aged 34, married with two children, Tom aged 8 and Sarah aged 3. He has recently gone into partnership with two other chartered accountants.

List his protection needs.

2   FACTORS ON WHICH A CLIENT'S PROTECTION REQUIREMENTS DEPEND

2.1   The **need for protection** and the **amount of cover** will vary from client to client depending on their particular needs. The factors which effect their needs are:

(a) Age
(b) Dependants
(c) Income
(d) Financial liabilities

Age

2.2   In this section we will look at the effect of age on protection needs.

Age	Death	Sickness	Redundancy
Under 18	Unnecessary	Unnecessary unless employed	Unnecessary unless employed
18 - 25	Only if the client is married, has a partner or has debts	Yes if employed or self employed	Yes if employed
25 - 40	Very important, if the client is married, has a partner with children and a large mortgage	Very important for reasons given above	Yes, think of the mortgage
40 - 50	May not be so important if children have left home and the mortgage is paid off *but* this is the age that some people are starting a *second* family	Still important especially as with increasing age there may be more chance of a claim	Yes, if there is still a mortgage

Age	Death	Sickness	Redundancy
50 - 60	May not be so important if children have left home and the mortgage is paid off *but* this is the age that some people are starting a *second* family!	Even more important than 40 - 50 and they may now start thinking of long-term care cover	Yes, if there is still a mortgage
60 +	Protection of assets, not income. Clients now think about preserving the estate against inheritance tax	Need turns to health protection and long-term care	n/a

Note. The above are 'stereotype scenarios'. Every client must undergo a full fact-find to diagnose his/her particular circumstances whatever his/her age.

Dependants

2.3 Quite a lot needs to be found out here.

(a) If a client has **no dependants,** then he may have no need for protection.

(b) Care must be taken to make sure that there are no **unlikely dependants,** for example a mother, father, aged relative.

(c) If the dependants are **children,** the factors to consider are their age and the length of their dependency upon the family, eg are they likely to be involved in further education?

(d) In some cases a **handicapped child or young person** could be a dependant for the whole of his/her life.

(e) The client's circumstances need to be **regularly reviewed**. Another child could be born or the client remarry and start a **second family.**

Income

2.4 This is important in deciding the level of protection needed.

(a) The client's **current income** is vital in deciding what level of premiums he can afford. Although there may be a need for many forms of protection it may be impossible to provide these if the income is small. The client's needs must then be prioritised.

(b) The **level of the client's income** is very important. Obviously he or she will want his family to maintain a similar standard of living following his death.

(c) A good guide to deciding the level of protection required on death is a **multiple of current salary, say four or five times.**

(d) In arriving at the amount of protection required, do remember that some clients (although these are rare) have sufficient **capital assets** so they have no need of additional protection.

(e) When considering the amount of sickness cover required, the normal method is to take account of the **vital outgoings of the household**, such as mortgage, council tax, heating and lighting and to ensure that sufficient income will be provided to cover these.

BPP PUBLISHING

(f)   In the case of sickness cover it is important to remember that **state benefits** should be taken into account and also that the insurer will have a maximum benefit he is prepared to offer.

Financial liabilities

2.5   The obvious liability is the **mortgage**. To ascertain the level of protection required it is important to know the type of mortgage, is it interest only, ie with the total capital value outstanding, or repayment with a reducing debt.

2.6   Some clients may have **personal loans and credit card liabilities** which may be high. These will still have to be repaid on death or during periods of low income arising through sickness or redundancy.

Question 3

Which factors would be taken into consideration in ascertaining the client's needs in the following situations.

(a)   A single man aged 43 with a repayment mortgage of £75,000 and no dependants.

(b)   A married man of 48, with no children, wishing to protect his income against long term sickness.

(c)   A married man aged 36 with two children aged 5 and 8 (both being privately educated) and a mortgage of £90,000.

Chapter roundup

- Recognising a client's need for protection requires a thorough knowledge of his financial background.

- His needs will vary throughout life depending on age, liabilities, dependants and standard of living.

- You must be aware of all the needs of the various age groups.

Quick quiz

1   Which of the following types of cover/advice is needed by an 18 year old student?

   A   Whole of life assurance
   B   Income protection
   C   Advice on a building society account
   D   Advice on budgeting

2   Which is the most important factor to take into account when advising a partnership against loss of income in the event of a partner's long-term illness?

   A   Value of office property
   B   Turnover
   C   Years in business
   D   Number of staff

3   Which of the following statements are true and which are false?

   A   A 17 year old student needs redundancy protection

   B   A retired 70 year old needs income protection

   C   A 25 year old manager with a mortgage needs redundancy protection

   D   A 35 year old divorced woman with two children needs protection against death and long term sickness

4   Which of the following would be the *most* important factor when advising a company about protection cover for a key employee?

   A   His length of service
   B   The amount of income he generated for the company
   C   His sickness record
   D   His age

5   In which of the following circumstances is business protection cover *not* required?

   A   A B & C and Co, window cleaner
   B   A director of a family company
   C   A schoolteacher
   D   An architect who is a partner in his firm

The solutions to the questions in the quiz can be found at the end of this Study Text. Before checking your answers against those solutions, you should look back at this chapter and use the information in it to correct your answers.

Answers to questions

2   (a)   Protecting his wife and children in the event of his death.
    (b)   Protecting his income in the event of long term sickness or critical illness
    (c)   Protecting himself against the death or long term sickness of either or both of his partners.

3   The factors to be taken into consideration are as follows.

    (a)   *Financial liability* of the mortgage.

    (b)   *Income.* The level of protection needed can be ascertained from his current income and outgoings.

    (c)   (i)   *Dependants* - wife and children.
          (ii)   *Income* - to ascertain the level of protection required for both death and sickness.
          (iii) *Financial liability* - both mortgage and school fees.

Chapter 2

KNOWLEDGE OF THE RANGE OF PROTECTION PRODUCTS

Chapter topic list	Syllabus reference
The providers, features, benefits, limitations and tax treatment of:	
1 Term assurance	A 2.1
2 Whole of life	A 2.1
3 Health and general protection insurance	A 2.1
4 Business protection insurance	A 2.1

Introduction

In the last chapter we identified the need for protection. In this chapter we will study the various policies which can be used to satisfy these protection needs.

1   TERM ASSURANCE

KEY TERM

Term assurance provides cover for a fixed term with the sum assured payable only on death. There are no investment benefits or payment on survival.

The providers

1.1   There are a number of different providers of term assurance.

Provider	Offer	Example
Life offices - mutuals	Life insurance	Standard Life
Life offices - proprietary	Life insurance	Axa/Sun Life
Composite offices	Both life and general insurance	Eagle Star
Industrial life offices	Small premium and sum assured business with premium collection from home	Pearl
Friendly societies	Small premium and sum assured business	Tunbridge Wells Friendly Society

Provider	
Lloyds of London	Although normally thought of as providers of cover for large risk general insurance, the Lloyds market will write short term life cover. They are likely to be competitive for large sums assured or proposers with unusual occupations, hobbies etc.

Level term assurance

1.2

Product features	Policy benefit	Policy limitations
<ul><li>A fixed term policy.</li><li>A guaranteed sum assured paid only on death during the fixed term.</li><li>No benefit on survival.</li><li>No surrender value.</li><li>Level premiums throughout term.</li></ul>	Cheap cover for family and business protection.	<ul><li>Fixed term means no flexibility. The client may want to extend cover but this is not possible.</li><li>No continuing insurability, ie the client may be ill at the end of the term of the contract and unable to obtain further cover.</li><li>No investment element.</li><li>The fixed sum assured does not take into account the effect of inflation.</li></ul>

Increasing term assurance

1.3

Product features	Policy benefit	Policy limitations
<ul><li>A fixed term policy.</li><li>A guaranteed sum assured increases either by a set percentage, eg 5% pa or by the RPI (Retail Prices Index) throughout the term of the policy.</li><li>Sum assured paid only on death during the term.</li><li>No benefit on survival.</li><li>No surrender value.</li><li>Level premiums throughout the term if the sum assured increases by an agreed amount, otherwise the premium increases with RPI.</li></ul>	Cheap cover for family or business protection which keeps pace with increasing asset values or inflation.	<ul><li>Fixed term means no flexibility. The client may want to extend cover but this will be impossible.</li><li>No continuing insurability, ie the client may be ill at the end of the term of the contract and unable to obtain further cover.</li><li>No investment element.</li></ul>

Renewable term assurance

1.4

Product features	Policy benefit	Policy limitations
• A five year policy (though not always) with the option to renew for further tranches of five years but with an eventual expiry date of age 60 or 65. • A guaranteed sum assured paid only on death during the fixed term. At renewal the sum assured cannot be increased (but see renewable increasable term assurance at 1.6). • Premiums remain level for the first five years. At each five year renewal they rise according to age. • There is no underwriting requirement on renewal of the term. • No benefit on survival. • No surrender value.	Cheap cover for family or business protection but with the option to extend cover *without further medical evidence*.	• Although the policy gives the flexibility of extending cover, nevertheless it has to cease at age 60 or 65 and does not protect for the whole of life. • No investment element. • The fixed sum assured does not take into account the effect of inflation.

Renewable increasable term assurance

1.5   This policy has all the features and benefits outlined above *plus* the ability to **increase the sum assured** either by a fixed percentage or the RPI.

1.6   In this case the policy does keep pace with increasing asset values or inflation.

Convertible term assurance

1.7

Product features	Policy benefit	Policy limitations
• A fixed term policy. • A guaranteed sum assured paid only on death during the fixed term. • A valuable option to convert all or part of the sum assured at any time during the term of the policy to another contract, such as a whole of life, endowment or further term assurance *without any further evidence of health*.	Cheap cover for family and business protection with the option to extend without further medical evidence and if necessary provide protection for life (by use of a whole of life policy on conversion).	• No investment element. • The fixed sum assured does not take into account the effect of inflation.

Product features (continued)

- No benefit on survival.

- No surrender value.

- Level premiums throughout term until conversion. Upon conversion the premium charged will be that applicable to the policy selected and the client's age at that time.

Question 1

Re-read the section on term assurance so far and consider the following.

(a) The reason which makes convertible term assurance attractive.

(b) The reason which makes renewable term assurance attractive.

(c) The reason why it is important to have some element of increase available in the sum assured.

Decreasing term assurance

1.8

Product features	Policy benefit	Policy limitations
<ul><li>Fixed term.</li><li>Sum assured reduces by an agreed amount, usually an equal amount over the term.</li><li>Sum assured is paid out only on death during the term.</li><li>No benefit on survival.</li><li>No surrender value.</li><li>Level premiums throughout term.</li></ul>	Cheap protection cover usually used in conjunction with the repayment of a reducing debt.	<ul><li>Fixed term means no flexibility. The client may want to extend cover but this is not possible.</li><li>No continuing insurability, ie the client may be ill at the end of the term of the contract and unable to obtain further cover.</li><li>No investment element.</li></ul>

Mortgage protection policy

1.9

Product features	Policy benefit	Policy limitations
<ul><li>Fixed term.</li><li>Sum assured reduces to reflect the outstanding capital under a repayment mortgage.</li></ul>	Cheap protection cover used in conjunction with a repayment mortgage.	<ul><li>Fixed term means no flexibility. The client may want to extend cover but this is not possible.</li></ul>

Product features	Policy benefit	Policy limitations
• Sum assured is paid out only on death during the term. • No benefit on survival. • No surrender value. • Level premiums throughout term.		• No continuing insurability, ie the client may be ill at the end of the term of the contract and unable to obtain further cover. • No investment element.

Gift inter vivos policy

1.10

Product features	Policy benefit	Policy limitations
• This policy is designed to provide cover for inheritance tax (IHT) for a client who has made a potential exempt lifetime gift (PET). You will remember from your studies in FP1 that if a client makes such a gift he has to survive for seven years for it to be outside the estate for inheritance tax purposes. If he dies in the meantime there is tax to pay on a tapering basis as noted below.	Cheap protection cover designed for a specific need - inheritance tax liability.	• Fixed term means no flexibility but most policies offer a legislation option which gives scope for change if the liability changes because of a change in the law. • No continuing insurability, ie the client may be ill at the end of the term of the contract and unable to obtain further cover. • No investment element.

Years between gift and death	*% of full IHT charge*
1 - 3	100
3 - 4	80
4 - 5	60
5 - 6	40
6 - 7	20

• The sum assured under the policy reduces in line with the reduction in inheritance tax liability.

• It is a fixed term seven year policy.

• Level premiums are paid throughout the term or in some cases a single premium can be paid.

• The sum assured is paid only on death during the term.

• There is no surrender value.

Question 2

(a) Why can a mortgage protection policy be used only with a repayment mortgage?

(b) What type of protection policy would a client have to use with an interest only mortgage?

Level family income benefit

1.11

Product features	Policy benefit	Policy limitations
• A fixed term policy. • Providing a *tax-free income* from the date of death for the balance of the term. • Option on claim to commute the income for a tax-free lump sum. • No benefit on survival. • No surrender value. • Level premiums throughout term.	Cheap cover for family providing a tax-free income particularly useful for young families.	• Fixed term means no flexibility. The client may want to extend cover but this is not possible. • No continuing insurability, ie the client may be ill at the end of the term of the contract and unable to obtain further cover. • No investment element. • The fixed sum assured does not take inflation into account.

Increasing family income benefit

1.12 To overcome the problem of inflation, it is possible to effect a family income benefit policy where either:

(a) the **benefit increases each year by a set percentage**, say 5% or the RPI (in which case premiums also increase); or

(b) the **benefit remains constant**. When a claim arises the benefit increases by an agreed amount.

Question 3

We have now looked at all the various types of term assurance. Before continuing re-read the section to make sure you understand the main features of each contract.

If you have access to life assurance quotations, it may be a useful exercise to obtain quotations as follows and compare the cost so that you will properly understand the costs and benefits of the policies:

Quotations

Male aged 32 next birthday	*Monthly premium*
Level Term Assurance 20 years sum assured £50,000	....
Convertible Term Assurance 20 years sum assured £50,000	....
Mortgage Protection Assurance 20 years sum assured £50,000	....

BPP
PUBLISHING

Tax treatment of life policies: protection and investment

1.13 For the **individual**, the following points should be noted regarding tax.

    (a) For tax purposes it is important to establish if a policy is **'qualifying' or 'non-qualifying'** (see paragraph 1.18 below) so far as the individual policyholder is concerned.

    (b) If tax is to be paid on the proceeds of a life policy, it is **income tax**. If the policyholder is the original beneficial owner or he has acquired the policy by assignment, not for money or money's worth, then he will not be subject to capital gains tax.

    (c) If someone 'buys' a policy, then on realising its value there could be a charge to **capital gains tax**.

    (d) Policyholders will be liable to an income tax charge only when a **chargeable event** has occurred which gives rise to a **chargeable gain**.

    (e) Examples of **chargeable events** are:

        (i) death of the life assured (the death of the second life assured in the case of a joint life second death policy);

        (ii) total surrender of the policy;

        (iii) maturity of the policy;

        (iv) assignment of the policy for money or money's worth.

    (f) Policyholders with qualifying policies will *not* be taxed on the benefits on the occurrence of a chargeable event as listed above so long as the policy has **not been made paid up, surrendered or assigned for money or money's worth within the first ten years of the policy** (or three-quarters of the term of an endowment policy, if shorter).

    (g) If a policy is **non-qualifying** or it has been altered in some way to make it non qualifying, eg surrendering the benefits in year 5, a chargeable event occurs which may be subject to tax. The chargeable gain will be calculated taking into account the amount received, ie maturity value or surrender value less the premiums paid. This amount is then divided by the total number of years that the policy has been in force (known as *top slicing*). The resulting sum is added to a policyholder's existing income to see if it brings him into the higher rate tax bracket (40%). If so, the whole gain is subject to tax at 18% (40% – 22%). For the method of calculation see Chapter 6.

1.14 Some policies still benefit from **Life assurance premium relief (LAPR)**

    (a) Currently there is no tax relief allowed on life assurance premiums if the policy was effected after **13 March 1984**.

    (b) Life assurance **tax relief** is still available for qualifying policies taken out **prior to 14 March 1984**. The current rate of relief is 12.5% of the premium up to the greater of £1,500 per annum or one sixth of income.

    (c) Premiums are paid **net** to the insurance company in a similar way as personal pension contributions for the employed.

    (d) Relief can be lost if the policy ceases to be **qualifying** or if the benefits are increased or the term extended. It is important to remember this if a client is being advised to amend a **pre-1984 policy**.

1.15 Corporation tax on income and capital gains is paid by the **insurance company** on its life fund regardless of whether policies are qualifying or non-qualifying. Contrast this with the treatment of an authorised unit trust, were gains within the fund are not taxed.

1.16 It is important to establish **whether or not a policy is qualifying** in order to be able to advise the client on the tax implications. As the majority of clients are basic rate tax payers it does not matter whether their policies are qualifying or non-qualifying as they will not be subject to the higher rate tax charge.

1.17 In many instances the **non-qualifying policy can offer greater flexibility** as it is not restricted by the qualifying rules concerning term and alterations. It is important that the student should understand the qualifying rules for each type of policy and these will be outlined in the remainder of the chapter.

Tax treatment of term assurance

1.18 For a term assurance to be **qualifying**, the following rules must apply.

   (a) **Where the term is for 10 years or less**

       (i) The term must be for at least one year.

       (ii) The policy must secure only a capital sum on death - no other benefits.

   (b) **Where the policy is for a term over 10 years**

       (i) The policy must secure only a capital sum on death - no other benefits.

       (ii) The premiums must be paid annually, or more frequently, for at least 10 years or 75% of the term, whichever is shorter.

       (iii) The total premiums paid in any one year must not exceed twice the total premiums payable in any other year and one eighth of the total premiums payable over the whole term.

   If these rules are followed, with the exception of a mortgage protection policy which is exempt, then the policy is treated as 'qualifying' for tax purposes. The effect of this is that no further tax is paid on the proceeds from the policy. Note that a policy which is initially qualifying can become non-qualifying.

1.19 If the proceeds of a term assurance are not **written in trust**, then they will form part of the deceased's estate. If the estate is worth in excess of £234,000 then **inheritance tax** may be payable. Similarly premiums paid for such a policy, if large enough, ie over the annual gift exemption or normal expenditure exemption, could be treated as potentially exempt transfers for inheritance tax purposes.

Exam focus point

The student should be aware that the remarks on qualifying and non-qualifying rules in this section apply to the proceeds of all types of insurance policy, not just term assurance.

Question 4

It is important to understand the section on qualifying policies. Re-read this and study the definitions of 'chargeable event' and 'chargeable gain' then answer the following questions.

(a) Is there any difference for a higher rate tax payer if they hold a qualifying or non-qualifying policy?

(b) Is it important that a basic rate tax payer should have a qualifying policy?

(c) If a client holds a qualifying policy taken out in 1975 that needs amending, in what aspect must you take particular care in giving advice?

(d) List the chargeable events.

(e) Why do you think the tax charge to a higher rate tax payer is 18% on a surrender of a gain in the tax year 2000/2001?

2 WHOLE OF LIFE

> **KEY TERM**
>
> A **whole of life policy** provides protection for a client for life. The sum assured is paid on death at any time.

The providers

2.1 The same service providers offer whole of life policies as offer term assurance (see earlier), with the **exception of Lloyds of London**.

Whole of life with profits

2.2 **Product features**

(a) A sum assured payable on death at any time.

(b) Term of policy - whole of client's life.

(c) Surrender value is available. This may be low or non-existent in the early years because of the costs of setting up the contract.

(d) **Charges**. The expenses of the policy are taken into account when calculating the premium to be paid. The premium level required for a policyholder of a certain age takes into account mortality, investment and expenses. These charges are not explicit. They are difficult to disclose in key features documents and therefore there has been a move away from the traditional with profits to unitised with profits schemes, where charges are visible.

(e) **Investment value**. The policyholder pays an extra premium to allow him to participate in the with profits fund.

(f) **Investment** - the traditional with profits system works as follows:

   (i) The insurance company guarantees a sum assured to which reversionary bonuses once added cannot be removed.

   (ii) Because of these levels of guarantee, the investment managers have to keep a high level of gilt edged securities (gilts) in the life fund. These can restrict the performance of the life fund.

   (iii) Each year the actuaries value the fund by comparing the assets and liabilities and declaring a **surplus**, part of which goes to reserve. The balance is then declared as a bonus.

   (iv) The ability to place monies to reserve allows the actuaries to smooth out performance. The with profit bonus rate may not look very competitive in years of good stock market returns. However, in years of poor stock market returns the reverse is true.

   (v) If there is a long period of poor investment return, as in the early 1990s, the insurance company may be forced to use up a part of its reserve to maintain the bonus level or reduce the rate and become uncompetitive.

   (vi) It must be stressed that there is no guarantee of the bonus rate from year to year.

(g) The bonus declared can be classified as follows.

Reversionary bonus. These bonuses are normally declared annually as a percentage of the sum assured (this is important, and different to a unitised with profits arrangement) and once added to the sum assured cannot be taken away. The bonus is either *simple*, say 4%:

	Sum assured	Bonus	Claim value
Year 1	£10,000	£400.00	£10,400
Year 2	£10,000	£400.00	£10,800
Year 3	£10,000	£400.00	£11,200

or *compound*, say 4%:

	Sum assured	Bonus	Claim value
Year 1	£10,000	£400.00	£10,400
Year 2	£10,000	£416.00	£10,816
Year 3	£10,000	£432.64	£11,248.64

In the first example, the simple bonus in always calculated on the guaranteed sum assured, whereas with a compound bonus rate, the bonus is calculated on the sum assured plus existing bonus and therefore builds up faster.

Terminal bonus

(i)   Terminal bonuses were introduced in the early 1970s to counteract the new contract, the unit linked policy. The claim on a unit linked policy truly reflected stockmarket performance and it was felt that the traditional with profits policy with only a reversionary bonus, and the smoothing effect of this, did not truly represent the client's share in the fund's performance at the time of a claim.

(ii)   The terminal bonus is added to a claim on death and reflects the life fund's performance in the previous year.

(iii) In the past terminal bonuses have been exceptionally high and even today can represent 50 % of a final claim value.

(iv)   Some insurance companies also make an allowance for terminal bonus in surrender values, particularly if the policy has been in force for some time.

(v)   It must be stressed that terminal bonuses are *not a right*. Insurance companies have been known not to pay them or to reduce them in times of poor investment performance.

Interim bonus is the rate of bonus which applies between bonus declaration dates. The interim bonus applies to claims and maturities which apply in this period.

Product benefits

(a)   Protection throughout life.

(b)   Investment element to help keep pace with inflation.

(c)   Medium risk investment, although the bonus rate cannot be guaranteed, once added to the policy the reversionary bonus cannot be removed.

Product limitations

(a)   The main purpose is life cover so the only access to benefits is through surrender. The surrender value is unknown and may be low in the early years (or non existent).

(b)   Unknown charges.

(c)   Restricted investment opportunities.

(d)   Lack of flexibility, fixed sum assured.

Question 5

Before proceeding to the unit linked policy make sure that you thoroughly understand the working of the traditional with profits system. Make sure you can answer the following questions.

(a) How do the actuaries decide on the level of bonus?
(b) Is the bonus level guaranteed from year to year?
(c) Can bonuses once added be taken away?
(d) How does a claim value reflect investment performance close to the date of payment?
(e) Why is a traditional with profits policy advisable for a cautious investor?

Whole of life unit-linked

2.3 Product features

(a) On death at any time a guaranteed death benefit or the value of the investment units, if greater, will be paid.

(b) Choice of level of death cover, **maximum, standard** or **minimum**. This level of death cover can be changed throughout the life of the policy.

(c) The client decides the 'mix' between death cover and investment at the outset (this can be changed later). Each monthly premium is used to buy units in a selected fund at the offer price (see (g) Investment) and sufficient units cancelled to buy the level of death cover required. So, the client requiring maximum death cover will have a minimal investment element and one selecting minimum death benefit a greater emphasis on investment.

(d) The client selecting standard or minimum life cover builds up a 'reserve' against the **premium review.** Premiums are reviewed on a periodic basis, often after the first 10 years, then perhaps every five years and when the client reaches 70 + on an annual basis. The aim of the premium review is to ensure that there is sufficient reserve to enable the death cover to continue at the same level without increasing the cost or reducing the level of cover. Students should realise that the cost of the life cover will increase with age.

(e) A surrender value of the investment units is available.

(f) **Charges.** The charges on a unitised scheme are easily visible. They are as follows.

   (i) **Unit charge.** Each time units are purchased they are bought at the offer price and sold at bid price - the difference is known as the bid/offer spread and is usually 5%/6%. An example of unit pricing is as follows:

Fund	Offer price	Bid price
Managed	249.5	237.0

   (ii) **Annual management charge.** This is the cost of managing the money and is usually a 1% of the value of the fund.

   (iii) **Policy fee.** The insurance company will charge a monthly administration fee, eg £2.00 per month which may be indexed in some way so that charges are inflation proofed.

   (iv) **Initial charges.** Insurance companies have to devise means of extracting the setting up costs from unit-linked policies. As they have to meet most costs at the outset of the policy, eg paying commission, they need to recoup the money from the policyholder as quickly as possible. This can be done in one of two ways.

      (1) **Low allocation.** During the initial period, often the first two years, only a small amount, or in some cases, a nil amount, of money is allocated to investment units.

(2) **Initial units**. The insurance company create *special* units called initial units. The client's investment premiums for the initial period are invested in these units which carry a higher charging structure and are therefore never worth as much as the **accumulation units** which are purchased thereafter.

(g) **Investment**. The client has the choice of a number of funds into which to invest his money depending on the risk profile. Some insurance companies offer as many as 13 funds. It must be stressed that unit-linked funds offer no guarantees; even the low risk funds, because of charges, could show a loss. With the exception of unitised with profits units all unit prices can fall as well as rise. Examples of funds available are as follows:

(i) **Lowest risk**

(1) **Cash or building society**. These funds have a performance linked to current interest rates and are a safe haven for very short term investments or for a client switching between funds and waiting for an investment opportunity.

(2) **Fixed interest funds**. These funds will invest in UK Government securities, local authority and possibly overseas bonds. Although safe, changes in interest rates could show a loss to a client who had invested at a 'wrong' time.

(3) **Unitised with profits**. In this instance the unit price is guaranteed never to fall. It rises in line with the declared reversionary bonus rate (which will differ from the traditional with profits rate, eg traditional with profits rate 3.0% on sum assured and 4.5% on accumulated bonus, unitised rate 6.75%). A terminal bonus may be paid. Some offices always keep the unit price at 100p and declare additional units but the overall effect is the same. Many companies apply a market level adjustment factor if units are encashed at a time when the underlying asset values of the fund are low.

(ii) **Low - medium risk**

(1) **Managed funds**. In this instance the client places the investment in the hands of the fund manager who spreads his investments between equities, fixed interest, property and cash. The risk profile is lower because of the spread of investment type. Not all funds hold property and the actual structure of the portfolio should be ascertained by the potential investor as they vary from company to company.

(2) **Property**. The managers invest in a portfolio of commercial and industrial properties such as factory units, offices and shops. Although property values rise and fall during economic cycles, this is a reasonably steady long term investment. There can however be a problem if there is a run on encashments because of the illiquidity of the assets. Usually there is a proviso that the settlement of sale proceeds can be deferred by up to six months.

(iii) **Medium - high risk**

(1) **International funds**. These funds invest in equities worldwide, normally in the well developed stockmarkets of the UK, Europe, America and Japan. Thus, risk is spread but there can be a problem from currency fluctuations.

(2) **UK equities**. These funds invest in a portfolio of UK shares with a mix between income and growth stocks.

BPP PUBLISHING

(iv) **High risk**

Specialist funds. These funds invest in specific geographical areas such as the Far East, Europe, America, Japan or specific higher risk situations, such as smaller companies, technology or special situation companies.

Product benefits

(a) Protection throughout life.
(b) Investment element to help to keep pace with inflation.
(c) Choice of investment fund and risk level.
(d) Flexibility to change protection and investment according to changing financial needs.
(e) Known charges.
(f) Access to an easily understood surrender value of units.

Product limitations

(a) The main purpose is life cover so the only access to benefits is through surrender.

(b) No guarantee on investment performance.

(c) Premium review may be a disadvantage. If performance is poor, premiums may have to rise or the level of cover fall.

(d) The surrender values in the early years may be low if maximum cover has been selected.

Question 6

The concept of a Unit-Linked Whole of Life is difficult. If you are not familiar with this, we undernote a number of examples

Example 1. Male aged 35 with £100 per month to spend. His prime objective is to buy life cover for his family.

If he effects maximum death benefit he will purchase cover of £588,569.

The illustrative cash in values assuming rates of return of 5% and 10% are

After year	5%	10%
10	£1,840	£2,440
15	Nil	Nil
20	Nil	Nil
25	Nil	Nil

What does this example show you about the value of the policy at the end of 10 years? Most of the premium has been used to buy the life cover and very little has gone to investment

What do you think will happen when there is a premium review? The premium will have to increase or the cover reduce.

Example 2. In this case the male aged 35 requires the policy for investment *and* life cover. He spends the same £100 per month.

He purchases standard cover with a death benefit of £200,557.

The illustrative cash in values assuming rates of return of 5% and 10% are

After year	5%	10%
10	£8,360	£10,200
15	£13,600	£19,600
20	£17,800	£31,600
25	£19,300	£46,500

In this instance you will see that there is a reasonable reserve at the end of 10 years so hopefully the policy can continue without review.

Question 7

Investment and charges

(a) Make sure that you revise the differences between the traditional and unitised with profits concepts.

Remember the traditional with profits policy will provide a guaranteed sum assured plus additional bonus.

The unitised contract provides a death benefit or the value of the with profits units if greater. In the early years the value of the with profits units will be low because it will only be the growth on the money invested.

(b) List the medium to high risk funds.

(c) Which funds do you think would be most suitable for the average whole of life investor who wants a mix of protection and medium risk investment?

(d) What is the offer price?

(e) How do insurance companies extract their setting up charges from a unit linked whole of life policy?

Whole of life low cost or minimum cost

2.4 Product features

(a) A sum assured payable on death at any time is made up of two elements:

(i) Whole of life with profits (traditional)
(ii) Decreasing term assurance

(b) The aim of the policy is to give maximum cover at minimum cost.

(c) In designing the policy, the actuary assumes a conservative with profits bonus rate which will be added to the whole of life sum assured. The decreasing term assurance decreases at the same rate as the assumed bonus rate.

Example

Year	W Life SA	Bonus	DTA	Total cover
1	£40,000	-	£60,000	£100,000
2	£40 000	£200	£59,800	£100,000
3	£40,200	£201	£58,599	£100,000

(d) If the bonuses are greater than assumed there should be a surplus on claim plus, hopefully, a terminal bonus will be paid. If the bonus is less, a shortfall can occur.

(e) A surrender value is available. It may be low or non-existent in the early years because of the costs of setting up the contract and the fact that only part of the contract, the whole of life element, is an investment policy.

(f) Charges - the expenses of the policy are taken into account when calculating the premium to be paid. The premium level required for a policyholder of any given age takes into account mortality, investment and expenses. These charges are not explicit.

(g) Investment value - Sum Assured plus bonus. For bonus details, see Paragraph 2.2(g) above.

Product benefits

(a) Protection throughout life.

(b) High level of cover at low cost.

(c) Part of the policy has an investment element to keep pace with inflation.

(d) Medium risk investment, although the bonus rate cannot be guaranteed, once added to the policy it cannot be removed.

Product limitations

(a) The amount paid out on a claim is not guaranteed if the bonus rate added to the whole of life policy is less than assumed.

(b) Unknown charges.

(c) Restricted investment opportunities. There will be growth only if the bonus rate is better than predicted or the terminal bonus high.

(d) Lack of flexibility, fixed sum assured.

Whole of life non profit

2.5 **Product features**

(a) A guaranteed sum assured payable on death at any time.

(b) Term of policy - whole of client's life.

(c) Surrender value is available; it may be low.

(d) Charges - the expenses of the policy are taken into account when calculating the premium to be paid.

(e) No investment value.

Product benefits

(a) Protection throughout life.
(b) High level of cover at low cost.

Product limitations

(a) Fixed sum assured - poor value for money.
(b) Unknown charges.
(c) Fixed sum assured - no protection against the effect of inflation.
(d) Lack of flexibility - fixed sum assured.

Whole of life - universal

2.6 **Product features**

(a) This is a unit-linked whole of life with further options. As well as cancelling units to buy life cover, they can be cancelled to buy:

    (i) permanent health insurance;
    (ii) critical illness insurance;
    (iii) personal accident benefits;
    (iv) hospital income benefit.

(b) The aim of the policy is to cover all the policyholder's protection needs in one policy, with the flexibility to move from protection to investment to suit changing needs.

(c) The policy is non-qualifying for tax purposes.

(d) The policy offers other options such as deleting lives assured (useful in divorce cases) suspending premiums in the event of unemployment, increasing cover on marriage and the birth of a child.

(e) The levels of death benefit selected are as in a unit linked whole of life policy: maximum, minimum and standard.

(f) There are regular premium review dates. These are more relevant because normally there is a high level of protection and low investment, so the chances of premiums rising or protection falling are greater.

(g) Investment - the same fund choices are available, see 2.3 (g) Investment.

Product benefits

(a) Protection throughout life for all types of situation, income and capital.
(b) Investment element to keep pace with inflation.
(c) Choice of investment fund and risk level.
(d) Flexibility to change protection and investment according to changing financial needs.
(e) Known charges.
(f) Access to an easily understood surrender value of units.

Product limitations

(a) The main purpose is life cover so the only access to benefits is through surrender.

(b) No guarantee on investment performance.

(c) Premiums may have to rise or cover fall at premium review dates.

(d) A non-qualifying policy may be a problem for a higher rate taxpayer if surrender values are higher than premiums. This is not common however.

(e) May be too complicated for client to understand and appreciate all options.

Tax treatment of whole of life policies

2.7 For **general rules concerning qualifying policies**, see Paragraph 1.13. The qualifying rules for whole of life policies are as follows.

(a) The **sum assured** must not be less than 75% of the total premiums payable if death were to occur at the age of 75.

(b) The policy must only secure **capital benefits** on death or disability.

(c) Premiums must be paid for a period of **10 years or more (or earlier death).**

(d) Premiums must be **evenly spread** so that the premiums paid in any one twelve month period are not more than twice the premiums paid in any other twelve month period nor more than 1/8th of the total amount of premiums payable over the first ten years of the policy.

Question 8

Before leaving Whole of Life policies, please make sure you can answer the following questions.

(a) Which two types of cover are used to make up a Low Cost Whole of Life Policy?

(b) If a client wanted £100,000 life cover for the rest of his life, which policy would have a reasonably priced premium, fixed for life and some investment element?

(c) If a client wanted to cover all his protection needs under one policy, which contract would you recommend?

(d) Which Whole of Life policies have premium review dates?

BPP PUBLISHING

3 HEALTH AND GENERAL PROTECTION INSURANCE

3.1 In the last section we have looked at the type of policies which can be used to provide a benefit, usually a lump sum, in the event of death. Now we consider the types of policy needed to provide a client with a benefit if he is unable to work through **sickness**, or if he needs **medical expenses or long- term care**.

3.2 Sometimes these benefits can be provided by an **individual policy** and sometimes an employee may be fortunate enough to belong to a **group arrangement**. We will look at both individual and group policies in the following sections.

Providers

3.3 Health and general protection insurance are provided by the following bodies.

(a) **Mutual and proprietary life companies**, eg Friends Provident and Eagle Star both write Permanent Health insurance.

(b) **Composite insurance companies**, eg Commercial Union write long term care, and Norwich Union offers Permanent Health insurance, Private Medical insurance and Personal Accident insurance.

(c) **Specialist general insurers**, UAP write Permanent Health cover.

(d) **Specialist insurers** (often **provident associations**) such as BUPA and PPP (Private Patients Plan) write medical expenses insurance.

(e) **Lloyds** could be used for special personal accident risks.

Permanent Health insurance (PHI) Income Protection - individual

3.4 **Product features**

(a) The policy provides an income commencing after a deferred period for an insured who is unable to work through sickness or injury.

(b) The insured chooses the deferred periods to fit in with his needs if self-employed, or his contract of employment. The periods are 4, 13, 26, 52 or even 104 weeks.

(c) The policy has a fixed term usually to retirement age 60 or 65.

(d) The policy, as its name implies, is permanent and once underwritten, the premiums cannot be increased or claims refused regardless of the number of legitimate claims. Some insurance companies have introduced **reviewable premiums** which increase in line with **overall claims**.

(e) There is a **maximum insured income** limit. This used to be 75% of earnings in the year prior to disability less a single person's state sick pay and any other disability benefits. However, following the change in the taxation of benefits, insurance companies have reduced the maximum insured income. Levels of cover vary but may be in the region of 60% - 66% of previous income.

(f) The benefits can be level or increase at a fixed amount or by the RPI.

(g) If the insured can return to work only part time or, if through illness, he can take only a lower paid job, then a proportionate benefit is paid.

(h) Premium rates are based on occupation. There are four categories by risk, ie professional sedentary categories are 1 and high risk manual 4. Some insurance companies include a **super class A** category for professionals such as solicitors and accountants. Some policies state that a change of occupation must be notified and the premium rate may change.

(i) Insurers normally insure only those resident in the UK because of the problems associated with tracking permanent health claims abroad.

(j) Investment- two types.

    (i) **Pure protection** - no return at the expiry of the policy.

    (ii) **Unit-linked** - A whole of life policy with units cancelled to buy PHI protection, the balance is invested in a unit-linked fund to provide a benefit on encashment.

(k) Premiums used to remain constant throughout the term of the policy. Some insurers still operate on this basis but reviewable premiums have been introduced in line with **overall claims experience**, not personal claims experience.

Policy benefits

(a) A guaranteed level of income in the event of long term sickness regardless of number of claims and future changes in health.

(b) Small investment return possible with a unit-linked policy.

Policy limitations

(a) Higher level of premiums for higher risk occupations.

(b) Higher level premiums for women who have statistically a higher claims record for permanent health insurance.

(c) Some policy exclusions apply, eg:

    (i) Pregnancy, childbirth and any complications
    (ii) Disability arising from war or invasion, whether or not war is declared
    (iii) Injury sustained in a criminal act
    (iv) Drug or alcohol abuse.

(d) Care must be taken over the definition of 'Disability' in the policy wording. Some are very harsh and will pay a benefit only if the insured is so disabled that he cannot carry out *any* occupation, eg a solicitor who had a nervous breakdown would still be expected to obtain some form of manual work.

(e) More stringent underwriting than for life assurance. A client may receive an exclusion on his policy for a pre-existing condition.

Permanent health - group arrangements

3.5 Some employers provide their employees with Permanent Health insurance through a group arrangement. Normally such a scheme would be non-contributory.

3.6 **Product features**

(a) Premium rates would depend on the size of the group, location, risk levels of work, age and benefit profile.

(b) Normally benefits would be fixed as a percentage of salary and may take into account State benefits.

(c) Benefits would cease at normal retirement age.

BPP PUBLISHING

(d) If there is a company pension scheme, provision may be made to include pension scheme contributions (both employer and employee) and national insurance contributions as part of the benefit.

(e) The employee continues in the employ of the company whilst sick and this enables him to remain in the pension scheme and possibly to continue to enjoy lump sum death in service benefits.

(f) The deferred period would be agreed to fit in with company sick pay policy.

(g) Employees would automatically join the scheme so long as they were actively at work on the renewal date and had been so for the previous 2 months. In large schemes there would be no need for medical evidence. In smaller schemes there may be an element of free cover, that is automatic cover irrespective of the member's state of health.

Product benefits

(a) From the employer's point of view, he is providing an extra 'benefit' to his employees.

(b) The employee can enjoy a benefit in the event of sickness for which he normally has not had to contribute.

(c) The employee may get cover even if he is medically unfit.

Product limitations

Employee is restricted by the amount of cover decided by the employer.

Tax situation on Permanent Health insurance

3.7 Individual policies

(a) The benefits payable are not normally taxable. They cannot, however, be treated as 'relevant earnings' for personal pension contributions.

(b) There is no tax relief on premiums paid by an individual.

(c) If the policy is a unit linked policy and on maturity/surrender the value exceeds premiums a higher rate taxpayer will suffer tax under the non-qualifying rules.

3.8 Group policies

(a) In this case the income is paid to the employer who pays the sick employee through the PAYE system as he remains an employee of the company. This means that pension contributions can continue. The income is therefore subject to tax.

(b) An employer will obtain tax relief on the contributions paid to the schemes as a business expense and the employee will not be taxed on them as a benefit in kind.

(c) If a controlling director is included in the scheme, the premiums paid for his benefits may be allowed as a business expense so long as he has similar and not better benefits than the rest of the group.

Question 9

(a) You are claiming under an individual Permanent Health policy. How will your benefit be taxed?

(b) How would the tax treatment alter if you had been a member of a group scheme?

(c) How will a Permanent Health policy deal with someone who can return to a less well paid job due to their illness?

(d) How would you respond to the client who said 'I don't want a Permanent Health policy because I am very fit, unlikely to claim and if I do not claim, I will have lost all my money'

Redundancy insurance

3.9   In the 1994 Budget the Chancellor announced measures to reduce the dependence upon the DSS for **mortgage payments of those who are unemployed**. From April 1995 anyone who is unemployed with an existing mortgage will get no financial assistance for the first two months and only 50% of the interest for the following four months. From October 1995 new borrowers have received no benefit from the state for the first nine months.

3.10   **Product features**

(a)   This policy provides an income in the event of redundancy.

(b)   Normally policies are linked to mortgages and offered by building societies as part of a mortgage package.

(c)   Benefits commence after a deferred period and normally pay out only for a maximum of two years.

(d)   Benefits may be restricted to a percentage of earnings subject to an overall maximum.

Policy benefits

Peace of mind that there will be income to pay the mortgage in the event of a short term redundancy situation.

Policy limitations

There are a number of exclusions under the policy, in particular no cover will be available unless the policy has been in force for 6 months before redundancy occurs.

Benefits are limited to the mortgage payments. Clients need greater protection but insurers have retreated from offering fuller cover because of the claims problems caused by the recession.

3.11   **Taxation of redundancy policies**

(a)   No tax relief on premiums
(b)   The benefits payable are not taxable.

Personal accident and sickness policies

3.12   **Product features**

(a)   This is a general insurance product offered on an **annual** basis. Thus the insurer has a right to refuse to renew in the event of a change in circumstances or adverse claims experience or he may increase the premiums.

(b)   The policy offers **lump sum benefits** in the event of:

(i)   death by accident;
(ii)   loss of one or two limbs as a result of an accident;
(iii)   irrevocable loss of sight of one or both eyes as a result of an accident;
(iv)   permanent total disablement as a result of an accident.

(c)   The policy offers **weekly benefits** in the event of:

(i)   temporary total or partial disablement as a result of an accident;
(ii)   temporary total disablement caused by illness of any kind.

(d)   The sickness benefit is paid after a very short deferred period, say 7 days, and continues for a maximum of 52 weeks.

Policy benefits

The important benefit is the short-term sickness benefit. This is very useful for the self employed who must have immediate income in the event of inability to work through sickness.

Policy limitations

(a) The policy is renewed annually, premiums can be increased or cover refused.

(b) The sickness benefit runs only for a maximum number of weeks and then ceases irrespective of recovery.

Group personal accident policies

3.13 Sometimes employers run **group personal accident policies** for the employees on a non contributory basis. The cover may be restricted to accidents which occur whilst at work rather than the 24 hour cover offered by the individual policy.

3.14 **Taxation of accident policies**

(a) Premiums paid by individuals do not attract tax relief.
(b) Premiums paid by employers can be treated as a business expense.
(c) Lump sum benefits paid are tax-free.
(d) Sickness benefit and weekly benefits are tax free as for individual PHI (see earlier).

Critical illness or dread disease

3.15 **Product features**

(a) Capital sum paid on diagnosis of a specified medical condition.

(b) Examples of such medical conditions: Heart Attack, Cancer, Renal Failure, Organ Transplant, Stroke.

(c) Critical illness policies can be 'stand alone' or added to whole of life, endowment or term assurance.

(d) Level premiums are paid.

Policy benefits

Useful to provide a benefit in the event of a diagnosed illness, particularly for mortgage cover.

Policy limitations

Clients may not understand the medical conditions giving rise to a claim. An understanding of the definition of disease is important.

3.16 **Taxation of critical illness policies**

(a) There is no tax relief on premiums.
(b) The lump sum benefits are not taxable.

Medical expenses insurance

3.17 **Product features**

(a) The schemes pay for the cost of medical treatment both as an in and out patient for those seeking private medical care. The cover includes consultants fees, surgeons, anaesthetist fees, nursing, private ambulance and room charges.

(b) Some policies will provide a cash payment if NHS treatment is received.

(c) Cost is based on number of family members needing cover and the hospital band required. Hospital bands depend on the area and the facilities available: for example, central London hospitals are the most highly graded.

(d) Some insurers are able to provide cheaper cover by including exclusions within their policy such as no outpatient cover or no cover if the treatment can be received on the NHS within 6 weeks.

(e) Premiums are reviewed annually and increase with age and *overall* claims experience.

(f) Many insurers do not seek medical evidence on new applicants. They simply impose a moratorium that they will not cover any treatment arising from a pre-existing condition. However, once the insured has had no treatment for the complaint for two years full cover is restored.

Policy benefits

Speedy attention and medical treatment as a private patient. This is of particular use to the self-employed or people running a small family business. It means that there is the minimum of inconvenience caused by a medical condition requiring treatment.

Policy limitations

Very few unless selected by the client such as an excess or a restriction on benefits to reduce cost.

3.18 **Taxation of private medical insurance**

(a) There is no tax relief on premiums.

(b) There is no tax on the benefits because they are paid either directly to the provider or to the client as recompense for an account paid, so there is no element of capital gain or income.

Group private medical insurance

3.19 Some employers provide **group medical insurance** for their employees. This is particularly relevant for the key employees, such as directors or managers where it is important to get medical problems dealt with swiftly and the executive back to work.

3.20 Some group schemes insure only the employee with the option for him to pay for cover for his **family**. Others are more generous and cover the family.

3.21 Care must be taken if an employee is **leaving** such a scheme. Usually there will be an option to continue the cover without suffering the moratorium covering existing illness. The premium will increase but this option is very valuable.

3.22 **Taxation of group medical insurance**

(a) The employer will be able to treat the premiums as a business expense for tax purpose. If the employee pays for the additional family benefit, there will be no tax relief in respect of his contributions.

(b) The premium paid on behalf of the employee will be treated as a benefit in kind.

(c) The benefits will not be taxed.

Long-term care insurance

3.23 There is a growing need for this type of cover because of the Government's problems in **funding** the cost of care for the elderly.

3.24 **Product features**

(a) The policy provides for the costs of those needing care in a nursing home or at home. Although this is normally the elderly it must be remembered that the policy would pay for the care of a younger policyholder who was forced into a nursing home because he had an illness such as multiple sclerosis or motor neurone disease.

(b) Premiums can be paid regularly, ie monthly, or by single premium, or a mixture. For example a person reaching retirement age and receiving a lump sum from a pension fund may use part of this to fund long term care.

(c) A claim will be paid only if the policyholder is unable to carry out a function of daily activity without help, such as washing, using the toilet, feeding himself, moving around the home or climbing stairs. He must be unable to carry out two of these activities before a claim can be considered. A higher benefit will be paid out depending on the level of incapacity.

(d) The insurer will normally work with the family and the doctor to design the most helpful package for the elderly person. To begin with it may be acceptable to have nursing help in the house, before progressing to a full time nursing home.

(e) Benefits can be designed to increase, which is essential.

Note. There is another product where *immediate benefits* can be provided. A capital sum is used to purchase an impaired life annuity. A higher income is paid out from the annuity because having taken medical evidence, the actuaries appreciate that the annuitant is unlikely to live long.

Product benefits

(a) Because of the cost of long term care, every client at retirement should consider such a policy to provide the cost of nursing home care.

(b) If the benefit is not available, the house and other family assets may have to be sold to support the nursing home fees. Many middle-aged children may well be prepared to pay the premiums for such a policy on behalf of their elderly parents in order to protect the family estate and assets.

Product limitations

(a) It is impossible to predict the level of cover required in possibly 30 years time. An inflation-proofed type of policy is essential but even this may not be enough as the demand and costs of care rise.

(b) The costs of the premiums will inevitably rise because of the claims experience. The client may be locked into a policy with spiralling premiums. This may be in retirement when he can ill afford the increasing costs yet feels vulnerable without the cover.

3.25 **Taxation of long-term care cover**

(a) Currently there is no tax relief available.

(b) Benefits are paid directly to the care provider so do not form part of the policyholder's income and therefore are tax-free.

Question 10

In the second half of this chapter we have looked at protecting the client in the event of sickness and redundancy. Although in an ideal world it would be a good idea for all clients to have all the types of cover we have discussed.

(a) *Prioritise needs*. List the policies in descending order of importance.

(b) Which policies would be most important for the self-employed?

(c) Some of the policies we have looked at have maximum benefits. See if you can remember what they are.

(d) A client who is married and earning £20,000 is provided with group life assurance of £80,000, accident and sickness cover and private medical insurance for himself and his wife:

  (i)   do you think he needs any other cover?
  (ii) will he be taxed on any of these benefits?

(e) A large firm of accountants decides to introduce a Group Permanent Health Scheme. What will the advantages be and what will the taxation of benefits be

  (i)   for the employees; and
  (ii) the partners?

4 BUSINESS PROTECTION INSURANCE

4.1 In the case of a business it is important to ensure that the business can continue irrespective of the **death or long-term illness of one of its directors,** partners or other key person. Let us consider four situations.

Sole trader

4.2 In this instance it is almost **impossible to safeguard the continuity** of the business in the event of the death or long term illness of the sole proprietor. He, (or she) is the key to the business. Without him/her there is little of value to preserve.

4.3 The answer is to **protect the family,** providing a substantial lump sum death benefit through term assurance or whole of life and critical illness cover. Sickness for a sole proprietor means an instant reduction in income, if he can no longer clean windows, produce accounts or whatever. It may therefore be necessary to take on a short term personal accident and sickness policy complemented by a permanent health policy with a long deferment period.

4.4 **Medical insurance** is also essential, if it can be afforded, so that the business is not left for too long while the owner undergoes and recovers from an operation.

Partnership

4.5 The **size** of the partnership can be from two in the case of say a builder to hundreds in the case of international firms of accountants or actuaries. The **Partnership Act 1890** is the legislation which controls partnerships. In this Act the rights and liabilities of partners are set out. If there have been no alternative arrangements made, in writing, then on the death of a partner, the partnership must be dissolved; therefore it is very important that a **partnership agreement** is in place.

> **KEY TERM**
>
> The **partnership agreement** should deal with all aspects of the partnership; for example what happens if a partner is ill, retires, dies or leaves.

4.6 As far as protecting the partnership is concerned, the agreement should include clauses stating that each individual partner must **insure his own life** in the event of a critical or long-term illness. He will normally continue to be eligible to draw profits in full or part for some time, at the end of which period he will have to retire from the partnership. The deferred period under the Permanent Health insurance policy should be agreed to fit into this situation, eg if profits are paid for two years, then the Permanent Health insurance policy has a 104 week deferred period.

4.7 They should also insert a clause which deals with **share purchase**. There are three options (see Paragraph 4.9).

Company directors and shareholders

4.8 A company is formed and registered with the Registrar of Companies. The operation of the company is controlled by its Memorandum and Articles of Association. The Memorandum contains the company's name and registered address and its objects. There will also be details of the shares issued. The Articles of Association establish how the company will conduct its day to day business. In the Articles there will be set out the method of the **sale of the shares of a shareholding director on his retirement or death**. There are a number of different methods of share purchase discussed below.

4.9 There are three **methods of share purchase for partners or directors.** These are applicable to both partnerships and companies.

(a) A **buy and sell agreement**. On a partner or director/shareholder's death, the remaining partners or directors must buy the deceased's share of the firm from his estate who in turn must sell it. The sale price may be arrived at using a previously agreed method of valuation.

Inheritance tax implications. On the death of the partner or director, his share of the firm forms part of his estate for inheritance tax purposes.

No business property relief applies for inheritance tax purposes because it is a binding contract for sale.

(b) The **double option agreement,** or **cross option agreement**. In this instance, if the deceased's estate wishes to sell or the surviving partners, shareholders/directors wish to buy then the other party must comply.

Inheritance tax implications. Again on the death of the partner or shareholder/director his share of the firm forms part of the estate but this time because there is no binding contract for sale, 100% Business Property Relief for inheritance tax purposes can be claimed.

(c) **Automatic accrual.** This is more appropriate to partnerships. In this case on the death of a partner no value falls into his estate and his share of the business automatically passes to the surviving partners.

Inheritance tax implications. All partners have given up their right to a capital payment on death as a commercial transaction. The value automatically accrues to the remaining partners and no inheritance tax liability exists.

4.10 If a **buy and sell or double option agreement** is in place then life policies will be needed to provide the surviving partners, director/shareholders with the necessary funds to buy out the deceased partner/shareholder. There are two methods.

(a) Policies can be taken out on a '**life of another**' basis but this becomes cumbersome if there is a large partnership/company, particularly when partners or shareholder/directors leave and new ones join.

(b) Each partner or shareholder/director takes out a policy on his own life written **in trust for his partners or fellow shareholders/directors**. The choice of trust wording is important and it is possible for the policies to be written for the benefit of the partners of X Y Z partnership at the date of death and in this way avoid the necessity for alterations each time a partner leaves or joins.

4.11 If **automatic accrual** applies then under the partnership agreement each partner should be obliged to make adequate life assurance provision for his spouse and/or dependants to compensate for the loss of the value of his share of the business.

4.12 **Type of life policy**

(a) The type of policy will normally be **term assurance written to an agreed retirement age**. Some form of increasing cover policy is advisable as hopefully the value of the partnership/company will increase, so increasable, or renewable increasable term assurance would be very suitable.

(b) The use of **pension term assurance** may be a possibility for partners and will allow for tax relief on premiums paid so long as they are aware that the premium will have to be deducted from the maximum amount they are allowed to pay for their pension contribution each fiscal year.

(c) Some partnerships and companies may prefer to use a **unit-linked whole life policy** because of the possibility of a surrender value at some future date.

Question 11

(a) Re-read this section, make sure you understand the difference between a sole trader, a partnership and a company.

(b) Consider the importance of life assurance as business protection. If there was no life assurance in place how would the directors or partners raise the money to pay out the spouse or dependants?

(c) What are the inheritance tax implications of a Buy and Sell Agreement, a Double Option agreement, Automatic accrual.

Key man cover

4.13 In all firms there are **key men and women** (eg the export manager who has just completed an excellent deal in Germany, or the computer programmer who has devised a new program which will make enormous savings in production). The company will suffer financially through the death or sickness of such a person, so the company needs to insure their lives against **sickness or death**.

4.14 Deciding on a suitable **level of cover** is difficult. In coming to a conclusion, the company must take into account the following matters.

(a) Past profits and possible future projections of the company.
(b) How much, financially, the loss of the keyperson would affect profitability.
(c) The cost of recruiting and training a replacement.

4.15 There are three possible ways of deciding on the **amount of cover**, multiple of salary multiple of profit or contribution to profitability.

(a) **Multiple of salary**. In this case the company looks at the keyperson's total remuneration package and insures for five or ten times this sum.

(b) **Loss of profits**. In this case the company is trying to quantify the loss of profits which may be suffered. This could be, say, 5 times profit net of expenses, or the average of the last two years' gross profit.

(c) **Contribution to profitability**. This is calculated as follows

$$\frac{\text{Key person's remuneration}}{\text{Total salary bill}} \times \text{Average gross profit for two years} \times \text{Recovery years}$$

4.16 The **tax situation** will change depending on the type of policy used as shown below.

(a) **Term assurance**

(i) If the premiums qualify to be allowed as a business expense then the policy proceeds will be taxed as a trading receipt. If this is the case the employer must take this into account when deciding the level of cover required.

(ii) It may be possible to effect a policy which will pay the sum assured to the company over a number of years. Each year the proceeds will be taxed as a trading receipt but this may help to spread the load.

(iii) If tax relief has not been allowed then the proceeds will not normally be taxed.

(iv) It is important that companies clear the situation with their local Inspector of Taxes at the outset of the contract.

(b) **Whole of life**

(1) The premiums will not be allowed as a business expense.

(2) The Finance Act 1989 introduced legislation which affected policies held by companies. Any gain made under such a policy (which normally will be surrender value less premiums paid) will be subject to tax on the gain.

4.17 Although in the proceeding paragraphs we have concentrated on the situation in the event of **death**, it must be remembered that it is equally important to have **Permanent Health** and **Critical Illness cover** in place.

Question 12

(a) The student should make sure that he clearly understands the different taxation of a term assurance or whole of life used for keyman purposes.

(b) Why do you feel that a multiple of salary basis of calculation of the sum assured for keyman insurance is less satisfactory than the loss of profit calculation?

Chapter roundup

- In this chapter we have looked at the products which can be used to protect a family in the event of the death of the main breadwinner.

- Similarly we have looked at the products suitable to provide an income if someone cannot work through illness or redundancy.

- Closely linked to providing an income in the event of sickness is the provision of speedy medical attention via private health insurance.

- We have also studied the products needed to protect the company or partnership in the event of the death or long term sickness of a director, partner or keymen/women.

Quick quiz

Multiple choice questions

1 What sort of tax is paid on the proceeds of a qualifying life policy?

A Capital gains tax
B 18% tax
C Income tax at the policyholder's highest rate
D None

2 If you wanted to provide your family with long term protection against your death which of the following would you effect?

A A term assurance
B A whole of life policy
C Permanent Health insurance
D Long term care insurance

3 Which of the following is a low risk fund?

A International Equity
B Tracker fund
C Fixed Interest fund
D Property

4 Why would you suggest that a policyholder should have an increasing sum assured under a term assurance policy?

A To earn more commission
B To give him a greater maturity value
C To keep pace with inflation
D To improve the surrender value

5 If the client wanted a unit-linked policy to give him as large a death cover as possible, which would you suggest?

A A unit linked whole of life with minimum death cover
B A non profit whole of life
C A unit-linked endowment
D A unit-linked whole of life with maximum death cover

6 If you pay a premium into a unit-linked whole of life policy, which of the following events happen?

A The premium is used to buy units in a chosen fund

B The increased premium allows the policyholder to participate in the with profits fund

C The premium is used to buy units in a chosen fund and then some are cancelled to buy the life cover

D The premium simply buys life cover

7   Which of the following share purchase agreements will give rise to the greatest inheritance tax liability?

    A   Buy and sell agreement
    B   Double option agreement
    C   Automatic accrual

In the following questions mark each option as TRUE or FALSE.

8   A term assurance

    A   Can be made paid up
    B   Can be assigned to a bank
    C   Will pay out on death during the term
    D   Has no investment value

9   Peter James took out a 10 year Family Income Policy in 1995 for a benefit of £10,000 per annum. He dies in 2000. What happens?

    A   The policy pays out £10,000 per annum until 2010
    B   The benefits can be paid out as a lump sum which will be more than £50,000
    C   The benefits can be paid out as a lump sum which will be less than £50,000
    D   The policy pays out £10,000 per annum until 2005

10 Which of the following policies have premium review dates?

    A   Unit linked Whole of Life
    B   Traditional Low Cost Whole of Life
    C   Decreasing Term Assurance
    D   Universal Whole of Life

11 A higher rate taxpayer or his estate could suffer an income tax charge in which of the following circumstances?

    A   If he surrendered his qualifying policy in year 4
    B   If he surrendered his qualifying 25 year endowment policy in year 20
    C   If he assigned his policy for cash, by means of a sale, in year 5
    D   On the death claim under a universal whole of life policy

12 A policyholder says he wants to cash in his 25 year low cost endowment in year 23 (2000). Which of the following would occur?

    A   He would lose the life assurance tax relief
    B   He would possibly lose terminal bonus
    C   He would lose life assurance cover
    D   If the performance had been good he may have enough to pay off the mortgage

13 Which of the following are methods of funding the setting up costs of a unit-linked whole of life policy?

    A   Policy fee
    B   Capital units
    C   Reduced unit allocations
    D   Annual management charge

14 In the event of the death of a partner or shareholder/director which of the following statements are true?

    A   Unless there is a partnership agreement, the partnership may have to be dissolved

    B   The shareholder's widow could demand her seat on the board

    C   Business relief for inheritance tax purposes will only arise if a Buy and Sell agreement is in force

    D   A spouse could be left with no benefit from the business if an automatic accrual arrangement existed.

The solutions to the questions in the quiz can be found at the end of this Study Text. Before checking your answers against those solutions, you should look back at this chapter and use the information in it to correct your answers.

Answers to questions

1   (a)   Convertible term assurance is attractive because of the ability to covert to another form of life assurance with no evidence of state of health. For example a client suffering from an incurable illness could convert to whole of life assurance and protect his family for life.

(b)   One of the main limitations of term assurance is fixed term. The attraction of renewable term is the flexibility to extend the term of the cover.

(c)   Term assurance policies are primarily used to protect families and business assets. In both cases the value of these assets is likely to increase over the years. For example, if a client is earning £20,000 today and needs £80,000 of cover, this will look hopelessly inadequate in 20 years time when he is earning £100,000 and needing protection of say £400,000.

2   (a)   The sum assured under a mortgage protection policy reduces. If a client has an interest only mortgage, the capital outstanding remains constant, therefore a mortgage protection policy would not produce sufficient cover on death.

(b)   Under an interest only mortgage, the full amount of the loan will always be outstanding on death, therefore the client will need a level term assurance for the full amount of the loan because this would not reduce throughout the term.

3   *Quotations* (*Note:* These are examples of quotations which may be obtained. The aim of the exercise is to demonstrate the difference in the cost of the different types of product.)

Male aged 32 next birthday	*Monthly premium*
Level Term Assurance 20 years sum assured £50,000	£9.20
Convertible Term Assurance 20 years sum assured £50,000	£10.20
Mortgage Protection Assurance 20 years sum assured £50,000	£6.20

4   (a)   A non-qualifying policy will always give rise to a chargeable event and the possibility of a 18% tax charge. A qualifying policy will only give rise to such a tax charge if it is altered to give rise to a chargeable event.

(b)   No, because even though a chargeable event may occur under a non qualifying policy, as he is a basic rate tax payer there would be no tax to pay.

(c)   Make sure the client does not lose his right to life assurance premium relief on premiums. This relief is currently enhancing the benefits of his policy.

(d)   Chargeable events:

(i)   the death of the life assured;
(ii)   the maturity of the policy;
(iii)   the surrender of the policy;
(iv)   the assignment of the policy for money or money's worth.

(e)   The Insurance Company's fund will have suffered tax. The higher rate tax payer will be asked to pay 18% (40% – 22%) tax on his gain.

5   (a)   The bonus level is decided by the actuaries after they have valued the life fund's assets and liabilities. Some monies are placed in reserve and the balance is used to pay the bonus.

(b)   No, the reversionary bonus depends on the surplus in the fund and the amount the actuaries are prepared to take from reserve, if any. The terminal bonus depends on short term investment performance.

(c)   No, the reversionary bonus, once added to the sum assured, cannot be removed. However the terminal or claims bonus is not guaranteed to be paid.

(d)   By the use of a terminal or claims bonus.

(e) The method has a high level of guarantee because the reversionary bonus once added cannot be taken away irrespective of future investment returns. The means of bonus declaration gives a smooth 'upwards' investment return without the 'highs and lows' of unit linked performance.

7 (a) *No answer applicable*

(b) Managed, property, international.

(c) Unitised with profits or managed.

(d) The price at which you buy the units in a fund.

(e) Either by the use of low or nil allocation of premiums to units or by creating a special class of unit for the first two years called *initial units*.

8 (a) Whole of Life and Decreasing Term Assurance.
(b) Low Cost Whole of Life.
(c) Universal Whole of Life.
(d) Unit Linked Whole of Life and Universal Whole of Life.

9 (a) The benefit will be tax free.

(b) The benefit will be paid to you through the PAYE system and will be taxable.

(c) By paying a proportionate benefit.

(d) The client needs a unit linked PHI policy because there is a chance he will receive the value of his investment units at expiry .

10 (a) Permanent Health, Redundancy, Accident Insurance, Critical Illness, Medical Insurance.

(b) Permanent Health or Accident and Sickness.

(c) Permanent Health and Personal Accident Insurance - say, 60% of previous year's earnings.

Redundancy cover may be limited to covering the mortgage and an overall limit on benefit.

(d) (i) Yes, Permanent Health Insurance and Critical Illness.
(ii) Yes, Private Medical Insurance as a benefit in kind.

(e) The staff can enjoy an income in the event of long term sickness. The benefits will be paid through the PAYE system. The partners will have individual policies. The benefits will be tax-free.

11 (b) If there was no life assurance in place, they would need to raise capital by sale of assets, which may not be appropriate, or by asking for a loan from the bank which again could be a problem if they were in the middle of a difficult business cycle.

(c) Buy and Sell Agreement - the value of the share of the business forms part of the estate and no business relief is available.

A Double Option Agreement - the value of the share forms part of the estate but 100% business relief is available.

Automatic Accrual does not give rise to inheritance tax so long as it is a commercial and reciprocal arrangement.

12 (b) The loss of salary basis is satisfactory as a method of providing funds to recruit and train a replacement but it does not take into account the loss of profit because of the absence of the keyperson. As a quantitative method it may be flawed because the keyperson may have been underpaid in relation to the profit he brought to the company.

Chapter 3

USE OF PROTECTION PRODUCTS

Chapter topic list	Syllabus reference
1 Who receives the benefit?	A3.1
2 Use of term assurance	A3.1
3 Use of whole of life policies	A3.1
4 Use of protection for ill health and redundancy	A3.1
5 Priorities	A3.1

Introduction

The syllabus expects you to be able to apply the products explained in Chapter 2 to satisfy client needs in particular circumstances.

In this chapter we summarise the uses of the policies we have previously discussed. Before we do this, it is important to remember that choosing the right policy is only part of the process. It is also important to ensure that any policy is written in the right way so that it achieves its purpose.

1 WHO RECEIVES THE BENEFIT?

1.1　**Policies written in trust**. In deciding the uses of these policies it is also very important to ensure that the benefits fall into the right hands. The only way that this can be achieved is by writing the policies in trust. In this way the benefits are paid to trustees who in turn pay the proceeds to beneficiaries.

1.2　Remember, of course, that if a policy is written in trust it ceases to be the property of the policyholder. He or she pays the premium but is not entitled to the benefits. If a client is protecting his income in the event of a long term or critical illness he will not want to write these benefits in trust as they are needed for his own use.

1.3　**Policies which are assigned**. It is not possible to write a policy in trust for the family if it is also being used to cover a loan and has to be assigned to a bank or building society. In this instance, the client would need cover for the loan *and* for the family. Then the policy for the family could be written in trust.

1.4　**Joint life first death policies**. In some instances it makes sense for the policy to be written on two lives, for instance if a mortgage has been taken out by two people. The policy will then pay out on the first death to repay the mortgage.

1.5　**Joint life second death policies**. Conversely, if clients are engaged in inheritance tax planning which involves the whole estate passing between husband and wife on the first death, the policy needs to be written on two lives but paid out only when the second one dies. It is only then that the inheritance tax will be payable and the proceeds from the policy required.

2 USE OF TERM ASSURANCE

2.1 In general terms, term assurance is a policy for those seeking **high levels of protection for a particular period and reason**.

2.2 **Level term assurance**. This might be used by the following.

(a) The **family man** of whatever age with wife and children needing **protection** for his dependants. The term will usually run to retirement age.

(b) A **married woman** with husband and children needing family protection. The term will usually run to retirement age.

(c) A **divorced man or woman with dependent children**. The term selected will usually run until the children have finished full time education. This may be up the to age of, say, 22.

(d) A man or woman with an **outstanding loan**, such as an interest only mortgage being repaid by a pension or ISA/PEP mortgage. The term would equal the period of the loan.

(e) A **self-employed person** or a person in non-pensionable employment who would use pension term assurance for the above reasons and claim tax relief on contributions. Similarly if he was in a company pension scheme he could make use of FSAVC life cover (See Chapter 10).

(f) **Partners** wanting business protection against the death of one partner.

(g) **Directors (shareholders)** of a small family business wanting protection against the death of a co-director.

(h) A **company** wanting to insure the life of a key employee.

2.3 **Increasing term**. This might be used by the following.

(a) The family man of whatever age with wife and children needing **family protection which will increase with inflation**. Term usually to retirement age.

(b) A **married woman** with husband and children needing family protection which will increase with inflation. Term usually to retirement age.

(c) A **divorced man or woman** with dependant children, term usually until children will have finished full time education, this may be up to age, say, 22. Increasing cover to protect against inflation is essential.

(d) **Partners** wanting business protection against the death of one partner. The value of the partnership will grow, so too should the cover.

(e) **Directors (shareholders)** of a small family business wanting protection against the death of a co-director. Again increasing cover to protect against the increasing value of the business is important.

(f) A **company** wanting to insure the life of a key employee if it is felt that his loss will increase financially over the years.

2.4 **Convertible term**. This cover might be used by the following.

(a) The **family man** of whatever age with wife and children needing long term protection but who is **unsure of long term needs**. He is buying the option to convert to a whole of life to give protection for life, further term assurance or a savings type endowment policy **without medical evidence**.

(b) A **married woman with husband** and children needing a family protection policy could later convert to a savings plan or whole of life if she had a medical problem.

(c) A **divorced man or woman with dependent children** needs protection until the children are, say, 22. He/she may then want to convert to a savings plan for his/ her own use with **no medical evidence**.

(d) Men or women who have a **potential inheritance tax liability**. When they are young they may not be able to afford the large premium required for whole of life cover. Thus, initially they cover the liability with term assurance and convert at a later stage, when their income may have increased, to whole of life.

2.5 **Renewable term**. This policy might be used by the following.

(a) a person covering a **short-term borrowing** who is not sure of future requirements and feels he may need to use the renewable option;

(b) a young person needing **very cheap cover**. The cost for the first five years will be cheap and by the time he comes to the first renewable option, when the premium will increase, he may have more money to spend.

2.6 **Family income benefit**. This policy might be used by the following.

(a) The **family man** of whatever age with wife and children needing family protection. The term will normally extend until the children have finished full time education. A husband may feel happier leaving his wife or partner with an income to meet her outgoings rather than a lump sum which will need investing.

(b) A **married woman** with husband and children needing family protection. The term will usually run until the children have finished full time education, not forgetting university. In this instance the level of cover should be sufficient to fund the employment of a nanny or housekeeper. This would be particularly useful if the partner happened to be a higher rate tax-payer because the income from this policy would be tax-free.

(c) A **divorced man or woman** with dependent children. The term should run until children have finished full time education.

(d) If children are being **privately educated**, it would be appropriate for a husband and wife to take out a joint life first death policy. The income should be sufficient to meet the annual school fees bill from the date of the first death to the end of the policy term which in turn should coincide with the end of full time education.

2.7 **Decreasing term assurance**. This policy might be used by a man or woman wishing to repay a reducing debt but note that this is an inadequate general protection policy because of the reducing cover.

2.8 **Mortgage protection policy**. This policy might be used by the following.

(a) Clients with a **repayment mortgage** need this policy to provide a sum sufficient to repay the outstanding capital on death. In most cases the sum assured should be sufficient. If, however there had been a considerable increase in interest rates there is a slight chance that the claim value would be insufficient.

(b) If a couple are repaying a mortgage, they would need such a policy written on a **first death basis** so that the mortgage could be repaid on the first death.

2.9 Gift inter vivos policy

(a) As explained in Chapter 2 this is a specific policy for paying inheritance tax on a **potentially exempt lifetime gift** (a PET). Obviously the policy would be on the life of the person who had made the gift.

(b) If the person had made a gift to a trust, the **trustees** would need to insure the donor's life.

Question 1

Re-read the section so you know the uses of term assurance policies.

(a) Which policies have been designed for specific purposes ?
(b) Which policies provide some form of inflation-proofing?
(c) What is 'insurability' and which term assurance policy provides the greatest level of insurability?

---

3 USE OF WHOLE OF LIFE POLICIES

3.1 **Whole of life policies** provide permanent **life cover** and in some cases an **investment element**.

3.2 In some instances there can be a dilemma as to the **most suitable type** of cover, term assurance or whole of life. In the past unscrupulous salesmen sold whole of life, which had a much higher level of commission, when in fact a simple term assurance would have sufficed.

3.3 The **criteria to adopt** in recommending term or whole of life cover are the following.

(a) **The cost of the cover.** Term assurance will almost always be cheaper. Unit linked whole of life using maximum cover could be almost as cheap but the client needs to beware because it is likely that the premium will be increased upwards in the future.

(b) **The reason for the cover.** If it is specific cover for a short period, term assurance is most probably more appropriate. However, if there is likely to be a need for long term protection and investment, then whole of life may be the answer.

(c) **The age of the client.** If the client is older, say, over age 60, a term assurance is normally inappropriate because the cost will be much the same as for whole of life and the client may as well have the lifelong cover.

Whole of life non profit - use

3.4 This type of policy is **little used**. It is poor value for money and offers no increase in potential benefit to compensate for inflation.

3.5 It could be used for an **elderly client** who had a known, and fixed, inheritance tax liability. The cost of the cover would undoubtedly be cheaper than whole of life with profits cover. The policy would have the further advantage of a fixed premium which would not be available with a unit-linked whole of life policy.

Whole of life with profits - use

3.6   A person wishing to provide a **tax-free lump sum to a beneficiary on death** could use such a policy. The policy would normally be written in trust and could be for the benefit of a partner, children, grandchildren, nieces, nephews, or godchildren.

3.7   The benefits would increase with **bonus additions** which would make it a worthwhile investment and also keep pace with inflation.

3.8   Because of the smoothing effect of 'with profits' the **investment risk would be low to medium**.

3.9   The policy would be useful for a person who had a **large estate** and a **potential inheritance tax liability**. As the value of his/her assets would undoubtedly increase, it is important to have a policy with an increasing value, such as 'with profits', to offset the increase in potential inheritance tax liability.

Unit-linked whole of life - use

3.10   This could be used by the family man or woman initially wanting high life cover for the family. He/she would need **maximum cover**.

3.11   Later he/she could turn to a **minimum cover** and build up an investment fund which could, if necessary, be surrendered, perhaps at retirement, to give a tax free lump sum so long as it remained a qualifying policy.

3.12   The middle aged man or woman who is interested in critical illness cover may wish to consider a whole of life with '**add on critical illness protection**'. In this case a lump sum would be paid out, on the diagnosis of the dread disease, or on death, or on both occasions depending on the wording of the policy. In some instances it is possible to have different levels of cover for critical illness and death cover.

3.13   Unit-linked whole of life is very useful in **business protection cover**. A partner or director can have the flexibility of changing the level of cover required to meet the changing needs within the partnership or company. The investment element means that the policy can if necessary be assigned to the retiring partner or director to provide continuing life cover without medical evidence.

Universal whole of life - use

3.14   The **young family man** can use the policy to buy cover for death, critical illness, income in the event of sickness and medical expenses insurance all in one package.

3.15   Older clients may like the **flexibility** of picking certain key protections they require such as medical expenses and permanent health insurance (PHI).

3.16   This type of policy can be useful in **business protection cover for keymen**. It is possible to insure all the benefits needed, death cover, critical illness and PHI under one policy. If one keyperson leaves the business and is replaced by another, it may also be possible to change the life assured without losing any investment benefit which has been built up in the policy. This can be done because it is a non qualifying policy.

4 USE OF PROTECTION FOR ILL HEALTH AND REDUNDANCY

Permanent health insurance - use

4.1 A **single employed man or woman** needs this cover. In most cases of protection we think primarily of people with dependants. When you are protecting income it is just as important, if not more important, for single people to protect their income in the event of sickness because they have no one upon whom they can lean financially in their time of need.

4.2 A **married employed man or woman**. In both cases he/she would need to study his/her contract of employment to ensure that his/her permanent health cover started when his/her employer ceased to pay him.

4.3 A **single or married self-employed person**. If he/she cannot work his/her income stops immediately. Care must be taken with those who have recently set up in self-employment because the Permanent Health insurance benefit is based on income in the previous fiscal year. In some instances this may be nil!

4.4 A **houseperson** can obtain limited cover. This is useful as the income can be used to hire someone to help with household tasks during the period of illness.

4.5 **Keyman, partnership and director cover.**

4.6 A client who had a **limited benefit from a company scheme**. This benefit could be made up to the maximum allowable by use of a separate policy.

Critical illness - use

4.7 Again, **single people** are very vulnerable in the case of a critical illness because they may have greater need of money to buy in help.

4.8 **Family men or women**, whose families would have financial problems in the event of a critical illness.

4.9 A man or woman who can see from his/her family history that there is a **good chance of a critical illness** happening to him/her. Obviously this will be taken into account in the underwriting but the younger he/she obtains the cover the more likely he/she is to be accepted.

4.10 Business protection. A business can suffer dramatically if a key person has a sudden heart attack. The need for this cover in business protection is now being properly recognised.

Long-term care - use

4.11 Those in their 50s who are **planning retirement**. Retirement planning should be considered in two tranches, the **active phase** when the client should be able to take holidays and enjoy hobbies and the **less mobile phase**.

4.12 There is now a **generation of clients** who have seen the financial effects of providing long term care for their parents. Alternatively they may have seen their parents coping with debilitating illnesses of old age which they suspect they too may suffer in time

4.13 Families with a history of **longevity**.

4.14 Families carrying out **inheritance tax planning**. Without a long term care plan in place the planning could be a waste of time as there may be few if any assets left after paying out huge nursing home fees.

4.15 **Single clients** who will have no family to care for them in their old age.

Redundancy cover - use

4.16 Anyone with a mortgage who is currently employed.

Personal accident and sickness - use

4.17 **Self-employed man or woman** to whom the short deferred period sickness cover is very useful.

4.18 Cover is cheap, so if a client is desperate for **extra life cover** it is better to have death by accident cover than nothing at all.

4.19 Accident lump sum death benefit is useful for the **client who travels a great deal**.

4.20 Lump sum death by accident cover is useful for a **young family man** who wishes to increase his life cover but cannot afford to do this. A substantial amount of accident cover will be very cheap and in the young there is a greater chance of death by accident than by natural causes.

Medical expenses insurance - use

4.21 It is useful for the **single man or woman** who has no one available to care for them in times of illness.

4.22 A **married man or woman** with or without children who need speedy medical care, particularly if they have an important career, will benefit.

4.23 Clients who are in the **30+ age group**. Medical expenses insurance is expensive and therefore there needs to be a reasonable level of disposable income to meet the cost of the cover.

4.24 Very useful for the **self-employed** who need to obtain medical attention so they can get back to work quickly. It is essential for anyone with a level of responsibility either at home or work where it is vital that the medical process can be undertaken quickly and with the minimum of inconvenience.

4.25 **Older clients** with high disposable incomes who prefer the comfort of private medical care and are concerned that the waiting list for some chronic conditions is very long.

5 PRIORITIES

5.1 Although in an ideal world every client should be protected by all the policies we have discussed, most clients have only **limited resources**. The financial adviser must carry out a **full fact find** and ascertain income and expenditure so that he knows how much is available to be spent as premiums for protection cover.

5.2 In all financial planning it is essential to leave **enough income** to cover current and future outgoings and to remember that sometimes premium payments will continue into retirement. Will the client still be able to afford them and be willing to pay? For example with long-term care cover, it is important to ensure that a client has properly funded a pension before worrying about long term care. It is no good providing for the later years if there is no pension for the earlier years of retirement.

5.3 For the **family man or woman** the priority list must be:

(a) life protection with continuing insurability options if possible;

(b) redundancy cover, if employed;

(c) sickness or permanent health cover;

(d) critical illness;

(e) private medical expenses insurance;

(f) long-term care.

5.4 For the **single man or woman** the priority list could read:

(a) life cover for debts;

(b) redundancy cover;

(c) sickness or permanent health cover;

(d) critical illness;

(e) private medical expenses insurance;

(f) long-term care.

5.5 It is important to realise that each case must be considered on its particular facts. There is no hard and fast rule about priorities or the protection policies a client needs.

Question 2

Make sure you understand the use of all the protection policies, then see which protection contracts you would advise in the following situations and how the policies should be written (stating the beneficiaries). Look back at Section 1 of this chapter which describes the options of writing policies on a life of another basis or in trust.

(a) Peter is 35, he has a wife, who does not work aged 28 and two children aged 3 and 1. He has a repayment mortgage of £50,000. He works for a small building firm, they offer no pension scheme or death in service benefits. His salary is modest.

(b) Andy is the same age. He is married. His wife Sarah works part time. They have two children aged 4 and 2. Andy is a self employed signwriter (sole trader). He has an interest only mortgage of £60,000 which he is repaying by means of a personal pension.

(c) Charles is also aged 35. He has just been promoted to the position of marketing director for a multinational company which means he will travel a great deal. His wife Harriet is a solicitor (employed). They have two children aged 4 and 1 and Harriet's salary pays for the nanny. Both Charles and Harriet are members of their company pension scheme which provides for death in service lump sum of 4 times salary and a spouse's pension. They have an interest only mortgage of £110,000 which they are repaying by means of a personal equity plan/ISA. Harriet knows that she will inherit a great deal of money when her father dies.

(d) Stephen is aged 35. He is a chartered accountant. He and a friend have recently left a large national firm of accountants and they are about to set up their own practice. Because of the uncertainty of the venture, Anne, his wife, is going back to work as a nurse. Their children, aged 7 and 9, are being privately educated. They have an interest only mortgage which they intend to repay by means of a low cost endowment.

Chapter roundup

In this chapter we have considered the following.

- The means of getting the protection benefits in 'the right hands'.

- The uses of the various type of protection policy protecting against both death and loss of income.

- The fact that people in different circumstances have different protection needs.

- Prioritising protection needs.

Quick quiz

Multiple choice questions

1   Which of the following policies most nearly meets the needs of a young family man needing life assurance protection?

    A   Gift inter vivos policy
    B   Level term assurance
    C   Endowment assurance
    D   Reducing term assurance

2   A man aged 35 wants £10,000 of life cover. Which of the following policies will be cheapest at the outset?

    A   Non profit whole of life
    B   10 year level term assurance
    C   Minimum cost Whole of Life
    D   Renewable term assurance

3   A man is about to board a plane and is worried about protecting his family in the event of a crash, which type of policy does he need?

    A   One year term assurance
    B   Death by accident
    C   Critical illness
    D   Redundancy cover

In the following questions mark each option as TRUE or FALSE.

4   A   A mortgage protection policy will be used to cover an interest only mortgage in the event of death

    B   A level term assurance will be used to provide cover in the event of death if the client has a PEP/ISA mortgage

    C   A mortgage protection policy would be used to provide cover in the event of death for a repayment mortgage

    D   If the lending rate reduces significantly over the term, the mortgage protection policy may not pay out sufficient in the event of death during the term.

5   A   A convertible term assurance policy may be a useful policy for inheritance tax planning
    B   The 'income' of a househusband can be insured for PHI purposes
    C   A family income benefit policy would be useful to insure the life of a househusband
    D   The lives assured can be changed under a universal whole of life policy

6   A   Long-term care cover will be taken out by someone with a terminal illness

    B   A critical illness policy will provide a benefit in the event of a terminal illness

    C   A permanent health insurance policy may pay out a benefit if the policyholder has a terminal illness

    D   Critical illness cover can be added to a term assurance

---

7   A   Private medical expenses insurance is more important for the self-employed than the employed

  B   Critical illness cover is no use to a single person

  C   Private medical insurance is not available to the over 60s

  D   Permanent health insurance is more expensive for those who have dangerous occupations

---

The solutions to the questions in the quiz can be found at the end of this Study Text. Before checking your answers against those solutions, you should look back at this chapter and use the information in it to correct your answers.

Answers to questions

1   (a)   Mortgage protection, family income benefit, gift inter vivos.

   (b)   Increasing term assurance, increasing family income benefit cover.

   (c)   Insurability is the ability to have continuing life assurance irrespective of your state of health. The only policy which can do this satisfactorily is a convertible term assurance, because if it is converted to whole of life it gives cover for life.

2   (a)   Peter needs:

   (i)   Protection for the family. This could be a *family income benefit policy* for say 20 years until the youngest child reaches 21 or a lump sum *term assurance* for the same period with the sum assured inflation-proofed by RPI linking if possible.

   The suggested method of writing the policy could be in trust for his wife with the proviso that if she predeceased him then the children benefited.

   It may be possible for Peter to effect *pension term assurance* and claim tax relief on the premiums but if he does so, the choice of policy and options may be restricted.

   (ii)   To insure his wife's life on a 'life of another basis' for *family income benefit* for a sum assured, sufficient to pay for some home and child care in the event of his wife's death while the children were young.

   (iii)   To cover the outstanding debt on his mortgage by means of a *mortgage protection policy*. This will be on Peter's life only or a joint life, first death if the mortgage has been effected on a joint basis.

   The policy should not be written for another person's benefit as the proceeds will be needed to pay off the mortgage and may need to be assigned to the lender.

   (iv)   To provide *redundancy cover*, if there is sufficient disposable income.

   (v)   To provide sickness cover. It would appear that Peter's employer is most probably unable to pay him for long periods if he were sick. Peter probably cannot afford Permanent Health Insurance and anyway he could be in an expensive category on grounds of occupation. A *personal accident and sickness policy* could be considered to give short term protection.

   (b)   In this instance although the personal circumstances are similar to Peter's the great difference is that Andy is self-employed so he must insure his income if he is unable to work, because his income will stop immediately he cannot work and his state benefits are likely to be less than Peter's.

   Andy will need:

   (i)   Family protection and the same policies as for Peter would appear to be appropriate. As he is self-employed, *pension term assurance* may be appropriate and would enable him to claim tax relief on the premiums.

   (ii)   To cover the loss of his wife's income in the event of death by means of say a *family income benefit policy* written on a 'life of another basis'.

(iii) To protect the income in the event of sickness is vital. The best solution may be a *personal accident and sickness* policy which runs for 2 years and a permanent health policy with a two year deferred period.

(iv) To protect the mortgage by level term assurance for a lump sum of £60,000 claiming tax relief on premiums as pension term cover.

(c) Charles and Harriet have most probably got enough life assurance protection through their company pension scheme. However there are a number of other areas they should consider covering.

(i) Charles travels a great deal and if his company has not already done so he should be covered for a large amount of *death by accident* cover. This should be written in trust for his wife and children.

(ii) Harriet should protect her income in the event of being unable to work through sickness by *Permanent Health insurance* with a deferred period to fit in with her contract of employment. This would then ensure that the nanny could be paid even if Harriet was not working through illness.

(iii) Similarly Charles's income should be protected against sickness by *Permanent Health insurance*.

(iv) It would seem essential if they were ill that they had *private medical expenses insurance* to ensure that they could be treated when convenient to fit with their work schedule and to ensure that they could get back to work 'in the fast lane' as quickly as possible.

(v) Harriet is likely to inherit money in the future which suggests that she will have a potential inheritance tax problem. A *convertible term assurance* would be useful to give additional family protection now but which could be converted at a later date with no evidence of health to provide cover for inheritance tax mitigation.

(vi) If they have not already done so, they should cover the mortgage with a joint life, first death *term assurance* for a sum assured of £110,000.

(d) In this case, we must look at business and private cover.

(i) *Business cover* - the partners will need to cover each other's lives with *term assurance*, hopefully increasing by the RPI, to ensure that there are funds available on the death of one partner. As there are only two partners it would be simple to write the policies on a life of another basis.

(ii) It is important that the partnership income is protected in the event of either partner suffering a critical illness or a long term illness so *Critical Illness and Permanent Health insurance* are very important.

(iii) Obviously the family must be protected. This is a case where *Unit-linked whole life* may be appropriate, initially with a maximum amount of life cover. However there is a good chance that Stephen's business will prosper and later he can reduce his life cover to standard or minimum and put more of the premium to investment. It may even be that he will have an inheritance tax problem and the whole of life policy could be used for inheritance tax planning purposes.

The policy should be written in trust, possibly a discretionary trust which allows beneficiaries to be appointed from a wide class (this gives greater flexibility to meet the changing uses of the policy).

(iv) Anne's income is obviously very important to the family budget in the early years of the business, so the loss of her income in the event of death or sickness should be protected possibly by short term, say five year *family income benefit* policy and a *personal accident nd sickness policy*.

(v) If disposable income allowed, a *family income* benefit to cover the school fees would be advisable, possibly written on a joint life first death basis.

(vi) If Stephen is running his own business, it is important that if he or his family need medical treatment this can be done as quickly as possible so that his ability to earn an income is disturbed as little as possible. Private medical expense cover is very important. Perhaps the cost could be contained by taking a policy which paid out only if the NHS could not provide the treatment within 6 weeks.

BPP PUBLISHING

Chapter 4

COMPARING PROTECTION PRODUCTS AND PROVIDERS

Chapter topic list	Syllabus reference
1 Selecting the type of product	A 4.1
2 Comparing different providers of the same product type	A 4.2
3 Comparing different providers of a particular product	A 4.3

Introduction

So far we have looked at the choice of protection products, their features and uses. Now we move on to decide which protection product to choose for a particular client and having made this choice which provider is most suitable.

The general public often appears to believe that this process simply involves putting one finger in the air and putting it down on a list of products and insurance companies. In this chapter you will learn that it is a more complex process. Let us look first at selecting the type of product.

1 SELECTING THE TYPE OF PRODUCT

1.1   The factors to be considered in **selecting a product** are:

(a) Price
(b) Surrender values
(c) Charges
(d) Commission structure
(e) Tax treatment

Price

1.2   Although the syllabus lists price or premium level as the second most important item, it is believed that in many cases, **price is of paramount importance**. Often clients want the maximum amount of cover at the cheapest rate.

1.3   A known cost for future budgeting is important. Therefore, a term assurance with a **guaranteed level premium** for the rest of the term, or a modest RPI increase, may be preferable to a unit-linked whole of life, which on maximum cover may start out looking as cheap as term assurance but, because of the premium reviews, there is a chance of increases in the future, eg **unit-linked whole of life** for a male of 35 with maximum death cover of £100,000 costs a monthly premium of £ 20.11 whereas **term assurance** for the same man for a sum assured of £100,000 for 25 years costs a monthly premium of £21.89.

1.4   In the case of permanent health, medical expenses, long-term care and critical illness

52

insurance, price may not be of paramount importance. The **terms of the policy, definitions of disability and the insurance company's history of paying claims** may be more relevant.

1.5 If a client has an **adverse medical history** or **hazardous occupation**, account must be taken of the possibility of a loaded premium.

1.6 The **sex** of the client can have an effect on cost. In life assurance the premium for a woman is usually lower than for a man of the same age on account of improved mortality for women. However, statistics show that women have longer periods of sickness and therefore their premiums under Permanent Health insurance are more expensive.

1.7 We will now look at the **levels of premium** for various types of cover.

(a) **Term assurance - level**. The costs will vary with age, sex, term and sum assured. See examples below.

	Monthly premium
Male age 25 sum assured £100,000 term 10 years	£9.30
Male 25 sum assured £100,000 term 20 years	£12.00
Male 35 sum assured £100,000 term 10 years	£15.20
Male 45 sum assured £100,000 term 10 years	£31.30
Male 45 sum assured £200,000 term 10 years	£61.40
Female 45 sum assured £200,0000 term 10 years	£36.70

Sometimes insurance companies are able to offer special rates for very large sums assured say £500,000 +

(b) **Term assurance - with convertible option or increasing sum assured**

The costs will increase if you include options such as a conversion right, or an increasing sum assured.

Example male aged 25

Level term assurance, 10 year term	sum assured £100,000 costs £9.30 per month
Convertible term assurance, 10 year term	sum assured £100,000 costs £10.50 per month
Increasable term assurance, 10 year term	sum assured £100,000 costs £12.50 per month

(c) **Term assurance - mortgage protection**

If the policy has a reducing sum assured as in a mortgage protection or decreasing term assurance, premiums are lower than for level term.

Thus £100,000 level term assurance for a male aged 35 for 25 years will cost £21.89 per month and a mortgage protection for the same man for the same term and same initial cover only £17.30 per month.

(d) **Term assurance - renewable term**

This can be very cheap cover initially because it is only costed for the first five years. Costs go up with age when each renewable option is exercised, so overall it can be much more expensive than level term for the whole period.

The adviser must, as a result of his fact find, decide whether this type of policy is really in a client's best interest. If he needs long term cover, it may not be. It may be better suited for someone who needs cheap short term cover but with an option for flexibility in the future.

(e) **Term assurance - family income benefit**

Although this is cheaper cover it must be remembered that at the outset the insurance company is potentially taking on a large risk. For example under a 10 year family income benefit policy with an income of £10,000 pa, the initial cover is £100,000. The cost of this cover for a man of 25 is £6.53 per month. This example has been used so that the student can make a direct comparison with level term assurance of £100,000 for the same term, monthly cost £9.30. The family income benefit policy is cheaper because each year the *total* cover reduces.

Note. Although most term assurance has a guaranteed fixed premium level for the term of the contract, in recent years reviewable term premiums have been introduced by some companies. These are often cheaper at the outset but the client has an uncertain premium future.

(f) **Whole of life**

In this instance the premium will depend on the type of policy selected. Whole of life non profit will be the cheapest and whole of life with profits the most expensive because the client is 'buying the right' to participate in the with profits fund.

(i) If a client is trying to maximise cover and minimise cost, he may decide to use either a low cost whole of life or the maximum cover under a unit-linked whole of life.

(ii) Premiums remain constant throughout the life of the policy for the traditional non profit, low cost and with profit whole of life but are reviewable for unit-linked whole of life.

(g) **Permanent health insurance**

In this instance the level of premium will depend on a large number of factors.

(i) Age.

(ii) Sex. Remember that permanent health insurance premiums are more expensive for women.

(iii) Period of deferment. If the client wishes to reduce the cost, he may be well advised to increase the deferred period.

(iv) Level of income required.

(v) Term of policy.

(vi) Occupation.

(vii) Medical history.

Note. Some permanent health policies give the policyholder a guaranteed level premium through the life of the policy (this is getting rarer). Others have reviewable premiums which allow the insurer to review the premiums in line with overall claims experience. The latter type of contract often commences with a lower premium than the guaranteed premium but of course the client has an unknown premium level for the future.

The following example shows the effect on the premium of selecting different deferred periods.

Example. Male age 35 assume Class 1, occupation benefit £10,000 pa, deferred periods 4, 13, 26, 52, 104 weeks, cover ceases at age 65.

Deferred period	Monthly premium
4 weeks	£31.83
13 weeks	£20.41
26 weeks	£15.03
52 weeks	£13.85
104 weeks	£11.84

(h) **Personal accident and sickness policies**

In this instance the same level of sickness benefit can be obtained as for Permanent Health insurance for a cheaper premium but the student must remember the **limitations on the cover**. Premiums will depend on the following.

(i) Level of cover

(ii) Occupation

(iii) Previous medical history and claims experience

This is an annual renewable policy like general insurance cover and the premiums can increase at renewal or cover can be withdrawn.

(i) **Redundancy cover**

Premiums will depend on level of cover required. There will be a set rate per unit of benefit regardless of age.

(j) **Medical expenses insurance**

Premiums will depend on the following.

(i) Age - rates are banded according to age

(ii) Number of members of family covered

(iii) Level of cover required

(iv) Any excess or restriction on cover accepted

(v) Hospital grade required

Premiums will normally increase at renewal by an overall amount for all Scheme members depending on the Insurer's total claims experience over the last twelve months, not the individual's claims experience. A further increase will occur as a client moves up an 'age band'.

(k) **Critical illness**

Premiums will depend on the following.

(i) Whether the cover is 'stand alone' or added to term, whole of life or an endowment policy

(ii) Age and sex

(iii) Sum assured

(iv) Previous medical history of client and family

Example of cost - male aged 35, cover £100,000 throughout life (maximum cover), monthly premium £27.08

(l) **Long-term care**

Level of premium will depend on the following.

(i) Age

(ii) Level of cover required

Question 1

A man aged 30 wants protection for his family, list:

(a) the most inexpensive policies he could effect;

(b) the most expensive.

Surrender values

1.8 One of the factors to be taken into account when recommending protection products is to ensure that the client appreciates that in most cases he is buying pure cover. There is **no investment element**; it is rather like insuring a car. In that instance if you have no accidents, no claims are paid out and in effect the premiums are wasted. It is the same with term assurance, permanent health insurance (unless unit-linked) medical expenses insurance, redundancy insurance and personal accident and sickness. Unless a claim arises, there is no return to the client or the family. Some clients do not like this idea and would prefer to feel that there was some return, however small. These clients should consider unit-linked policies, if available.

1.9 We will now consider the situation of **surrender values** for each type of product.

1.10 (a) Life cover - surrender values

    (i) There is no surrender value on a term assurance.

    (ii) If a client wants an investment value incorporated in his protection cover, he will need a whole of life policy.

    (iii) The surrender value under a traditional non-profit or with-profits whole of life contract is likely to be nil or low in the first two years of the term of the contract and is unlikely even to meet the premiums paid for some considerable number of years. Disclosure and key feature documents make it easier for clients to see the effects of early surrender on these policies.

    (iv) If the client selects a unitised whole of life policy (unitised with profits or a unit linked fund) with minimum or standard cover, part of each monthly premium will be invested in units which in turn can produce a surrender value. However, if maximum cover is selected there is unlikely to be a surrender value of any size unless there have been exceptional investment returns.

    Note. It may be in a client's best interest to split his protection and investment needs in order to give greater flexibility than can be achieved by trying to combine both requirements in a whole of life policy.

(b) **Permanent health - surrender values**

Some insurance companies offer unitised permanent health policies. These contracts work like unitised whole of life policies. Premiums are invested in the chosen fund and units cancelled to buy the permanent health cover. A small unit value may grow up depending on investment performance. This could produce a surrender value if the policy were cancelled or at the end of the term of cover.

Charges and commission

1.11 The adviser must take into account **charges and commission** when recommending a product. The introduction of full disclosure makes this easier as all insurance companies now have to annotate their charges in real terms and also the commission paid to the adviser.

Charges

1.12 (a) **Term assurance**

In this case, charges are built into the overall premium rate. When calculating the rate the actuary will have taken into account mortality, interest and charges. The charges will include the costs of putting the business on the books; items such as payment of medical fees, administration, documentation and agent's commission. The premium will also include a charge for the ongoing cost of administration, premium collection, payment of claims etc. Obviously the offices with the most efficient administrative systems should be able to offer the most competitive premium.

Thus, as far as term assurance is concerned, charges are of little importance other than the effect they have on the overall premium and the adviser will no doubt be choosing the cheapest premium.

(b) **Whole of life**

Traditional whole of life policies such as non profit, with profits and low cost, will have the charges taken into account when the actuary calculates the premium rate in a similar way to the term assurance as described above.

In the case of a unit linked whole of life the charges will be:

(i) **Unit charge** - each time units are purchased they are bought at the offer price and when sold a bid price applies - the difference is known as the *bid/offer spread* and is usually 5% - 6%. An example of unit pricing is as follows:

Fund	Offer price	Bid price
Managed	249.5	237.0

(ii) **Annual management charge**. This is the cost of managing the invested funds and is usually a percentage of the value of the fund, say 1%

(iii) **Policy fee**. The insurance company will charge a monthly administration fee, eg £2.00 per month which may be indexed in some way so that the charges are inflation proofed

(iv) **Initial charges**. Insurance companies have to devise means of extracting the setting up costs from these policies. As they have to meet these costs at the outset of the policy, eg paying commission, they need to recoup the money from the policyholder as quickly as possible. This can be done in one of two ways as follows.

(1) **Low allocation**. In, say, the first two years only a small amount, or in some cases, a *nil* amount is allocated to investment units.

(2) **Initial units**. The insurance company creates *special* units called initial units. The client's investment premiums for the first two years purchase these units which carry a higher charging structure and are therefore never worth as much as the accumulation units which are purchased from year three onwards.

Commission

1.13 **Commission is usually based on the level of premium** paid. As we have seen the premium paid for a whole of life with profits policy is much greater than that for the equivalent cover under a level term assurance. Consequently the commission will be higher on the whole of life with profits. Therefore an adviser must be very confident of his reasons for his recommendations if he suggests a higher commission-paying contract.

BPP PUBLISHING

1.14 The **key features document draws** the client's attention to the level of commission and there may be room for negotiation between the client and the adviser as to the level of commission he will take. In some instances, particularly with an investment type contract, such as whole of life, the benefits or unit allocations can be improved by giving up a certain amount of the commission.

1.15 Although LAUTRO (Life Assurance and Unit Trust Regulatory Organisation) has now ceased to exist and was replaced by the PIA, nevertheless levels of commission are normally referred to as a **percentage of LAUTRO**, 100% of LAUTRO being the normal level with certain agents being eligible for higher levels.

1.16 Each insurance company offers a huge range of **commission options** such as:

   (a)   140% LAUTRO with small renewal commission;
   (b)   100% LAUTRO and increased renewal;
   (c)   60% LAUTRO and further increased renewal commission;
   (d)   8% Level commission throughout the term of the contract.

1.17 It must be remembered that many advisers, whether independent or tied, have a business to run and therefore must be **remunerated** for their work. They need to receive commission or a fee which covers the time expended on the particular case plus a profit and which is acceptable to the client.

1.18 There is a move for independent intermediaries to take a **fee for advice**. In these circumstances they will take no commission from the contract and allow the commission to be invested back into the policy to increase the benefits.

Tax treatment

1.19 In deciding which policy to select, the adviser must take into account the client's **tax situation** now. The adviser must also look into the future when the client may be surrendering a contract, or a claim arises through death. If there is a chance that at that time the client could be a higher rate taxpayer and a chargeable gain could arise, then he should only recommend a **qualifying policy**.

1.20 If however the client is always likely to be a **basic rate taxpayer,** then it does not matter whether the policy is qualifying or not and the policy should be selected on the other criteria, premium, surrender values, charges, commission and so on.

Question 2

Look back in Chapter 2, paragraph 1.18 and revise qualifying and non-qualifying policies.

Remember that even if a higher rate taxpayer has a qualifying policy there could still be a charge to higher rate tax. When might this arise?

2   COMPARING DIFFERENT PROVIDERS OF THE SAME PRODUCT TYPE

2.1 When an adviser has decided on the right product type for the client, his next job is to decide on the **appropriate provider**. The first thing he must do is look at the features and options available under the various contracts.

2.2   The first problem is to identify a provider for a **particular type of contract**, for example some predominantly unit-linked offices will not offer term assurance.

2.3   If there is likely to be an **underwriting problem**, it is useful if the adviser has experience of a particular life office's attitude to impaired lives. In some cases it may be a wise move to submit simultaneous proposal forms to a number of insurance companies, having taken into account premium rates and possible underwriting attitudes. For example an office which offers competitive rates may load an impaired life more than an office with a middle of the road premium.

2.4   We will now look at the different features which require attention for the different types of **protection policies.**

2.5   **Family income benefit - features requiring attention**

   (a)   What level of income is available and whether the benefit will increase during the course of the policy or just in claim.

   (b)   The adviser must see whether the benefits increase by a set percentage or the RPI.

   (c)   He must investigate the rules for commuting to a lump sum in the event of a claim.

2.6   **Convertible term assurance - features requiring attention**

   (a)   The adviser must ask whether the conversion options cease at a particular age.

   (b)   It is very important to know the range of contracts to which the policy can be converted. The wider the range the better.

   (c)   The adviser must be aware of the insurance company's investment performance. For example, if it allows conversion to a 'with profits' contract the adviser must ensure that the company has a good reputation for consistent 'with profit' performance.

2.7   **Whole of life with profits - features requiring attention**

   (a)   The adviser must be aware of the insurance company's 'with profits' past performance history, both reversionary and terminal bonus. He must know its current bonus trend over recent years and gauge the probability of consistent future performance.

   (b)   He must know if there are any options available and, if so, when they expire.

   (c)   He will need to know if there is a restricted premium payment period, ie to age 65 or 80.

   (d)   He must take a view on possible surrender values.

2.8   **Whole of life low cost - features requiring attention**

   (a)   The with profits history of the company is very important because the success of this policy depends upon the insurance company being able to maintain and hopefully improve the bonus levels.

   (b)   The split between the with profits whole of life sum assured and decreasing term sum assured is important. For the same premium value it is important to obtain as high a whole of life sum assured as possible because upon this depends the final claim value.

   (c)   It is also important to determine the age of the life or lives assured when the decreasing term assurance expires. If the adviser wants to achieve maximum cover at minimum cost then this is likely to be when the clients are well into their eighties. However, if the aim of the policy is to try and experience some investment growth from the 'with profits' element, it is important that the decreasing term assurance ceases earlier.

(d)   Possible surrender values must be considered.

2.9   Whole of life unit-linked - features requiring attention

(a)   Performance of all the unit funds to which premiums can be linked and in particular the funds which the adviser will recommend must be investigated.

(b)   The policy conditions concerning premium review and the dates upon which the review takes place are important.

(c)   The adviser needs to discover whether any market level adjuster could apply to the unitised with profits fund on early encashment.

(d)   The adviser needs to check the client's risk profile and to ascertain whether the policy has funds which fit this.

2.10   Universal whole of life - features which require attention

(a)   The adviser needs to check all the features applicable to unit-linked whole of life.

(b)   As the facility exists to link into non life products, the terms and conditions applying to these covers need to be investigated, in particular any restricting clauses which may apply to permanent health or medical insurance.

2.11   Permanent health insurance - features which require attention

(a)   The definition of disability is the key to a good permanent health policy. Ideally the adviser should recommend a contract which has a definition which will pay a claim if the policyholder is unable to carry out his own occupation, such as:

> 'Incapacity means that because of sickness or accident the Insured is able to perform no part whatever of the duties of the ordinary occupation stated in the schedule and is not following any other gainful occupation.' (Permanent Insurance Company Ltd.)

If the definition says 'unable to carry out any occupation', the chances of paying a claim are slim. The policyholder would virtually need to be in a coma!

(b)   The maximum levels of benefit allowed should be checked. Many insurance companies restrict cover for high earners.

(c)   The terms of premium waiver needs attention. It is important that it applies during a claim.

(d)   The terms of any 'option to increase cover' must be studied, eg the option to increase by 25% every four years without medical evidence.

(e)   The deferred periods offered by the insurance company are important. Some offices do not underwrite cases with a minimum deferred period of 4 weeks.

(f)   Some providers offer a combination of permanent health insurance and medical expenses insurance giving preferential rates on the medical expenses insurance if combined with the permanent health insurance. This may be useful for a particular client's needs.

(g)   Occupations are categorised for permanent health insurance. Different offices may use different categories for the same occupation. So with some investigations an adviser may be able to obtain a better rate for the client purely on the basis of occupation.

(h)   The insurance company's treatment of claims is important.

(i) Other factors the adviser should take into account are:

   (i) How does the company view proportionate benefits?

   (ii) Does the insurance company have a consultancy service to help claimants' recovery?

   (iii) What happens if the policyholder goes to work abroad?

   (iv) What are the general exclusions?

   (v) What happens if the policyholder changes job? Does he have to inform the insurance company and suffer a possible increase in premium?

   (vi) What happens during periods of a policyholder's unemployment?

2.12 Critical illness - features which require attention

(a) In selecting this cover the definition of dread diseases is of paramount importance.

(b) The adviser will need to ascertain whether the cover can be 'stand alone' or added to another policy.

2.13 Medical expenses - features which require attention

(a) The adviser needs to consider the classification of hospitals, particularly in the area where the client resides.

(b) Another important consideration is age bands and treatment of spouse and children. From a premium point of view, some offices offer a 'family' package. Others charge for each child separately which can be expensive for the big family!

(c) Most schemes now have a moratorium for existing medical complaints. Others may still require full underwriting and medical examination.

(d) The range of benefits, in particular whether there is an upper limit imposed on certain aspects of the cover, say, an overall maximum per operation or per annum.

(e) The adviser should investigate any restriction on cover; for example it may be possible to reduce the cost of benefits by accepting an excess.

(f) Other restrictions may be compulsory NHS treatment so long as the waiting list is less than six weeks or there may be no outpatient cover.

(g) The insurer's attitude to alternative medicine is important. Particularly, will the company pay for acupuncture, homeopathy etc?

(h) If the cover is world wide, this is a bonus because it saves the need for the client to cover medical expenses under holiday insurance.

2.14 Long-term care - features which require attention

The adviser should be considering the following:

(a) The definition of disability used in the contract.

(b) Choice of payment. Can it be either monthly or single or a combination, and are there facilities to purchase more cover at a later date?

(c) Because of the long term nature of the contract and benefit, it is important to establish any likely increases in premium, and whether any form of guaranteed premium rate can be obtained.

(d) Level of benefit and flexibility may be important, for example could a policyholder stay in his own home and have nursing care rather than having to go into a nursing home.

2.15 **Personal accident and sickness - features which require attention**

The adviser should be considering the following:

(a) The definition of disability used in the contract
(b) The extent of the cover
(c) The exclusions
(d) Periods of deferment
(e) Period of total cover

2.16 **Redundancy cover - features which require attention**

The adviser should be considering the following:

(a) Period of deferment
(b) Maximum amount of cover provided
(c) Any exclusions
(d) Maximum period of payment

Question 3

(a) What is the main factor you would take into account when comparing the providers of level term assurance?

(b) What are the factors you would take into account when deciding on a provider for a unit linked whole of life policy?

(c) Do you think that the premium is the most important factor in deciding which provider to use for permanent health insurance. Please list the other factors which you feel are relevant.

---

3 COMPARING DIFFERENT PROVIDERS OF A PARTICULAR PRODUCT

3.1 The following are the factors to **be taken into account**:

(a) Financial strength
(b) Quality of service
(c) Investment choice and performance.

Financial strength

3.2 Why is it important that an insurance company is **financially strong**? The **Treasury** insists that insurance companies are financially viable before they can be authorised. However, the strength of insurance companies does vary.

3.3 If the client is investing for a long period, it is important for the adviser to be confident that the insurance company **will still be there to pay out the claim**.

3.4 The FSA/PIA states that independent advisers should take financial strength into consideration when making their **choice of provider**.

3.5 Insurance companies are authorised by the **Treasury** under the Insurance Companies Act 1982.

3.6 The Act states that the insurance companies must make **returns to the Treasury** within 6 months of the end of their financial year or possibly more frequently if they are recently authorised or there reason to be concerned about their trading position.

3.7 The returns give **full accounting and actuarial valuations** for the life office.

3.8 From the return it is possible for the **free asset ratio** to be calculated. In simple terms the free asset ratio is the difference between the insurance company's assets and its liabilities. This is the **solvency margin**.

3.9 The level of free asset ratio is an indicator, to some extent, of the company's ability to produce **good 'with profit' returns** in the future. Companies with a higher content of fixed interest holdings in their portfolio can show a higher free asset ratio. However this may not subsequently result in good bonus declarations because real growth is normally achieved by a higher weighting in equities.

3.10 The assets are calculated at **market value**. Some of the rules are as follows:

(a) Equities listed on the world stock markets are valued at their mid market value.

(b) Unlisted securities, that is investments in very small companies, are valued by multiplying the maximum of the average profits earned in the last three years by a price/earnings ratio.

(c) Property and land must be professionally valued at least every three years.

(d) Equipment is valued at its cost price less depreciation.

3.11 **Valuation of liabilities**. The liabilities are the mathematical reserves in relation to the office's long term business and the short term liabilities. The actuary has to use an appropriate valuation basis, usually the net premium method. However different companies use different methods and apply different rates of interest. Because of the complexity of the matter it is often difficult for the non-actuary to analyse the free asset ratio tables which are produced.

3.12 When looking at tables of free asset ratios, it is important for the adviser to distinguish between the **proprietary and mutual companies**. The proprietary companies need a higher free asset ratio because they will pay out usually 10% of their profits to the shareholders, before payment to the with profit policyholders.

3.13 We have studied the free asset ratio mainly in the context of the ability of a financially strong company to continue to **maintain its bonus record**. It must also be appreciated that if a company has 'financial strength' this is an indication that it has its expenses under control and has the finances to undertake expansion in the market place.

Quality of service

3.14 **Service is of paramount importance in the financial services business**. The client does not have a product to admire or use. All he has is a promise demonstrated possibly by some documentation. If this is not correctly and efficiently produced, the client can doubt the validity of the contract and the promised ability to produce good returns.

3.15 Good service is required in the following areas.

(a) An adviser must be confident that he can obtain **accurate and swift quotations**.

(b) The adviser must have access to **well trained technical staff** so that the arrangement can be correctly established.

(c) Efficient **ongoing administration** is vital, particularly at the time of a claim.

(d) Correct **collection of premiums** is important. Clients like their premiums to be collected promptly.

(e) **Correct documentation.**

3.16 Now that **full disclosure** pinpoints the exact amount of money taken in charges by the insurance companies and the adviser, there is an even greater need for good administration and service to convince the client that he is getting value for money. Therefore it is a vital consideration to take into account when choosing a provider.

Investment choice and performance

3.17 As previously mentioned, if a client requires a unit-linked whole of life policy it is vital that the provider has a **range of funds with good performance**. It is in fact better to offer funds with consistent performance over long periods rather than 'the top of the charts one month' and then disappearing without trace thereafter!

3.18 A **choice of risk rated funds** is important as not all clients will wish to take high risk.

3.19 A choice of funds is important if the client is likely to **switch** from protection to investment at a later time in the history of a whole of life policy.

3.20 The ability to **move funds** with the minimum of administrative hassle and cost is useful.

Question 4

Re-read the section on *free asset ratio*. See if you can find a copy of the annual returns of the Companies Financial Strength printed in *Money Management*. This is useful (even if it is out of date) to give you an idea of the different free asset ratios between companies and the complexity of the figures.

Chapter roundup

Having completed this chapter, you should be aware of the following.

* The reasons for the choice of the different protection products to satisfy varying client needs.

* Then the method used by the adviser to analyse the various products of a similar nature.

* Finally, the choice of the right insurance company for the client.

Quick quiz

Select one answer to the following questions

1   What is the most important factor in choosing a term assurance?

    A   Cost
    B   Commission
    C   Service
    D   Charges

2   Which factor is *not* taken into account when calculating a whole of life non profit policy premium?

    A   Age
    B   Morbidity
    C   Interest
    D   Expenses

3   Under which of the following contracts do you think that investment performance is the *most* important feature?

    A   Unit-linked whole of life maximum cover
    B   Low cost whole of life
    C   Non profit whole of life
    D   Unit-linked permanent health insurance

4   In the selection of which of the following policies would the fact that the client was a higher rate tax payer be relevant?

    A   Medical expenses insurance
    B   Universal whole of life policy
    C   Accident and sickness policy
    D   Permanent health insurance

In the following questions mark each option as TRUE or FALSE.

5   In selecting a company to provide medical expenses insurance for a client, the adviser would take into account of which of the following factors?

    A   The type of hospital he would wish to use
    B   The age and number of dependants to be covered
    C   The client's place of birth
    D   The client's attitude to alternative medicine

6   Consider the premium charges for various types of cover. Indicate which are true and which are false:

    A   An Insurance company may give an improved rate for a large sum assured, say £2 million

    B   The premium for a female aged 35 for £50,000 convertible term assurance for 10 years will be less than for a male of the same age

    C   The premium for a male aged 35 for £5,000 permanent health insurance for 10 years will be more than for a woman of the same age

    D   Two men of the same age and state of health may obtain the same premium rate for life assurance but different rates for permanent health insurance

7   When deciding on an insurance company's financial strength, which of the following are true/false?

    A   A knowledge of an insurance company's free asset ratio is useful to form an opinion as to future performance of unit-linked funds.

    B   Tables of free asset ratios are easily understood because the figures are all based on the same assumptions.

    C   One of the ways of improving the free asset ratio of a company is to increase the equity holding in the portfolio.

    D   If a company is 'strong' it is an indication that it has good expenses management.

---

8   Factors which may be considered when recommending a suitable insurance company for Permanent Health insurance are as follows:

A   All Permanent Health policies offer a four week deferment period

B   The applicant's occupation may give rise to an increased premium for permanent health insurance purposes

C   All Permanent Health policies pay out for a maximum of two years

D   The definition of disability under a permanent health policy can vary depending on the client's occupation or from company to company

9   When considering which type of contract to recommend, the adviser will take into account the following:

A   There is unlikely to be a surrender value under a minimum cost whole of life policy in the first two years if full commission has been taken

B   There may be a surrender value under a level term assurance after 12 years

C   There is unlikely to be a surrender value under a unit-linked whole of life policy with minimum death benefit

D   There is unlikely to be a surrender value under a unit-linked whole of life policy with maximum death benefit

---

The solutions to the questions in the quiz can be found at the end of this Study Text. Before checking your answers against those solutions, you should look back at this chapter and use the information in it to correct your answers.

Answers to questions

1   (a)   Least expensive: level term, family income, personal accident and sickness

(b)   Most expensive: whole of life with profits, permanent health insurance, critical illness, medical insurance

2   A higher rate taxpayer with a qualifying policy could face a charge to higher rate tax if:

(a)   the premium payment was to alter in some way so that premiums paid in one twelve month period were greater than in another;

(b)   if the policy were to be surrendered say in year 5.

3   (a)   The main factor is the premium.

(b)   The factors to be taken into consideration are:

(i)   level of cover required;
(ii)   range of funds available from the provider;
(iii)   frequency of premium review.

(c)   Premium is not the most important factor. The other considerations should be:

(i)   definition of disability;
(ii)   the chosen insurance company's history of paying claims in a sympathetic manner;
(iii)   the insurance company's attitude to occupations and hobbies;
(iv)   deferred periods available, ie is there a four week deferred period?

Part B
Savings and investment

Chapter 5

SAVINGS AND INVESTMENT IN THE FINANCIAL PLANNING CONTEXT

Chapter topic list	Syllabus reference
1 Savings advice: circumstances and dependent factors	B 1.1, 1.2
2 Investment advice: circumstances and dependent factors	B 1.1, 1.2

Introduction

You are urged to understand the reasons for savings as set out in this chapter. This will help you at a later stage to fit the various products to the client's needs.

1 SAVINGS ADVICE: CIRCUMSTANCES AND DEPENDENT FACTORS

1.1 **Why does anyone save**? Why not spend all the money you earn? The answer is obvious. You may need money in the future for unexpected happenings, a future expenditure, the rainy day, or when you are too old or ill to work.

1.2 We will now look at a number of **different situations** and how the savings needs of these people may change.

(a) **Susan Thomas** aged 20 may wish to save for:

    (1)   A holiday
    (2)   A car
    (3)   The deposit on a house
    (4)   Money to get married

(b) **Dean and Halley Brown,** both aged 35, with two young children, may wish to save for:

    (1)   A holiday
    (2)   A second car
    (3)   A deposit on a bigger house or home improvements
    (4)   School fees
    (5)   Retirement
    (6)   The children to provide for a wedding, the first car etc
    (7)   'Rainy day' costs: the new roof, or new car or an unexpected tax bill

(c) **John and Pat Jones,** both aged 48, with children of 16 and 18, may wish to save for:

    (1)   A car for the children

    (2)   University costs for the children

    (3)   A holiday

(4)   Home improvements or the deposit on a bigger house

(5)   Money for the children to provide a deposit on their first house or money for a wedding

(6)   Retirement, maybe early retirement

(7)   A 'rainy day': they may anticipate that one of them may be made redundant or be unable to work through sickness

1.3   As you will see, most people have some of the same savings needs and some will vary with age and circumstances. You will also notice that the last example is for a couple aged 48. Once clients near retirement, their needs tend to change from savings to investment. By that stage in life it is hoped that the client will have accumulated, possibly through savings, capital which can then be turned into income for retirement.

Features of savings needs

1.4   Individual savings needs can be discovered from a thorough **fact find**.

1.5   Savings can be divided into **short and long-term needs**.

(a)   The **short-term savings need** is for the car, or the holiday for which the obvious type of investment is a deposit account, such as a bank or building society account.

(b)   **Longer term savings** needs will be for retirement, school fees or providing capital for the children as they reach adulthood. However, as you will see from our example, the Joneses have left it later than the Browns to start this saving, so the type of investment recommended, although for the same purpose, may be different. The Browns have longer to save and so will possibly choose an asset backed investment such as an individual savings account (ISA) or unit trust savings plan, whereas the Joneses may have a shorter period and should select safer deposit type schemes.

1.6   The client's own **aims and ambitions** for the future are very important but they must be realistic in line with the amount the client has available to save. Many clients have no concept of the amount of regular savings needed to accumulate, say, £40,000 in 20 years' time. They may well assume that this can be achieved by, say, a £50.00 per month contribution.

1.7   Another important feature is **access**. This will influence the choice of type of savings and is particularly relevant for any savings into an emergency fund. As its name implies, this is money which may be needed at very short notice, so there is no point in tying it up.

1.8   **How much can the clients afford**? It is important to analyse income and expenditure. Having agreed the disposable income, the adviser must discuss how much they are prepared to spend and how much to save. An adviser should never allow them to over-commit themselves to a long term contract with penalties.

1.9   The adviser should also be looking to the **client's future**. He should ask the question, will the client be able to afford more in the future? For example are there clear signs that the client's earnings may increase, say from a promotion at work or income may be available from another source? If this is the case, a savings plan where contributions either increase, automatically or by selection, may be appropriate.

1.10 If the client is approaching retirement age, or if he works in an industry where there is the likelihood of redundancy ahead, savings schemes should be flexible with **easy access to money**.

1.11 In advising on savings the attitude of the client to **risk** is very important. The client must have risk properly explained, and if his assets and the amount available to save is small then he must be guided to low risk deposit type schemes.

1.12 If the client has more money to save, then as with all investment advice, there should be a **spread of types and terms of investment**, for example:

(a) low risk
(b) higher risk
(c) easy access
(d) fixed term

1.13 If a client is saving in an asset-backed investment, such as a monthly premium unit linked endowment plan, or a unit trust savings plan, the client should be made aware of the very useful feature of such a scheme, the **pound cost averaging**. What does this mean?

This means that the client is investing a regular premium each month in, say, a managed fund. Each month his premium will buy units in this fund. However the price of the units will vary from month to month depending on the performance of the fund. Take for example the units purchased by a monthly contribution of £30.00 into the GT Far East and General Fund between August 1991 and January 1992.

Month	Bid price	Units purchased
August	208.40	14.395
September	201.20	14.911
October	210.50	14.252
November	201.40	14.896
December	181.40	16.538
January	182.30	16.456

As you will see the price varies, so the number of units purchased by the same monthly premium will vary from month to month. Over a long period the client will benefit from the fluctuations in the market by buying more units when the price is low and selling when the price is high!

1.14 **Existing investments and savings plans** must be taken into account when giving advice for a new savings scheme, any new recommendations must fit in, giving a good spread of type and risk.

1.15 **Tax situation**. Whatever the level of tax paid by the client, the income tax and capital gains implications of all investments must be considered and advantage taken of any tax incentives or reliefs available.

Question 1

James Harris invests £30 per month in a unit trust savings plan. The prices at certain dates were as follows.

BPP
PUBLISHING

Month	Offer price	No of units purchased
August	257.60	
September	263.00	
October	272.90	
November	280.00	
December	278.90	
January	291.00	

Calculate the number of units purchased on each occasion. Compare the total amount of units with the amount he would have purchased if he had invested a lump sum of £180 in November.

Question 2

(a) Consider a lady client of 56 who asks for savings advice. She is single and in a company pension scheme to which she contributes 5% of pensionable salary. She expects to retire at 65 but there have been redundancies and early retirement plans in operation and therefore she may go sooner. Her aim is to increase her income in retirement. She has some existing investments and savings plans.

What factors should you take into account when advising this woman?

(b) Paul Stone is aged 30, unmarried with no 'intentions of marrying in the near future'. He earns £35,000 a year as the marketing director of a large firm. He says he has disposable income for savings.

What factors will you take into consideration when advising this man?

2 INVESTMENT ADVICE: CIRCUMSTANCES AND DEPENDENT FACTORS

2.1 There are many ways in which clients **acquire capital sums for investment**.

(a) Maturing investment policies
(b) Inheriting capital
(c) Winning the lottery!
(d) Redundancy payments
(e) Tax-free lump sums from pension schemes
(f) The proceeds of many years of savings
(g) Existing portfolios

2.2 Let us look at a few examples of circumstances in which clients may need investment advice for capital sums.

(a) **Mr and Mrs Ellis**. Both aged 63. Mr Ellis has just retired. He has

£30,000 from the tax-free lump sum from his pension scheme,

£20,000 from the proceeds of a maturing endowment policy,

£30,000 in various building society accounts.

Mr and Mrs Ellis need advice on how to invest this capital in order to maximise their income in retirement.

(b) **Mr and Mrs Collins**. Mr Collins is aged 52 and has been made redundant.

He has been able to take early retirement benefit from the pension scheme. However, he will take on a part time job. This does not pay as well as the existing job but, together with his pension, he feels he can manage. He has

£20,000 from the pension scheme tax-free lump sum,

£28,000 lump sum redundancy payment,

£20,000 in the building society.

Mr Collins aims are to accumulate capital for the next eight years so that he can retire at age 60 with sufficient income. Therefore his aim will be short term capital appreciation with a view to converting to income-producing assets at age 60.

(c) **Mrs Simmons** is aged 48 and has just inherited £100,000 from her mother.

Mrs Simmons works part time but feels that she will now give up her job. Her husband is a director of the family business. His position is secure and he earns £45,000 per annum.

Mrs Simmons' aims are to invest her capital in a well spread portfolio to achieve some income now but capital appreciation for the future. She views this money as family money and hopes that at least some of the capital can be passed on to the next generation. Mrs. Simmons is prepared to take some risk with her investments because she has more capital and no particular short term needs.

In these three situations you will see greatly varying investment needs.

Features of investment needs

2.3 Individual investment needs can be discovered from a thorough **fact find**.

2.4 Investments can be divided into **short and long term needs**.

(a) The **short-term investment** need is an emergency fund for the new car, mending the roof, medical expenses etc. The obvious investment is a deposit type, such as a bank or building society account with easy access.

(b) **Longer term investments** may be for growth to provide for retirement, school fees or capital for the children. If a client needs total **security of capital** it may be that the only recommendation is a deposit type scheme. However, if a client is to preserve the real value of his capital over a long period, an asset backed investment, such as a share portfolio, unit or investment trusts, is the only one which, hopefully, should give a real rate of return above inflation.

2.5 To make financial sense the **income achieved from long-term investment should increase over the years**. Unfortunately, with changing rates of interest, it is not always possible to achieve this, as was seen in the late 1980s and late 1990s when interest rates fell, and many retired people relying on this income saw it reduce dramatically. The only way to achieve an increasing income is to use asset backed investments. Most income unit trusts have shown a steady upward growth in the value of their distributions whilst still maintaining and, in some cases, increasing the value of the underlying asset.

For example, if a client had invested £10,000 in Perpetual High Income unit trust in January 1990. Five years later it would have been worth £14,976 and the income would be £620. If, however, he had invested in a building society the capital value would still be £10,000 and the gross income approximately £620.

2.6 The clients' own **aims and ambitions** for the future are important, as is **access**. Similar considerations apply here as for savings.

2.7 On advising a client on investment, his **attitude to risk** is very important. If the client is unaccustomed to investment but wants to take some risk then a medium risk scheme should be recommended, possibly using a package which is more easily understood, for example a pooled investment such as a unit trust.

If the adviser is dealing with a husband and wife, or any two partners, he must remember to ascertain the attitude to risk of both partners. It may be different!

2.8 If clients indicate that they are prepared to take risk, then the different levels of risk must be explained and particularly the relationship between the amount of **risk and the potential reward**; for example, the risk with a managed fund, consisting of shares, gilts, fixed interest and possibly property, is much less than an emerging markets fund which may invest in the economies of South America, China and the Eastern European countries.

2.9 If the client is retired then great care should be taken to ensure that **capital is preserved** in order that a reasonable level of income can be maintained.

   (a) For those with **amounts below £20,000** to invest, a low-to-medium investment should always be chosen.

   (b) If the client has **a large capital sum** to invest then there should be a spread of types and terms of investment, for example:

      (i)   low risk
      (ii)   higher risk
      (iii) easy access
      (iv)   fixed term

2.10 The client's **tax position** is of vital importance. If a couple is being advised, it may be possible to invest capital in the name of the non-taxpayer or the lower taxpayer (having obviously ascertained their attitude to such a suggestion: some clients do not like the idea of investing in the partner's name even if it does save tax!)

Care must also be taken to utilise the tax-exempt investments and to ensure that the adviser has checked the capital gains tax implications of investments.

2.11 **Existing investments** must be taken into account and new ones recommended to fit into a well spread portfolio.

Question 3

On a scale of 1 - 5 list the risk ratings for the following situations, 1 being low and 5 very high.

(a) Woman aged 83 wishing to achieve increased income from her capital for nursing home fees.

(b) Man aged 25 who is single with a low mortgage, who has just won £25,000 on the football pools.

(c) Married man of 43 who wants to invest the proceeds of a maturing life policy of £10,000 to provide some capital for his children, possibly for a deposit on their first house in 15 years' time.

(d) Woman of 49 who has just received £30,000 as a redundancy payment but already has a better job. She is also a member of a company pension scheme, is married to a successful solicitor and has no children.

(e) Child aged 10 who has just inherited £2,000 from his grandmother.

Question 4

Before moving on from this chapter test yourself on the following.

(a) What is an asset backed investment?
(b) When would you use a deposit type investment?
(c) Describe the concept of pound cost averaging.

Chapter roundup

- In this chapter we have learnt of the varying savings and investment needs of the individual and studied how these can change with age and circumstances

- We have also become aware of the idea of asset backed and deposit investments and their risk profile.

Quick quiz

1   A single man of 30 is asking for advice on a long term savings scheme. Which of the following factors is the least important?

    A   Risk profile
    B   Ease of access
    C   Existing investments and savings
    D   Aims and ambitions

2   If a client only has assets of £10,000 in total, which level of risk would you recommend?

    A   Low
    B   Medium
    C   High

3   Which of the following statements are true and which are false?

    A   If you are advising a wife on investments, the adviser does not need any financial details about her husband's savings and investment schemes.

    B   Investments should be split between short and long term needs.

    C   There is a direct link between risk and reward.

    D   If a client needs a medium risk investment he should avoid pooled investments.

4   Which of the following statements are true and which are false?

    A   The shorter the term of savings the greater the need for security.

    B   An asset backed investment is backed by the Government.

    C   Deposits with banks and building societies are suitable for short term investments.

    D   Pound cost averaging is a method of taking advantage of the changing price of units by saving on a monthly basis.

The solutions to the questions in the quiz can be found at the end of this Study Text. Before checking your answers against those solutions, you should look back at this chapter and use the information in it to correct your answers.

Answers to questions

1

Month	Offer price	No of units purchased
August	257.60	11.646
September	263.00	11.407
October	272.90	10.993
November	280.00	10.714
December	278.90	10.757
January	291.00	10.309

Total units purchased during the period 65.826. If £180 had been invested in November 1993 only 64.285 units would have been purchased.

2 (a) Factors taken into account are:

    (i)   Age

    (ii)   Flexibility, she may need access to her savings if she has to retire early

    (iii)   Risk, she needs her investments safe

    (iv)   Knowledge of the existing investments need to be gained from a thorough fact find

  (b) Factors taken into account are:

    (i)   Age, he is younger than client (a).

    (ii)   Paul can tie his money up for longer.

    (iii)   Paul can take greater risk if he wishes, after full discussion of risk.

    (iv)   Paul will need a spread of investments.

    (v)   He must have some invested as an emergency fund, some for a fixed term.

    (vi)   Paul must invest in schemes with tax advantages because he would appear to be a higher rate taxpayer.

3 The first point to make is that we should say 1 - 2 is low, 3 - 4 medium and 5 high.

  (a) 1 because she must not risk her capital.

  (b) 3 - 4 or 5 depending on his attitude to risk. As he has won the money he may be prepared to take more risk.

  (c) 3 - 4 He needs security but also growth. Some form of packaged or pooled fund such as a unit trust in a medium risk fund may be the answer.

  (d) 4 - 5 There is no need for security, she could afford to take a risk to reap potentially greater reward.

  (e) 1 - 2 Small investments and investments for children should always be safe.

Chapter 6

SAVINGS AND INVESTMENT

Chapter topic list	Syllabus reference

Introduction

The syllabus expects you to have knowledge of the range of savings and investment products. This means that you need to know who provides such products, how they are treated for tax purposes, how risky they are, what charges are imposed and so on.

1 BANK AND BUILDING SOCIETY PRODUCTS

1.1 In general terms all these products can be referred to as **deposits,** ie the investor receives a rate of interest in return for depositing his capital with the institution.

1.2 The **rate of interest** received can be fixed or variable and the term of the investment can be fixed or open ended. It is worth the client noting the frequency of crediting interest into the account. A lower rate added to the account on a monthly or quarterly basis may have a better overall effect than a higher rate which is credited annually.

1.3 The key feature of these investments is that there is **no growth in the capital value unless the interest is allowed to roll up.**

BPP
PUBLISHING

Bank accounts

Providers

1.4 **Banks,** but remember that the choice is not restricted to the largest banks.

Tax treatment

1.5 The **interest on the accounts is paid net of 20% tax.** This can be reclaimed by non-taxpayers by completion of the green R85 form. Individuals who only pay tax at 10% can reclaim the excess 10% tax. There is of course **no charge to capital gains tax** as no capital gains as such are made, rolling up interest is not a capital gain!

Risk

1.6 The **risk** on a bank account is low because the capital invested is secure at all times. The risk cannot be said to be nil because there is a chance that the bank will become insolvent as happened with the Bank of Credit and Commerce International. In this event the client would have recourse to the deposit protection fund which pays out a maximum of £18,000.

1.7 Some clients may feel happier **spreading their capital** between a number of banks if they intend to deposit a large amount. However, they must realise that if they do this they may lose the incentive of the larger interest payments made to those depositing larger sums with individual banks.

Returns

1.8 The **returns on bank accounts** vary from account to account but are only interest payments and no capital gains accrue.

Contribution limits

1.9 There is no restriction.

Penalties and accessibility

1.10 These features will be investigated under the topic of the **individual accounts.**

Type of bank account

1.11 **Current accounts**

(a) Most clients will have opened a current account with a bank as a means of receiving their salary and making standing order and direct debit payments.

(b) These accounts will offer a cheque book, cheque card and cashpoint card facility. Internet bank accounts do not provide cheque book and cheque card, but do provide a cashpoint card.

(c) Interest - the traditional account pays no interest and makes no charges so long as the client does not become overdrawn.

(d) Some accounts pay interest but in return the client may have to pay for transactions. The rate of interest will be variable.

1.12 **High interest cheque accounts** - in this instance a high level of deposit must be maintained in order to receive the higher rate of interest which is normally tiered according to investment amount. Again this rate of interest will be variable.

1.13 **Access** - on all current accounts there is immediate access.

Penalties - withdrawal charges are unlikely on current accounts.

1.14 **High interest accounts**

Interest is paid on accounts with a tiered system depending on the amount invested.

Access and penalties. These apply - there is often a 90 day notice period. If this is broken a loss of interest results.

1.15 **Monthly income accounts**

The rate of interest is slightly lower than that credited on an annual basis to allow for the more frequent payments.

Access and penalties. Some accounts have instant access. Some have terms requiring notice to be given.

1.16 **Time deposits**

(a) This is a facility which is available to anyone who has a large amount to deposit for a short period, eg someone may have sold a house and is waiting to buy another.

(b) The bank will quote a guaranteed rate for a fixed period, say 1 or 3 months.

(c) The rates are directly linked to the rates available on the money market.

(d) The money is held for the agreed term. At the end the client is given the choice of taking the money away or investing for a further term. If he decides to invest for a further term, he is quoted a new guaranteed rate for the term selected.

Access. There is no access until the end of the agreed period.

Building society accounts

1.17 **Providers**

(a) **Building societies.**

(b) Apart from the remaining larger societies that have not converted to banks, there are many **small building societies** closely related to a particular geographical area. They may offer better rates of interest but a client living in another part of the country may be 'suspicious' because the building society is not familiar to him.

(c) **Postal and telephone-based accounts** are able to offer better rates of interest because all transactions are carried out by post or telephone. This of course cuts down the administrative costs for the building society.

Tax treatment, risk and contribution limits

1.18 The same considerations apply as for **bank accounts**.

Returns

1.19 The returns on building society interest-bearing accounts vary from account to account but no capital gains accrue. The **demutualisation** of a number of building societies led to 'windfalls' either in cash payments or shares for investors and borrowers. To curb speculation, most remaining building societies require new members to sign over their right to any windfall to a charity and some regionally based societies restrict new accounts to local residents.

Access and penalties

1.20 See **individual accounts** listed below.

1.21 **Types of building society account**

(a) **Instant access.** Highly suited for a client's emergency fund. Interest is tiered depending on amount invested.

Access and penalties. No restrictions.

(b) **Notice accounts.** These pay a higher rate of interest than an instant access account. For example, in April 2000 the Nationwide Building Society would have paid 3.15% gross on a deposit of £5,000 for instant access and 4.40% for a similar amount deposited with 90 days notice.

Access. Normally the client must give 30, 60 or 90 days' notice of a withdrawal otherwise he will lose interest.

(c) **Monthly interest accounts.** These accounts are favoured by the retired for the regular monthly income facility. Rates are tiered according to the amount invested. However, the rate is a little lower than the notice account because the interest is paid monthly. Using the same building society as before in April 2000, the Nationwide would have given a rate of interest of 4.18% on an investment of £5,000 in a monthly interest account as opposed to 4.40% if the interest was added annually.

Access and penalties. Normally there are access restrictions of 30, 60 or 90 days.

(d) **High interest cheque accounts.** Some of these accounts start to pay interest only if a reasonable deposit remains in the account. Even so the rate is low compared with the rate which could be received on a notice account. In some instances a high initial deposit must be made. Cheque books, card and cashpoint facilities are available.

Access. Instant.

(e) **Fixed rate accounts.** Building societies offer fixed rate bonds (also offered sometimes by banks). These give a fixed rate of interest for a selected number of years, say 1, 2 or 3 with a guaranteed return of capital. Interest would be paid monthly or annually.

Some bonds are known as escalator bonds. These are fixed rate bonds but the interest rate rises each year, normally over a five year period with the guarantee of the return of the capital at the end of the term. The advantage of these bonds is an increasing income which could be useful if inflation begins to take a hold.

Access. Usually none within the selected period.

Tax Exempt Special Savings Accounts (TESSA)

1.22 These schemes came into operation in January 1991 and ceased on 5 April 1999: from this date, no new accounts can be opened but existing accounts can continue for their five year life. A TESSA is a **five year tax exempt savings plan**.

1.23 **Providers**

   (a) Banks
   (b) Building societies
   (c) Incorporated friendly societies

Returns

1.24 The return on the scheme is the payment of gross interest so long as the investment is kept for five years and the interest, if withdrawn, is only taken net leaving the balance to roll up.

1.25 The **interest rate** offered by institutions is normally variable but it is possible to obtain a fixed rate TESSA from a restricted number of institutions.

1.26 Some schemes offer a final bonus for those who remain loyal for the full five years.

Contributions limits

1.27 Contribution limits were as follows.

   (a) The maximum total contribution per person, over the age of 18, was **£9,000** over the five year period.

   (b) The maximum in year one was £3,000, £1,800 in year 2, 3 and 4 and a balancing £600 in the final year. £1,200 more could be invested in the final year if the full allocation had not been made in previous years.

   (c) Investors holding TESSAs for 5 years were able to roll-over the full £9,000, but not the accumulated interest, into a further tax exempt account within 6 months of maturity. Provided this account was left for a further 5 years, all the interest was tax free.

   (d) On 6 April 1999 TESSAs were replaced by the deposit section of the Individual Savings Account (ISA). No new TESSAs can be opened from that date but existing arrangements, whether new or roll-over accounts, can be maintained for their full five year term. At the end of the term, either type of account can be rolled over into the ISA without affecting the permitted ISA contribution for that year. Once again only the capital may be rolled over. Such accounts are known as TESSA only ISAs.

   (e) Some building societies offer 'feeder accounts'. The client invests the full £9,000 initially and each year the provider automatically feeds the amount for that year into the TESSA account. Gross interest will be earned on the TESSA account and net interest on the 'feeder account'.

Accessibility and penalties

1.28 If the client is to enjoy the gross interest, then he must not withdraw from the scheme within the five year period. However if he is dissatisfied with the level of interest, it is possible to **change providers**, although some institutions charge a transfer fee.

1.29 If the client attempts to withdraw the total income rather than the allowable 80% of the gross income during the period of the scheme the **tax exempt status will be withdrawn**.

Tax treatment

1.30 **Income is credited gross for all taxpayers,** but see Paragraph 1.29 above.

Risk

1.31 **Risk is low**, other than the inherent risk of the institution becoming insolvent. However, because of the small amounts involved, the investments would be completely covered by the compensation schemes.

Save as you earn schemes

1.32 The **basic SAYE scheme was withdrawn** in the 1995 Finance Act. Advisers may meet clients still contributing to these schemes. They were tax free savings schemes for up to £20 per person giving a tax free return of 8.3% over a five year period or 8.26% over a 7 year period.

1.33 However the **SAYE linked share option schemes** still remain. Under these schemes the employee is granted an option to buy company shares in three, five or seven years' time at 80% or 90% of the market price of the shares when the scheme commenced. The employee then saves on a monthly basis for three, five or seven years to produce the capital to buy the shares.

2 NATIONAL SAVINGS PRODUCTS

2.1 **Provider** - the Government.

Risk. Very low because the money is invested with the government and all schemes guarantee the return of the capital invested.

2.2 We will consider return, tax treatment, accessibility, penalties and contribution levels under each individual type of scheme.

Types of National Savings scheme

2.3 The National Savings products can be divided into **three main types**.

(a) Bank type accounts
(b) Income providing schemes
(c) Growth schemes

Bank type schemes

2.4

Feature	Ordinary account	Investment account
Return	Low rate of interest which is variable. This account is no longer marketed by NS since it is inferior to the Cash mini ISA.	Higher rate of interest. Interest is tiered between £20 - £100,000 (maximum). Rates will vary in line with overall interest rates.

Feature	Ordinary account	Investment account
Contribution levels	£10 - £10,000.	£20 - £100,000 per person.
Access and penalties	£100 can be withdrawn without notice (or up to £250 at a chosen post office). For larger amounts a few days' notice will be required.	30 days notice. Or without notice with 30 days interest penalty.
Tax treatment	The first £70 of interest is paid free of income tax (£140 on a joint account). Any additional interest amounts are paid gross but are liable to tax and must be declared.	Interest paid gross but liable to tax and must be declared.

There are also CAT-standard cash mini ISAs and TESSA-only ISAs provided by National Savings. These are subject to the normal CAT requirements.

Income providing schemes

2.5

Feature	Income bonds	Pensioner's bond
General description	Provide an income. No fixed term of investment.	Five-year bond or two-year bond, giving a guaranteed rate of income. Capital is returned at the end of five years. Available to those over 60, male and female.
Return	The bond provides a monthly income. The rate is variable. The interest rate is tiered according to the amount of the investment.	Guaranteed monthly income for five years.
Contribution limits	£2,000 - £250,000 sole or joint. (£1,000 for further purchases.)	£500 - £1,000,000 per person.
Access and penalties	Three months notice. Minimum withdrawal £1,000. Immediate withdrawal is allowed but with loss of 90 days interest.	60 days' notice with no interest in notice period (except at 5-year anniversaries). Alternatively, immediate withdrawal with 90 days loss of interest.
Tax treatment	Interest is paid gross but liable to tax and must be declared.	Interest paid gross but liable to tax and must be declared.

Growth schemes

2.6

Feature	Fixed rate savings bonds	Capital bonds
General description	Offer fixed rates of interest for periods of 6, 12, 18 or 36 months.	These are five year term investments with a rising rate of interest.
Return	Interest rates range from 5.85% to 6.65% depending upon term chosen and amount invested. The interest is rolled up. A monthly income option is available at lower rates.	A guaranteed rate of interest is paid on encashment. As at April 2000 the guaranteed rate was 6.15%%.
Contribution limits	£500 - £1,000,000 sole or joint	£100 - £250,000 per person.
Access and penalties	The NS guide says "allow a few days". No penalty for repayment at full term. Otherwise 90-day penalty. Repayment by BACS.	No interest is paid if capital is withdrawn in the first year, thereafter capital can be withdrawn on 8 working days' notice.
Tax treatment	Taxed at source at 20%. Non taxpayers and 10% taxpayers can reclaim tax.	Interest paid gross but liable to tax, it must be declared

National Savings certificates

2.7

Feature	Fixed rate issues	Index linked certificate issues
General description	Guaranteed rate of interest rolled up at the end of a term. There are five year and two year fixed rate bonds	Guaranteed rate of return based on inflation at the end of a term. There are five year and two year index-linked bonds
Returns	A guaranteed rate of interest 4.50% for 5 year bond and 4.75% for 2 year bond (April 2000) paid on encashment at end of term.	A guaranteed rate 2% pa compound plus inflation for five year issue and 3.15% pa compound plus inflation for two year issue paid on encashment.
Contribution limits	£100 - £10,000 per person plus no upper limit if reinvesting maturing certificates.	£100 - £10,000 per person plus no upper limit if reinvesting maturing certificates.
Access and penalties	Access on 8 working days' notice. No interest is given if the bond is encashed in the first year except reinvested certificates.	Access on 8 working days' notice. No interest or inflation proofing is paid if encashed in first year unless the certificate is a reinvestment.
Tax treatment	Interest is tax free.	Interest is tax free

Children's bonus bond

2.8 This is a savings certificate for a child with a **high rate of guaranteed interest**. It has a five year term.

    (a) **Return**

        (i)   A guaranteed rate is paid on encashment at the end of five years.

        (ii)   Interest rate available in April 2000 was 5.65% per annum.

    (b) **Contribution limits**. £25 - £1,000 for a child under 16 when bond effected.

    (c) **Access and penalties**. No interest if encashed in first year, otherwise 3.5% if repaid before 5th anniversary.

    (d) **Tax treatment**. Tax-free.

Yearly bond

2.9 This was withdrawn from 31 January 1995. It was a **one year monthly savings** plan with interest tax free so long as it was held for a total of five years.

Premium bonds

2.10 **Return**. A prize draw is held once a month. The prize could be from £50 to £1 million, from a prize fund each month.

    Contribution limits. £100 - £20,000 per person.

    Access and penalties. Withdrawal on 8 working days' notice.

    Tax treatment. Winnings are tax-free.

Question 1

(a) List the main differences between the National Savings income bond and the pensioners guaranteed income bond.

(b) In order to help you remember some of the key features of the National Savings products draw yourself up a schedule along the lines shown below.

Investment type	Term					Interest		
	None	1 yr	2 yrs	5 yrs	Other	Tax free	Gross	Net
Ordinary account								
Investment account								
Income bond								
Pensioners bond								
Capital bond								
Fixed rate bond								
Fixed rate certificate								
Index linked certificate								
Children's bond								
Premium bond								

Question 2

Before leaving the deposit type schemes, re-read the section and answer the following questions.

(a) Which type of account or scheme would appeal to someone wanting tax free growth?
(b) Which type of scheme would appeal to someone wanting a regular monthly income?
(c) Which schemes pay gross interest without the need to fill out a form R85?

3 GILTS

> **KEY TERM**
>
> A **gilt** is a government bond. This means that the investor is lending money to the government.

3.1 The government needs the money raised from gilts to help to cover its **spending deficit** which is not recouped from taxation.

3.2 The government promises to pay a **fixed rate of interest,** called the **coupon**, and to repay the capital at set times or redemption dates, for example:

(a) **Treasury 9% 2008**: the redemption date is 2008 and 9% interest is paid on every £100 of stock purchased;

(b) **Treasury 12½% 2003-5:** the redemption date will be somewhere between the two dates. The government can decide when to repay subject to the latest date and giving notice of repayment.

3.3 A gilt is a **low risk investment** if held to redemption because the investor knows that for every £100 nominal value of stock purchased £100 will be repaid by the government on the redemption date. The coupon will also always be paid.

3.4 Investors can choose their term to lend money to the government by selecting a **redemption date to suit their needs**. The redemption dates fall into three categories.

(a) **Shorts**: redeemed within 5 years
(b) **Mediums**: redeemed between 5 and 15 years
(c) **Longs**: redeemed at dates over 15 years

3.5 There are also **undated** or **irredeemable stock** available which simply pays a guaranteed rate of interest per £100 of stock purchased with no guarantee of repayment of stock. The government reserves the right to repay when ready, if ever!

Although the rates of interest look low, this is not necessarily so. Let us look at an example, say Treasury 2.5%. At a purchase price of £50.45 per £100 of stock (ignoring the spread between buying and selling prices, and commission costs), the amount which will be purchased for £10,000 is £19,821 of stock. Now work out the income receivable - £495.54 pa. This is not a bad buy, particularly for a non taxpayer, say an elderly person, wanting a high level of income. This is equivalent to 4.95% for as long as the stock is held.

3.6 The other type of government security is an **index-linked gilt**. In this instance, the interest rate and redemption value are linked to inflation.

3.7 The investor buying in the market is unlikely to pay £100 for £100 stock. As you will see from the extract from the *Financial Times* (Tuesday 11 April 2000) below, some stocks cost more than £100 and some are priced at less.

UK GILTS - cash market

Stock	Notes	Yield Int	Yield Red	Price £	+ or –	52 week High	52 week Low
Shorts" (Lives up to Five Years)							
Cn 9pc '00		9.00	–	100.00	....	103.43	100.00
Tr 13pc '00		12.78	6.01	101.74	–.01	109.54	101.74
Tr 8pc '00		7.91	6.23	101.11	....	104.74	101.08
Tr Fltg Rate '01		–	0.11	99.98xd	....	100.74	99.95
Tr 10pc '01		9.70	6.30	103.09	–.01	108.82	103.08
Cn 9½pc '01	✠	9.15	6.30	103.78	–.01	109.50	103.73
Cn 9¾pc '01	✠	9.35	6.30	104.33	–.01	110.39	104.27
Tr 7pc '01		6.93	6.32	101.00	–.02	105.03	100.05
Cn 10pc '02	✠	9.37	6.34	106.77xd	–.03	113.97	106.56
Tr 7pc '02		6.90	6.28	101.43	–.03	106.33	100.82
Cn 9½pc '02	✠	8.94	6.35	106.30	–.04	113.27	106.03
Tr 9¾pc '02		9.08	6.34	107.40	–.04	114.87	107.09
Ex 9pc '02	✠	8.47	6.35	106.27	–.05	113.33	105.74
Cn 9¾pc '03	✠	8.92	6.35	109.36	–.05	117.71	108.78
Tr 8pc '03		7.61	6.18	105.16	–.07	112.14	104.13
Tr 10pc '03		8.97	6.21	111.48	–.09	120.39	110.57
Tr 13¾pc '00–3	✠	13.46	6.00	102.16	–.01	110.72	102.16
Tr 6½pc '03		6.42	6.09	101.31	–.09	107.68	99.86
Tr 11½pc '01–4		10.99	6.29	104.66	–.02	111.71	104.66
Tr10pc '04	✠	8.81	6.21	113.54	–.11	123.30	112.33
Tr 5pc '04		5.18	5.94	96.57	–.11	98.80	94.53
Fnd 3½pc '99–4		3.82	5.73	91.68	–.10	95.40	89.41
Cn 9½pc '04	✠	8.32	5.88	114.23xd	+.11	123.19	112.17
Tr 6¾pc '04		6.52	5.88	103.47	–.13	110.43	101.32
Five to Ten Years							
Cn 9½pc '05		8.22	5.89	115.51xd	–.15	124.89	113.23
Ex10½pc '05	✠	8.66	5.89	121.20	–.17	131.91	118.78
Tr 12½pc '03–5	✠	10.41	6.21	120.06	–.11	131.56	119.37
Tr 8½pc '05		7.54	5.81	112.79	–.19	121.83	110.08
Cn 9¾pc '06	✠	7.98	5.67	122.20	–.22	132.09	118.84
Tr 7¾pc '06		7.01	5.76	110.56	–.17	118.93	107.25
Tr 8pc '02–6		7.73	6.47	103.46	–.05	109.57	102.84
Tr 7½pc '06		6.83	5.72	109.74	–.19	118.08	106.40
Tr 11¾pc '03–7	✠	10.35	6.34	113.56	–.05	123.41	113.29
Tr 8½pc '07		7.29	5.67	116.67	–.23	125.90	112.94
Tr 7¼pc '07		6.58	5.60	110.14	–.22	118.57	106.17
Tr 13½pc '04–8	✠	10.67	5.88	126.55	–.14	138.62	125.47
Tr 9pc '08		7.30	5.53	123.27xd	–.24	133.87	118.77
Tr 8pc '09	✠	6.64	5.23	120.49	+.94	128.33	114.68
Tr 5¾pc '09		5.52	5.20	104.12	–.28	110.89	99.10
Ten to Fifteen Years							
Tr 6¼pc '10		5.75	5.19	108.61	–.31	115.43	103.35
Cn 9pc Ln '11		6.83	5.23	131.79	–.37	140.80	126.26
Tr 9pc '12		6.70	5.18	134.42xd	–.39	143.17	128.45
Tr 5½pc '08–12		5.47	5.43	100.48	–.25	108.71	95.68
Tr 8pc '13		6.24	5.08	128.18	–.38	135.51	122.43
Tr 7¾pc '12–15		6.40	5.32	121.05	–.39	129.41	115.84
Over Fifteen Years							
Tr 8pc '15		5.97	4.87	134.03	–.46	139.80	127.70
Tr 8¾pc '17		5.96	4.76	146.75	–.51	152.40	139.82
Ex 12pc '13–17	✠	7.25	5.23	165.57	–.23	178.18	157.92
Tr 8pc '21		5.52	4.64	144.89	–.50	151.64	137.64
Tr 6pc '28		4.80	4.45	124.90	–.51	132.62	116.63
Undated							
Cons 4pc	✠	4.94	–	80.90	–.46	86.94	73.95
War Ln 3½pc		4.77	–	73.40	–.40	78.83	67.14
Cn 3½pc '61 Aft.	✠	4.10	–	85.40	–.40	90.83	79.14
Tr 3pc '66 Aft.	✠	5.29	–	56.67	–.26	60.59	51.78
Cons 2½pc	✠	4.84	–	51.62	–.25	55.55	46.78
Tr 2½pc		4.90	–	51.06	–.28	54.87	46.70

Index–Linked	Notes (b)	Yield (1)	Yield (2)	Price £	+ or –	52 week High	52 week Low
2½pc '01	(78.3)	3.13	3.86	206.55	+.08	206.55	201.90
2½pc '03	(78.8)	3.34	3.68	202.20	+.15	206.01	200.50
4⅜pc '04	(135.6)	2.74	2.99	128.68xd	+.14	134.12	127.26
2pc '06	(69.5)	2.30	2.47	230.94	+.50	238.67	229.47
2½pc '09	(78.8)	1.95	2.07	216.79	+.36	220.21	208.87
2½pc '11	(74.6)	1.97	2.07	230.69	+.42	234.02	219.11
2½pc '13	(89.2)	1.91	2.00	195.71	+.33	197.50	183.57
2½pc '16	(81.6)	1.86	1.93	217.78	+.38	220.12	203.03
2½pc '20	(83.0)	1.77	1.84	220.81xd	+.30	224.25	203.17
2½pc '24	(97.7)	1.64	1.69	195.93	+.35	199.43	176.32
4⅛pc '30	(135.1)	1.55	1.60	195.67	+.41	199.61	174.35

Prospective real redemption rate on projected inflation of (1) 5% and (2) 3%. (b) Figures in parentheses show RPI base for indexing (ie 8 months prior to issue) and have been adjusted to reflect rebasing of RPI to 100 in February 1987. Conversion factor 3.945. RPI for July 1999: 165.1 and for February 2000: 167.5.

Other Fixed Interest

Stock	Notes	Yield Int	Yield Red	Price £	+ or –	52 week High	52 week Low
Asian Dev 10¼pc 2009		8.01	6.10	128	....	137$\frac{27}{32}$	123
B'ham 11½pc 2012		7.81	6.00	147¼	....	155½	140¾
Leeds 13½pc 2006		9.93	6.50	136	....	147	132¾
Liverpool 3½pc Irred.		5.09	5.10	68¾	....	73	55
LCC 3pc '20 Aft.		5.04	5.00	59½	....	64	50
Manchester 11½pc 2007		8.73	6.10	131¾xd	....	140½	127
Met. Wtr. 3pc 'B'		3.33	6.70	90	....	92½	85
N'wide Anglia 3⅞pc IL 2021		–	3.00	194	....	200½	174$\frac{31}{32}$
4¼pc IL 2024		–	2.95	189	....	196¾	169

● Source: Debt Management Office (DMO). All UK Gilts are tax-free to non-residents on application. xd Ex dividend. Closing mid-prices are shown in pounds per £100 nominal of stock. Int yield: Interest yield. Red yield: Redemption yield. Prospective real Index-Linked redemption yields are calculated by HSBC Greenwell from GEMMA closing prices.

3.8 The price of the stock on the market **varies according to demand**, which in turn is influenced by changes in interest rates, for example a rise in interest rates will mean a fall in gilt prices. Similarly a fall in the value of the UK currency, sterling, can mean a fall in gilt prices.

3.9 **Long-term gilts** are not affected so directly by rises or falls in interest rates, the influences on long-dated gilts are less tangible. It is the markets' feeling regarding long term inflation and political problems within the government. Thus, if the market feels that the government shows signs of containing inflation for some time to come, the value of long-term gilts will rise. If however there are reports of rifts in the Cabinet and low opinion polls, the price of long-term gilts may fall.

3.10 Although in this section we have referred to the UK Government's borrowing requirement through gilts, **other governments and international companies** need to raise capital through bonds and there is an enormous **Eurobond market**.

Question 3

Before proceeding, make sure you understand the concept of how much stock (nominal value) you purchase per £100 invested. Work the following examples.

(a) Exchequer 9% 2002 price £112 - stock purchased £.............

(b) Treasury $8\frac{1}{2}$% 2007 price £123- stock purchased £ ....

The providers

3.11 The government initially releases the stock for sale via the **Debt Management Office** (see **buying and selling mechanisms** below). Once on the market the stock can be bought and sold via a stockbroker or the Post Office.

Buying and selling mechanisms

3.12 When the government issues gilts it does so via the Debt Management Office (DMO) taking advice from **The Bank of England**. The DMO then sells on the stock to the dealers. Not necessarily all the stock is passed on to the market at the same time, so the DMO is able to control the market. This method of passing the gilts into the market is called the **tap**.

3.13 If it is a **very large new issue**, say £1bn, the DMO will organise a tender. In this case, mainly institutions will tender for the stock which is then released to them. The highest bidder receives stock first and it is distributed down until a minimum price is reached.

3.14 The DMO has organised **auctions**, similar to the tender, but in this case investors receive the stock at the price they bid and there is no minimum price.

3.15 If the investor buys via a **stockbroker** the charges are higher but the stock can be purchased or sold at an immediate and known price. The **Post Office** is a cheaper option but there is a delay in purchase or sale and the investor does not know the price at which he is dealing.

Income and capital growth prospects

3.16 The investor has a **guaranteed income and return of capital** from his stock. When he buys the stock he can calculate how much income he will receive and also his capital return. As we have seen from looking at the gilts available, the investor knows exactly how much income he will receive, eg Treasury 8.5% 2007 will pay 8.5% per £100 of stock. The 8.5% is known as the **coupon**.

3.17 However if the stock is currently priced at £123 for £100 of stock, this means that if you invest £100 you will buy £81.30 of stock and the income per annum will be £6.91 (6.9%). This is the interest yield or current yield or running yield (see yield column in the FT extract, noting that for simplicity we have rounded the price of the stock to the nearest pound). Similarly if you buy Exchequer $10^1/_2$% 2005 at 135 the current yield will be:

$$\frac{100}{\text{Current price}} \times \text{coupon} = \frac{100}{135} \times 10.5 = 7.78\%$$

Remember that the yield that is payable on the stock when you buy it remains until redemption. However the current or running yield would alter if the investor bought the stock a few days later at a different price.

3.18 The investor also knows exactly how much **capital** he will have returned if he holds the gilt until redemption. To this extent there is no risk, the loss or gain is quantified at outset.

3.19 It must be remembered that the stock is **traded** in the market and its value will move up and down, so it may be that at some time before 2007 the Treasury $8\frac{1}{2}$% stock may become more attractive to investors and the price will rise. The investor could then sell into the market without waiting for the redemption date and make a profit rather than waiting for redemption and making a loss.

3.20 We have looked at the income and capital gains situation, however there is a third situation to be considered. An investor who buys a low coupon gilt will expect to receive an income and make a capital gain if he holds the gilt until maturity. Others, as we have seen, will expect to receive a high income but suffer a capital loss They may wish to calculate their **overall return**, or yield from the investment. This is called the **yield to redemption** and again can be seen in our extract from the *Financial Times*. The calculation is a complex one making use of compound interest. As an example, an investor buying Exchequer $10\frac{1}{2}\%$ 2005 at 121 will suffer a capital loss of £21 for each £100 nominal value of the guilt at redemption. The market value of the gilt will therefore fall as the redemption date gets closer.

Risk and accessibility

3.21 As we have seen the investor can calculate in advance the income and capital gain or loss expected at maturity so this is a **low risk investment**.

3.22 **Access** is possible at any time because the stock can be sold through a stockbroker or the Post Office. However it must be pointed out that if it is sold on the market rather than being retained until redemption there is a risk element that the capital return may be less than expected.

3.23 The income from a gilt is paid half yearly. The **interest is paid gross**, with two exceptions. Existing gilt holders who receive interest net will not be affected unless they choose to switch to the gross payment method. Other gilt holders will be able to request that their interest is paid net.

3.24 There is **no capital gains tax** to be paid on any gain on a gilt held and then sold or redeemed by an individual. However there is no relief for any losses incurred.

Charges

3.25 If the stock is purchased via a stockbroker, **commissions** will be deducted. If the gilt is bought via the Post Office, the commissions are lower.

Question 4

Before moving on, make sure you know and understand the definitions of the following expressions in connection with gilts.

Yield to redemption	Coupon
Current yield	Tap
Shorts	Irredeemable stock

---

4 SHARES

What is a share?

4.1 When an investor buys a share in Marks and Spencer plc that is exactly what he has done; he has bought a share in the ownership of the company. He has a **right to vote** on major decisions of the company and to take a share in its profits. However the investor must take the good with the bad and he may have bought a share in a company where there will be no profits and in fact it may go into liquidation and he will probably then lose his investment.

4.2 It is useful to understand why **some companies are quoted on the stock market and some not**. If you look at Yellow Pages for your area at any trade, you will see a large number of

companies listed. These are private companies, owned by a family or one or two directors. These companies are, of course, not quoted on the stockmarket.

The issue of shares

4.3　If one of these small companies was very successful, it would initially expand by borrowing money from the banks but after a while, the directors may want to expand still further or increase their own wealth by selling some of their shares. While the company is **in private hands,** the value of these shares will be difficult to agree and the market for their sale will be small.

4.4　For these two reasons, **raising capital** and **releasing their equity in the business,** the directors may decide to float their company on the stockmarket and they can do this through a new issue. Normally the directors will continue to hold the majority of the shares. To obtain a full listing the company must normally offer at least 25% of the shares for public subscription.

4.5　Before the **listing** is obtained, the company must ensure that it is acceptable to the Stock Exchange. They will have to hire professional help to achieve this such as accountants, solicitors, a merchant bank and a stockbroker.

4.6　The Stock Exchange will require **extensive financial disclosure** of the company's affairs and the company must have a three year track record.

4.7　A **new issue of shares** can be dealt with in a number of ways. The most common methods by which a company issues shares and obtains a stock market listing for the fist time are:

(a)　**Offer for sale or offer for subscription**. In this case a fixed number of shares is offered to the public at a fixed price. If more people apply for the shares than the number available, there is either a pro-rata allocation of shares or a ballot.

(b)　A **placing**. This is often used for the sale of a small issue of new shares. In this instance the shares are not sold directly to the public. The company's merchant bankers agree a price and sell the shares to a number of institutions at this price. The institutions may hold the shares or sell some, or all, into the market.

(c)　**An offer for sale by tender**. Members of the public tender for shares, naming the price they are prepared to pay. When all the tenders are in, the merchant bank will agree a price at a sufficient level to sell all the shares. All tenders at that level or above will receive an allocation.

4.8　So far we have discussed how new companies raise capital by issuing shares to the general public for the first time. However, a company which is already listed may wish to raise more capital for expansion or possibly to reduce its bank borrowings. In this case the company will issue a **rights issue**. The shares are first offered to existing shareholders and the balance usually underwritten with a number of institutions.

4.9　You may also come across the term **scrip issue**. This is not an issue of shares to raise more capital. It simply gives the shareholder more shares without raising any new money, eg a 1 for 4 scrip issue, shareholders will receive one new share for every four they already hold. The company is simply converting its reserves into share capital. The market price of the shares will obviously fall because there are more shares but it makes them more marketable. A **scrip dividend** occurs when an investor is offered additional shares rather than taking a dividend in cash. It is in effect a way of the company retaining more capital.

4.10 Once quoted shares have been issued they can be bought or sold on the stockmarket. Obviously the price for the shares will **rise or fall with demand**. Clients will normally buy or sell their shares through a stockbroker.

4.11 The **London Stock Exchange** groups UK companies into 40 sectors. These are aggregated to produce the FT All Share Index. This index contains the largest number of shares, but not all shares. There is a smaller grouping, the FTSE 100, which is the 100 largest companies on the market (known as **blue chip companies**). Stock market indices can monitor market performance on a minute by minute basis by computers.

The London Stock Exchange includes the 'main market' which lists larger more established companies and the second-tier **Alternative Investment Market (AIM)** which lists the smaller, younger companies.

Types of share

4.12

Type of share	Features
Ordinary shares	The shareholder is entitled: (a) to a share of profit distributed as a dividend (b) the right to vote on matters affecting the company (c) in the event of a winding up, to a share of assets, but note that shareholders do not take precedence over the creditors
Preference shares	(a) These shareholders are placed ahead of the ordinary shareholders for dividend payments and in the event of a liquidation. (b) The dividend is usually a guaranteed amount but if the distribution to the ordinary shareholders is higher, the preference shareholders do not receive the increased amount.
Convertible preference shares	The dividend paid on these is usually less than the non-convertible preference share but there is the option to convert to ordinary shares in the future at pre-set dates and at pre-set prices.
Partly paid shares	In this instance shares are paid for in instalments. This was a feature of some privatisations. The outstanding instalment must be paid if the company goes into liquidation. (This is known as an **unpaid call**)
An unquoted share	This is a share in a private company which is not listed on the stockmarket. Marketability of these shares will be a problem.

Income and capital growth prospects

4.13 Shares give the investor the chance of increasing income and capital growth but there is **no guarantee** of either, and so it is a **high risk investment**.

4.14 The income that investors receive from a share is known as a **dividend**. Companies declare an interim dividend after six months trading and a final dividend after the end of their financial year. The amount of the dividend depends on their financial success during the year. The company will not distribute all its profit as dividend; some will be ploughed back into the business for future growth. If a large amount is retained, this is a good sign because it means that the dividend; is well covered. On the other hand if the company dips into reserves to maintain a dividend then this is referred to as an 'uncovered dividend'.

4.15 The investor's **dividend yield** on the share will depend on the dividend paid and also the price paid for the share, eg:

Dividend 20p, price 500p, yield $\dfrac{20}{500} \times 100 = 4\%$

However if Mr B had bought the same share for 400p his yield would be:

$\dfrac{20}{400} \times 100 = 5\%$

Please note that **as prices rise, yields fall**. Now calculate for yourself the dividend yield if the price of the share rose to 600p.

4.16 The investor will hope that the **dividends will increase each year** but there is no guarantee of this.

4.17 Investors are also hoping for **growth on the capital value of their shares**. In selecting a share, they normally take into account three measurements.

(a) Dividend yield
(b) Price/ earnings ratio
(c) Net asset value

4.18 The **price/earnings ratio** gives an indication of how high the price of the share is, compared to its current earnings, eg if the earnings are 30p per share and the current price is 400p then the P/E ratio is 400/30 = 13.33. If the share price reduces, so too does the P/E ratio. So, if the price falls to 200 the P/E ratio is 6.66. As share prices rise so too does the P/E ratio. So, a high P/E ratio is indicative that earnings are expected to rise or recover.

Risk and accessibility

4.19 The amount of risk which the investor takes depends upon the **type of company** into which he invests. If he buys shares in blue chip companies, such as British Telecom or Shell, the risk should be modest and the shares should be easy to dispose of in the market.

4.20 However if the investor selects **a smaller company or a company** which has been through a poor trading period (a **recovery stock**) then the risk is greater. Not only will the prices of these shares be more volatile, but there is also the chance that when the investor wishes to sell he cannot find anyone interested in buying and the price will reduce still further.

Tax treatment

4.21 With effect from 6 April 1999, dividends are received with a tax credit of 10%. Non-taxpayers cannot reclaim the tax. Lower rate and basic rate taxpayers will have no further liability. Higher rate taxpayers will be liable to a further 22.5% on the grossed up dividend. For example, suppose that a company pays a dividend of 9p per share. This is the net dividend, and the gross dividend will be 10p. Tax of 10% (1p) is deducted at source, and the shareholder receives a tax credit of 1p. Higher rate taxpayers will be liable to pay a further 22.5% (2.25p) in tax.

4.22 Any **capital gains on a share** may be subject to capital gains tax if the gain exceeds the annual exemption after allowing for indexation and tapering relief, if applicable.

Buying and selling mechanisms and charges

4.23 Shares will be bought and sold through a **stockbroker** who will have a set level of charges.

Question 5

(a) If possible buy or obtain a newspaper with share prices, such as the *Financial Times*. Open up at the financial pages and look at the listings of shares. See how they fall into categories and how they are priced.

(b) Ensure that you can calculate:

    (i) a dividend yield on a share priced at 250p with a dividend of 15p;
    (ii) a P/E ratio - price of share 200p; earnings 40p per share.

(c) Ensure that you know the meaning of:

    A placing
    Rights issue
    An unpaid call
    An unquoted share

KEY TERM

An **option** is the right to buy or sell a share in the future at a fixed price for which a premium is paid.

(a) A **call option** is the right to buy.
(b) A **put option** is the right to sell.
(c) The option market is for the experienced or professional investor.

---

5 CORPORATE BONDS

5.1

KEY TERM

Corporate bonds are interest-earning securities issued by corporations in order to raise short, medium or long term finance. The interest rate is normally **fixed**, (but in some cases is variable, related to the London Interbank Offered Rate or LIBOR). A bond has a known maturity value, payable at redemption.

Bonds are normally redeemed at par; ie bonds with £100 nominal value will be redeemed at maturity for £100. The market value of a bond before redemption will vary inversely with interest rates, consequently the owner of a bond will benefit from a capital gain if market interest rates fall, or will suffer a capital loss if market interest rates rise.

5.2 Corporate bonds are subject to the provisions of the Financial Services Act, therefore advisors must be authorised to advise on and arrange deals in these securities.

5.3 Corporate bonds often pay a higher yield than government bonds. This is because bonds issued by corporations are usually riskier than those issued by governments. Corporations

have limited resources from which to pay interest on their debt. Governments can always increase taxation to meet their liabilities.

5.4 Corporate bonds issued in the UK are also known as **debentures** or **loan stock**. Corporate bonds issued in the international bond markets are called eurobonds.

Features of corporate bonds

5.5 Corporate bonds have the following features.

(a) Companies need to borrow money. Sometimes this money is borrowed from banks in the form of loans. An alternative is to borrow from investors by issuing corporate bonds.

(b) A debenture is usually established under trust. Trustees are responsible for the operation of the debenture. In particular the trust deed protects the position of the lender in the event of the company winding up and limits the other debt the company can issue. Eurobonds are not established under trust, but protection is provided for bondholders in the form of covenants associated with the bond issue.

(c) The company issuing the loan will have to pay interest from pretax profits and also find the money to make the capital repayment on redemption. There is a risk that they will not be able to do this. Credit rating agencies such as Standard and Poor's and Moody's rate Government and corporate bond issues. Government bonds are generally given a high rating, AAA or AA. Corporate bond credit ratings range from AAA to D. Anything below BBB is considered speculative.

(d) The position of the bondholders in the event of the winding up of a company will depend upon whether the bonds are secured or unsecured. They may be secured on a fixed asset such as a property or by floating charge over the company's assets. Security on a fixed asset provides greater security.

Types of corporate bonds

5.6 There are a number of different types of loan stock.

(a) Secured loan stock (debentures)

(b) Unsecured loan stock. This is the least protected loan security in the event of default. In the event of such a default the holders only rank with other unsecured creditors (such as suppliers).

(c) A convertible loan stock offers the investor a fixed interest rate (usually lower than a straight fixed interest security) plus the option to convert into a quantity of the company's ordinary shares at a later date on a pre-stated formula. Its other features are as follows.

(i) It is almost always an unsecured loan stock.

(ii) It pays a fixed rate of interest until it is converted and on conversion it becomes a quantity of ordinary shares, in the company, ranking equally with all the other ordinary shares.

(iii) The attraction of this type of stock is that it offers the benefits of a fixed interest security. The interest must be paid to the loan stock holders before any dividend payment is made to the shareholders. In addition, it also carries the option of switching into ordinary shares if the company's results are good.

Prices and methods of buying and selling corporate bonds

5.7 *Prices.* The initial interest rate offered must be attractive to investors. After issue, bonds can be traded on the market and the price of the bond will vary according to interest rates, in the same way as gilts.

For example, if the debenture offers a coupon interest rate of 8% and market interest rates rise from, say, 8% to 10%, the price of the bond will have to fall to compensate fact that the bond will pay less interest (8%) than is currently available in the market (10%).

5.8 The credit rating of the company can affect the price. If the credit rating of the company falls bond holders will have greater concerns that the company will not be able to pay the interest on the loan or repay the capital at redemption. The price of the bond will therefore fall.

5.9 Corporate bonds are negotiable stock and can be purchased and sold via a stockbroker.

Risk

5.10 An investor in a fixed rate corporate bond takes the risk that market interest rates will rise while he is locked into the bond's fixed interest payment. He can then sell it on the market, but the bond's price will have fallen as its yield has become less attractive.

5.11 The investor may be concerned that the profits of the company will be insufficient to pay the interest and repay the debt at maturity. There is a higher risk of non-payment than with a government security. Investors will therefore expect to receive a higher return from corporate bonds in compensation. Large companies which are financially secure should not need to offer an interest rate much above the rate on government bonds (gilts). Smaller companies will have to offer very attractive rates to persuade investors to take the risk.

5.12 Another consideration is that although an investor may be happy to lend to the government over a period of, say, 25 years, he will only be happy with a shorter term loan to a company.

Uses

5.13 A corporate bond will be useful for a client wanting a higher income than may be achieved from a gilt. He must be made aware of the higher risk he is taking.

5.14 Convertible loan stock is useful for the client who is fearful of the equity market yet feels he needs some exposure to equities. In this way he has a secure income and if the company shares perform well he has the right to convert the bonds into equity.

5.15 As convertible loan stocks are complicated investments the less sophisticated client will be best advised to enter the market via a pooled investment such as a unit trust.

5.16 A zero coupon bond will be useful for a client who does not need income but requires capital in the future and does not wish to take undue risk to obtain this capital growth. The capital may be required for school or university fees. (A zero coupon bond is a bond that pays no interest, and at maturity is redeemed at par. Zero coupon bonds are always purchased for a price below par, ie at a discount to par. The interest earned by the investor is reflected in the size of the discount.)

Taxation

5.17 The interest income on corporate bonds is subject to 20% tax at source. Non taxpayers can reclaim this tax. Lower rate taxpayers can reclaim 10% tax. Basic rate taxpayers are deemed to have satisfied their income tax liabilities. Higher rate taxpayers are subject to a further 20% tax on their gross income.

5.18 If the bond is deemed to be a qualifying corporate bond, then it is an exempt asset for capital gains tax purposes. A qualifying corporate bond is a security which, amongst other things:

(a) represents a 'normal commercial loan'

(b) is expressed in sterling

(c) was acquired by the person now disposing of it after 13 March 1984

(d) does not have a redemption value dependent upon a published index of share prices in a stock exchange.

6 EMPLOYEE SHARE OPTION SCHEMES

6.1 An employer can set up a scheme, under which employees can choose to make regular monthly investments in special bank or building society accounts called sharesave accounts. (They used to be called SAYE or save as you earn accounts.) The maximum monthly investment is £250, and if a minimum is set it cannot be more than £5. The investments are made for three or five years, and a tax-free bonus is then added to the account by way of interest. The employee may either withdraw the money or leave it for another two years. If he leaves it in the account, another tax-free bonus is added.

6.2 At the withdrawal date, the employee may take the money in cash. Alternatively, he may use it to buy ordinary shares in his employer company or its holding company. The price of these shares is fixed when the employee starts to save in the account, by the granting to the employee of options to buy shares. The option price must be at least 80% of the market value at the date the options are granted.

6.3 The only tax charge is to capital gains tax, on the gain on the shares when they are finally sold. This gain is computed as if the employee bought the shares for the price he actually paid for them.

6.4 A scheme must be open to all employees and full-time directors, and on similar terms. Part-time directors may be included, but can be excluded. However, a minimum qualifying period of employment (of up to five years) may be imposed, and there may be differences based on remuneration or length of service.

6.5 Anyone who has within the preceding 12 months held over 25% of the shares of a close company which is the company whose shares may be acquired under the scheme, or which controls that company either alone or as part of a consortium, must be excluded from the scheme.

7 INVESTMENT TRUSTS

> **KEY TERM**
>
> **Investment trusts** are companies quoted on the London Stock Exchange whose business is investing in other companies' shares.
>
> An investment trust is the oldest type of **pooled investment**. The first investment trust was established in 1868.

7.1 The investment trust has a **fixed issued share capital** and the shares must be sold in the market so, if there is no demand, then the shares cannot be sold.

7.2 The schemes are known as **closed end funds**.

7.3 The investment trust shareholders have the **same rights as all shareholders**.

    (a) The right to a dividend if paid.
    (b) The right to vote on material matters affecting the trust.
    (c) The right to a share of the assets on a winding up.

7.4 Sometimes the shares of an investment trust sell at a **discount to net asset value**. What this means is that the assets less the liabilities of the trust divided by the number of shares on issue is greater than the current price of the share on the market. Similarly the shares can from time to time sell at a premium to net asset value (NAV).

7.5 The investment company, like all companies, has a **facility to borrow money**. In this instance the company is borrowing money to buy more shares and increase the value of the trust. If the borrowings are high, relative to its total capital value the company is said to be **heavily geared**. In a rising stock market a trust which is highly geared can perform well but in a falling market the effect of interest to be paid on the borrowings may be onerous. Investment trusts can be **geared to produce income or growth**.

7.6 Investment trusts invest in shares **in all parts of the world**. They can specialise in European shares, or Far Eastern, emerging markets, Indian or Chinese or the traditional UK market. The choice of funds is as wide, if not wider than for unit trusts.

Income and capital growth prospects

7.7 Investment trusts offer a strange animal, the **split level trust**, in which different types of share are issued: an income share which offers an entitlement to all the net income on the entire trust and a capital, or zero preference share, which offers the capital appreciation on the whole of the fund on winding up. This type of investment trust will have a limited life. As the fund is equity based there is a risk particularly on the value of income shares on redemption.

Risk and accessibility

7.8 The **level of risk** will depend on the underlying investment of the trust. If the investment is blue chip UK companies, the risk will be medium; if the trust is investing in the Indian sub-continent the risk will be greater.

7.9 **Accessibility** is similar to any share. If there is demand, the share can be sold. The greater the demand, the higher the price.

Tax treatment

The trust

7.10 The **trust** is taxed as follows.

(a) The trust itself pays **no capital gains tax**.

(b) **Prior to April 1999** the trust received franked income from dividends from UK shares and unfranked income from overseas securities, cash and fixed interest securities. Franked income ceased with the abolition of Advance Corporation Tax (ACT) in 1999. Dividends are now received with a **10% tax credit** and the trust has no further liability.

(c) Income from overseas securities, cash and fixed interest securities may be liable to **corporation tax**.

The investor

7.11 The **investor is taxed as for any other share**.

(a) With effect from April 1999 dividends are received with a tax credit of 10%. Non-taxpayers cannot reclaim the tax. Basic rate taxpayers will have no further liability. Higher rate taxpayers are liable to a further 22.5% on the grossed up dividend.

(b) Any **capital gains** on a share may be subject to capital gains tax if they exceed the annual exemption after allowing for indexation and tapering relief, if applicable.

Buying and selling mechanisms

7.12 Investment trusts can be purchased via a **stockbroker**. The trusts themselves also offer a dealing service for the private investor.

Charges

7.13 The **bid/offer spread** is around 5%, the **management charge** between 0.3% and 0.5% per annum. The overall charges of an investment trust are cheaper than a unit trust. Traditionally the directors have not paid commission to advisers, but this is now changing.

Question 6

List the main features of an investment trust.

Later in the course, you will need to refer back to these features to compare them with the features of a unit trust.

Study the extract from the *Financial Times* below, in particular the columns headed price, NAV and discount or premium and ensure that you understand the principle of discounts.

INVESTMENT COMPANIES

	Notes	Price	+ or -	52 week high	low	Yield	NAV	Dis or Pm(-)
Approved by the Inland Revenue								
3i	♣†	700½	+17½	718	450	1.5	676.4	-3.6
3i Smllr Quoted Cos	†	188	....	216	118	2.2	224.8	16.4
AIM Distribution		80	....	98	75	4.5	-	-
AIM Trust	♣	94	-1	97½	65½	1.0	124.0	24.2
AIM VCT		100	....	100	95	-	-	-
Aberdeen Asian Smlr	♣	63¾	....	65	25	0.2	82.9	23.1
Warrants		26¾	-¼	27	6	-	-	-
Aberdeen Convertible	♣s	109¼	....	133¾	94½	5.9	-	-
Aberdeen Emg Asia	♣	23½#	....	*28½	13½	-	-	-
Aberdeen Emrg Ecos	♣	57½	+½	63¼	26	-	71.4	19.5
Warrants		17¾	+¼	18	4½	-	-	-
Aberdeen European	Z	125#	....	155¾	92	0.8	-	-
Warrants		33#	....	67	27	-	-	-
Aberdeen High Inc	♣†s	122½xd	+½	137½	95½	6.5	121.0	-1.2
Aberdeen Latin Amer	♣	56¾	-¼	77	27¼	-	72.4	21.6
Warrants		18¾	-¼	25	5	-	-	-
Aberdeen New Dawn	♣	151	....	151¾	61½	1.1	174.6	13.5
Warrants		72½	+½	74½	8	-	-	-
B Warrants		38½	....	39	4½	-	-	-
C Warrants		5	....	5	1	-	-	-
Aberdeen New Thai	♣s	59¼	+¼	60	32¾	2.3	59.0	-.4
Aberdeen Pfd	♣M	164	-1	183	145	10.8	144.7	-13.3
5⅜pc RPI Deb 2007		£120½	....	£124½	£113½	-	-	-
Units 8 1/4pc Ln '23		£107½	....	£107½	£99½	7.7	-	-
Aberforth Smllr		265	+2½	265	155½	2.8	295.6	10.4
Warrants		162½	+½	163	73	-	-	-
Abtrust Scotland	♣	47	....	54½	44	2.8	62.1	24.3
Warrants		14½	....	15½	10	-	-	-
Acorn Income Fund		108	+1	108	101½	-	109.7	1.5
Advance Dev Mkts		109	+1	109	63½	-	116.0	6.0
Advance UK Trust		108	....	133	88	1.2	124.9	13.5
Advent VCT	♣F	77½	....	100	65	0.8	-	-
Advent 2 VCT	♣	77½	....	102	73	3.9	-	-

8 PERSONAL EQUITY PLANS (PEPS)

8.1 **PEPs** were introduced in 1986 to encourage share ownership. The attraction of the schemes was that both the income and capital gain were free of tax. The original maximum investment was £2,400. The maximum investment was increased and the scope of investment way widened. It is impossible to make any further contributions to PEPs after 6 April 1999 but those schemes which are in operation may continue and will enjoy the same tax treatment as the new individual savings account (ISA), which we will see later in this chapter.

8.2 The rules which are still relevant are as follows.

(a) The investor must be a UK resident over the age of 18.

(b) The underlying investments can be shares quoted on the UK (excluding AIM shares) or any EU stock exchange, or unit trusts units, or shares in investment trusts. The unit trust or investment trust must invest 50% of the fund in UK equities or shares quoted on EU stock exchanges. Only units in securities unit trusts may be held in a PEP. As an alternative, £1,500 can be invested in a unit trust or investment trust with more than 50% of its funds outside the EU, eg the investment could be in Japan or the USA. The balance over £1,500 must then be in qualifying UK shares or unit trusts or investment trusts which meet the 50% limit.

(c) General PEPs can include fixed interest corporate bonds with at least 5 years to maturity and convertibles of UK non-financial companies and preference shares in UK and EU companies.

(d) Only authorised managers can run PEPs.

(e) It is possible to switch between providers, even after 5 April 1999.

(f) Shares bought through a new issue can be transferred into a PEP within 42 days of issue.

(g) Single company PEPs must hold the shares of only one company. Employees could transfer in shares held in a 'sharesave scheme'.

(h) Shares received from insurance company/building society windfalls could be transferred into a PEP within 42 days in addition to the general PEP and single company PEP allowance.

Providers

8.3 **Approved managers**, normally stockbrokers, unit trust or investment trust managers.

Income and capital growth prospects

8.4 Both income and capital appreciation have good potential, depending of course on the selection of underlying shares, unit trust or investment trust. There is the opportunity for both **tax free income and growth**.

Risk and accessibility

8.5 **Risk** will depend on the scheme or shares selected. PEPs are normally equity investments and as such there is a risk. If a corporate bond PEP was selected there is still a risk of capital loss and variable income if the bonds have a variable coupon.

8.6 There is no minimum investment period to achieve the tax free status.

8.7 **Accessibility** is normally easy. The unit trust units, or investment trust or other shares are simply sold. With some unit trust PEPs, there is an early withdrawal penalty.

Tax treatment

8.8 **No tax is paid on income or capital growth for any taxpayers**. PEPs held after 5 April 1999 are exempt from income tax and capital gains tax and will benefit from a 10% tax credit on dividends from UK equities until 5 April 2004.

Buying and selling mechanism

8.9 The buying and selling process is related to the underlying investments. PEPs themselves are not bought or sold, merely established with an approved manager or cancelled or transferred.

Charges

8.10 There was a move towards lower charges on PEPs. Many nil up-front charge PEPs were launched; some had a set fee, say £90. Most have an annual management charge of 1% - 1.75%. A PEP with a nil up-front charge might impose a penalty on withdrawal within five years.

9 UNIT TRUSTS AND OEICs

9.1 In Section 1 of this chapter, we looked at the low risk deposit type of investment which gives security but no opportunity for real growth of capital. At the other end of the spectrum we have discussed shares and even shares in unlisted companies, where the risk of loss of capital is high but equally the rewards can be great.

The unsophisticated and small investor needs an investment which is pitched somewhere between these two extremes: **a scheme which allows him to take some risk but reduces his exposure by pooling his investments with others**. Such an investor also wants something which is easy to buy, sell and understand. This is the role of the **packaged**

product. We will now look at a number of packaged investments currently available, concentrating in this section on unit trusts and OEICs.

Unit trusts

Product features and structure

9.2　A **unit trust is an investment pool**. If investor A wishes to place £5,000 in the market he can only invest in, say, two shares. However if he pools his £5,000 with, say, 20 other investors, together they will have a fund of £100,000. This amount can be used to buy a portfolio of shares and therefore spread the risk. At the outset each investor will have a share in the fund of 5,000 units at £1 (not allowing for charges). As the value of the underlying portfolio rises, so too does the value of the units so, if the portfolio is worth say £250,000 in five years time, each unit will be worth £2.50 and each investor's holding worth £12,500. That, in simplistic terms, is how a unit trust works.

> **KEY TERM**
>
> A **unit trust** is an open-ended fund which means that there is no finite number of units in the trust. As more investors join, more units can be created. The manager is under an obligation to buy back units and these will then be sold on to new investors.

9.3　The unit trust will be established under a **deed of trust** which appoints trustees, often a bank. The deed sets out the trust's aims and objectives.

9.4　The investment of the fund is run by a **fund manager** who is responsible for the selection and management of the shares within the portfolio. Managers who run the overseas funds may be located in the country of their fund or alternatively travel to the country regularly to visit companies and keep in touch with economic and political changes.

9.5　The funds can **specialise in overseas markets** such as Europe, USA, Far East or Japan (usually higher risk funds) or be UK based with an emphasis either on income or capital growth.

9.6　In some funds it is possible to buy **income or accumulation units**. If accumulation units are purchased, the income is rolled up either in the price or by the issue of additional units. Looking under the heading '**Authorised investment funds**' in the *Financial Times* will give you an idea of the range of funds available to the investor.

9.7　To spread the risk still further, some unit trusts are '**funds of funds**'. This means a trust that buys units in other unit trusts.

9.8　**Tracker or index funds** are available. These funds mimic the performance of an index such as the FTSE 100. Such funds have lower charges because they are cheap to run. It is a computer operation. An expensive fund manager is not required.

9.9　One of the main drawbacks of a unit trust is that in a falling market the unsophisticated investor, who favours unit trusts, may rush to sell his holding. The manager will be obliged to buy back in the units and in order to repay the unitholders he may have to sell shares at an unfavourable price. Often his best holdings must be disposed, as these will be the only ones **easily marketable in a crisis**. This will reduce the price of the units still further and make it difficult for the fund to recover and show good performance in the following months.

9.10 Investments can be **lump sums** with a minimum of £500 or £1,000 per fund. It is also possible to **save on a regular basis**. The minimum monthly payment can be as low as £25.00.

Providers

9.11 The provider is the **unit trust manager**. Many of these are international companies with offices worldwide. Units can be bought and sold easily through a bank, building society, stockbroker, independent intermediary or by going directly to the provider. Commission is normally paid to the introducer and the investor does not normally buy the product cheaper by going direct.

Benefits

9.12 The benefit of a unit trust is that **the investor is able to spread his risk** by investing in a pool of shares. He is also able to spread his risk geographically by investing in, say, an international fund.

Risk

9.13 The **risk is spread,** particularly if a fund of funds is used. Such a fund would be appropriate for a first time investor.

9.14 The risk for most unit trust funds will be **medium to high** depending on the underlying shares in the portfolio. If, for example, the investor chooses a 'smaller companies fund' the performance is likely to be more volatile. In a bear market the fund manager may get stuck with shares which cease to be easily marketable and at worst, shares of companies which go into liquidation. Similarly, if the fund is invested, say, in the Far East, performance may be volatile and the ability for the fund manager to deal in a falling market may be difficult. Units trusts can be particularly vulnerable in such circumstances, since if investors sell units, the trust manager may be forced to sell assets at an unfavourable price. (With investment trust shares, the position is different, since when an invester sells, the shares are bought by someone else, and that number of shares in the investment trust is unchanged.)

Tax treatment

9.15 **The trust** is taxed in a similar way to investment trusts (see paragraph 7.10).

9.16 **The investor** is taxed as follows.

(a) Since 6 April 1999, dividends have been received with a tax credit of 10%. Non-taxpayers are no longer able to reclaim the tax. Basic rate taxpayers have no further liability. Higher rate taxpayers are liable to a further 22.5% on the grossed-up dividend.

(b) If a trust distributes interest rather than dividends these will be received net of 20% tax.

(c) Any capital gains on a share may be subject to capital gains tax if they exceed the annual exemption after allowing for indexation and tapering relief, if applicable. In the past it was possible to make use of a scheme known as a **bed and breakfast** transaction in order to minimise CGT liability. The scheme worked as follows: close to the end of a financial year the investor disposed of a holding of shares, the gain on which was just below the capital gains threshold. He then repurchased the units in the new tax year, establishing a new purchase date for future capital gains tax purposes. It is still possible to do this, **provided** that thirty days are left between the two transactions.

9.17 EXAMPLE: BED AND BREAKFASTING

	£
March 1987	
1,000 units purchased at offer price £5.00	5,000
March 2000	
1,000 units sold at bid price £9.00	9,000
Gain	4,000
April 2000 (30 days later)	
980 units purchased at offer price £9.18	9,000
April 2005	
980 units sold at bid price £15.00	14,700
Gain	5,700

Without the 'bed and breakfast' this gain would have been subject (under current rules and without allowing for indexation) to capital gains tax, as the total gain would have been £9,700.

Accessibility

9.18 The investor can sell units back to the manager at any time. Settlement will be made on production of the signed unit trust certificate in a matter of approximately **7 - 10 days** depending on the administration of the unit trust company concerned. In the case of non-certificated units (units issued with no certificate but confirmed in a contract note) a form of renunciation is completed.

Charges and penalties

9.19 The unit trust managers charge an amount up front. This is the difference between the bid price and the offer price (the bid/offer spread).

9.20 The spread is normally 6% or 7%. The **offer price** is the price at which the manager sells his units. This is the higher price and the **bid price** is the price at which he buys back his units or the price at which the investor sells.

9.21 At times when the manager wants to discourage sales he can **widen this spread**. In the crash of 1987, many funds moved to a bid basis.

9.22 The funds also have an **annual management charge** of between 1% and 2%.

Open-ended investment companies (OEICs)

9.23 **Open-ended investment companies** were introduced into the UK in January 1997. They are a very familiar type of investment in continental Europe.

(a) An OEIC is an **open-ended company** with a structure somewhere between an investment trust and a unit trust.

(b) The **company issues shares**. These are usually participating redeemable preference shares rather than ordinary voting shares. An OEIC can issue many types of share under one management and this is referred to as an 'umbrella fund'. Each share can invest in a different international sector. There is usually a wider choice of funds than with a unit or investment trust.

(c) The value of an OEIC share should normally reflect the **net asset value** (NAV) of the fund.

(d) OEIC shares trade at a **single price**. The charge is shown separately.

Question 7

It is important to understand the difference between a unit trust and an investment trust.

(a) List the differences.
(b) Which would be the more advantageous investment in a rising market?
(c) Which would be easier to sell in a market crisis?

---

10 INSURANCE BASED PRODUCTS

10.1 Products based on insurance policies are a very popular and useful form of **packaged product**.

KEY TERM

An **investment bond**, also called a single premium bond or unit-linked bond, is in fact a non-qualifying single premium whole of life policy. The money invested is used to buy units in a selected fund. Most insurance companies offer a wider range of funds from low to high risk.

10.2 Examples of the types of fund available are as follows.

(a) **Managed**. The fund manager decides the mix between equities, fixed interest and maybe property.

(b) **UK equity**. The fund manager invests in UK shares.

(c) **Distribution fund**. This provides, hopefully, a rising income from a fund which distributes its dividends. This type of fund is useful for the investor taking withdrawals from a bond. When taking a withdrawal from a distribution bond the investor is withdrawing dividends or interest, whereas when taking a withdrawal from another fund, he may be encashing units which could be eroding the original capital investment.

(d) **International**. This is a portfolio of shares of many economies.

(e) **Specialist funds**. European, Far Eastern, Japan, USA etc.

(f) **Unitised with profits**. These funds are very popular with the conservative investor. Apart from the initial charge they suffer no loss of capital. Bonuses are added each year either by an increase in the price of units or additional units. Some offices now offer a with profits only bond. Some offer the fund as part of a portfolio or on special short term offers.

(g) **Stock market funds**. These funds offer the investor a fixed term bond, usually 5 years with a guarantee of the greater of the return of the capital invested or the performance in the FTSE over the same period. This allows clients an exposure to the stock market with limited risk.

10.3 There is an ability to **switch between funds**. Normally the investor is allowed one free switch in each policy year and thereafter there is a fixed charge, such as £20.

10.4 Although the policy is a whole of life contract, there is normally only a **minimal amount of life cover**, such as 101% of the value of the units.

10.5 There is **no fixed term** to the investment.

10.6 It is possible to take a **regular income** by encashment of units. The normal withdrawal facility is 5% per annum of the original investment. This income can be taken, annually, quarterly or monthly and a tax charge can be deferred. See below for tax treatment.

10.7 The policy can be written in a **number of policies or segments** to allow more flexibility on partial encashment.

Benefits

10.8 The advantages of investment bonds are as follows.

   (a) The investment bond is primarily a **packaged investment for growth**.

   (b) There is a facility **to take an income by encashing units**.

   (c) It is **simple to operate**. The investor is not bothered with dividend vouchers and complications on the tax return.

   (d) There is a choice of a **wide range of geographical funds** and the ability to switch between economies with nil or minimal charge.

Tax treatment

10.9 If the policyholder is the owner of the bond on encashment, there is no **capital gains tax liability**.

10.10 The investment bond is a non-qualifying whole of life policy, so on encashment or on partial encashment (as with an income facility) a **chargeable event** will occur. This may give rise to a charge to higher rate income tax.

10.11 **Tax on withdrawals**

   (a) The investor is allowed to withdraw 5% of the original investment each year for 20 years (ie until the entire capital is returned). In this way he can defer taxation until final encashment.

   (b) If the investor takes no withdrawal for a few years he may make up the backlog, eg:

   (i) *Year 1*: 5% withdrawal taken
   (ii) *Year 2*: 5 % withdrawal taken
   (iii) *Year 3*: No withdrawal
   (iv) *Year 4*: No withdrawal
   (v) *Year 5*: 15% withdrawal

   However, if the annual allowance is exceeded, a tax charge may occur. Let us take the above example further.

   In Year 6, 25% withdrawal is taken. Total withdrawals amount therefore to 50% of the original investment. The allowance has been exceeded by 20% (ie 50% of original investment *less* 6 years at 5% pa (30%) = 20%).

   If we assume the original investment was £10,000, there is now a taxable gain of £2,000 irrespective of the underlying performance of the bond. The underlying value could now be £2,500 but there would still be a taxable gain which could be subject to tax.

BPP
PUBLISHING

10.12 **Tax on final encashment**. A chargeable event occurs, regardless of the investor's tax position. The question is not so much that a chargeable event has occurred but rather whether this will give rise to a tax liability.

To decide this, the following procedure must be undertaken. Let us assume an original purchase price of £10,000 and encashment value of £25,000.

Stage 1. Ascertain whether a gain has occurred, as below.

(a) If no income withdrawals have been taken:

Gain = encashment value – purchase price

Gain = £25,000 – £10,000 = £15,000

(b) If a regular 5% withdrawal has been taken for 5 years:

Gain = encashment value + value of withdrawals – purchase price

Gain = £25,000 + £2,500 – £10,000 = £17,500

Stage 2. As the gain has been made over a number of years, it is divided by the number of years the policy has been in force. This is called *top slicing*.

So, if the policy has been in force for 10 years the top slice in our example will be:

$$£15,000/10 = £1,500$$

Stage 3. This 'slice' is then added to the investor's taxable income for the fiscal year in which the chargeable event occurs to ascertain the rate of additional tax, if any, which is to apply to the chargeable gain. Let us have a look at some examples to see how this works.

(a) If the investor had a taxable income of £10,000, the 'slice' of £1,500 is added to this giving a total of £11,500.

Tax rate applicable to this level of income = 22%.

As the insurance company has already paid tax at this rate on the fund there is no tax to pay.

(b) If the investor had a taxable income of £0, the slice of £1,500 falls in the 10% band. The insurance company has paid tax on the funds, but the investor may not reclaim excess tax suffered.

(c) If the investor had a taxable income of £40,000, the 'slice' is added giving a total of £41,500.

Tax rate applicable to this level of income = 40%.

As the insurance company has already paid tax on the fund there is tax to pay of 40% – 22% = 18% on the whole of the gain. The tax on the gain is 18% of £15,000 = £2,700.

(d) Sometimes the 'slice' just puts the investor into the higher rate tax bracket.

If the investor has a taxable income of £27,000, the slice is added giving a total of £28,500.

The first £1,400 of the slice (ie up to the higher rate tax threshold of £28,400 - from 6 April 2000) is not subject to additional tax, because the insurance company has already paid tax on the fund. There is tax to pay of (40% – 22%) = 18% on the balance of the slice 18% of £100 = £18.

We now have to find an average tax rate to apply to the whole gain £18/£1,500 = 1.20%. Therefore tax to be paid = £15,000 × 1.20% = £180.00.

10.13 There are a number of important things to note.

(a) The **whole of the gain** is taken into account when determining whether an investor will lose his age allowance in the year of encashment.

(b) No '**top slicing**' occurs if the owner of the policy is a company.

(c) If an individual makes a **capital loss** it can only be deducted from taxable income for the purposes of higher rate tax.

10.14 EXAMPLE: TAX ON FINAL ENCASHMENT

Which type of taxpayer gets best results from an investment bond?

10.15 SOLUTION

A higher rate taxpayer will benefit most for the following reasons.

(a) The 5% withdrawal is a good method to defer tax.

(b) The 5% withdrawal for a higher rate taxpayer equates to 8.33% gross income.

(c) If a higher rate taxpayer is likely to become a basic rate taxpayer in the future, then, if he invests in a bond, he has the benefit of a high level of income while a higher rate taxpayer, if he uses the 5% withdrawal, and no tax to pay on encashment.

(d) If the client will always be a higher rate taxpayer he should keep the bond until death. If he dies in the early part of a tax year, say May, then it is unlikely that he will have sufficient income in the year of death to make the proceeds of the bond taxable.

(e) In a husband/wife situation, let us assume that the husband is the higher rate taxpayer. If the bond is written on a joint life second death basis, the tax charge may be deferred until after the death of the first life. If the survivor, the wife, is a basic rate taxpayer she can encash the bond after her husband's death, free of income tax.

Note. Every situation must be carefully worked out.

Accessibility

10.16 The bond has no fixed term, so it can be encashed in whole or part at any time. However, it is sensible to keep it in force for **at least five years** to recoup 'up front' charges.

Penalties and charges

10.17 Charges are as follows.

(a) The normal up-front charge on the bond is **a 5% bid/offer spread**.

(b) In addition there is **an annual management charge -** often 0.75% or 1% of the value of the fund.

10.18 There are two situations when penalties may be incurred on encashment.

(a) **Property funds.** The fund manager usually reserves the right to defer repayment for up to six months at the time of a property crash or 'run on the fund'.

(b) **With-profit funds.** In this instance if the investor withdraws when the market is 'down' the investment company reserves the right to apply a **market level adjuster** to the bonus element of the encashment value.

Maximum investment plans

> ### KEY TERM
>
> A **maximum investment plan** is a unit-linked 10 year qualifying endowment policy designed for the more sophisticated investor. Although premiums are higher than for a normal endowment policy.

10.19 Most insurance companies will give a **wide choice of funds**: managed, UK equity, Europe, USA, Japan, Far East, special situations, smaller companies.

10.20 Funds can be **switched** and new monies directed into different funds. There is normally one free switch per annum with a small fixed fee for further switches in a year. These schemes need to be actively managed to ensure maximum return.

10.21 Each premium buys **units in the chosen fund**. Units are purchased at the offer price and sold at the bid price. There is usually a 5% spread. In addition there will be an annual management charge of, say, 1%.

10.22 There will be a **minimum amount of life cover** as the basis of the scheme is investment. The life cover will have to satisfy the qualifying rules. For those under age 55 this means a death benefit of at least 75% of the premiums paid throughout the term. So, for a 10 year scheme with an annual premium of £1,000 the life cover must be at least £7,500.

Benefits

10.23 It is a **good savings medium** for the sophisticated investor wanting to use a range of funds with the facility to switch between these at low charges.

Tax treatment

10.24 (a) The **life fund** is subject to tax on interest and dividends received at 20% and to tax on capital gains.

(b) The **investor** will receive the proceeds free of income and capital gains tax at maturity.

(c) If the policy were to be surrendered early there could be a tax charge for a **higher rate taxpayer.**

Accessibility

10.25 **None**. This scheme should run for 10 years to achieve maximum return. It can be surrendered early, but there will be a penalty imposed by the insurance company and a possible tax charge if the investor is a higher rate taxpayer.

Penalties and charges

10.26 (a) There will be a **penalty on early encashment** to allow the insurance company to recover setting up charges.

(b) Normal **bid/offer spread** = 5%.

(c) **Annual management charge,** say 1%.

(d) **Up front charges** on the first two years' premiums will be made either by the purchase of capital units or low unit allocation.

Question 8

The charging structure for all unit-linked policies is similar, whether whole of life, endowment or maximum investment policy. Therefore before reading on, refer back to Chapter 4, Paragraph 1.12 and re-read the section on 'charges'.

Endowment policies

> ### KEY TERM
>
> An **endowment policy** is a savings and life assurance policy for an agreed period. The minimum period is 10 years with terms up to 20 or 25 years. A benefit is paid out at maturity or on earlier death. The policyholder may sell the policy on in the **traded endowment market,** as an alternative to surrender before the end of the term, if cash needs to be raised.

Types

10.27 **With-profits**. In this instance bonuses are added to the sum assured and once added cannot be withdrawn (re-read section on with-profits Chapter 2, 2.2(f)). Bonuses may be added annually (known as the reversionary bonus) and at the end of the term (a terminal bonus) depending on investment performance at that time.

10.28 **Non-profit**. In this case there is a guaranteed sum paid out at maturity or previous death. This policy is very poor value for money because it does not take into account inflation. Such policies are rarely found these days. At one time when mortgage monies were hard to find, insurance companies would lend money linked to non-profit endowment policies which were profitable to them!

10.29 **Low cost endowment**

(a) Many endowment policies have traditionally been used as a means of paying back an 'interest only' mortgage. The with-profits contract referred to above is expensive and so to reduce costs the insurance market invented a package called a low cost endowment. This is a combination of a **with-profits endowment** and **decreasing term assurance**.

(b) Bonuses will be added to the endowment sum assured at an assumed rate and the term assurance will decrease at the same rate. The result is that there **should** be sufficient cover to repay the mortgage at the end of the period. The word *should* is emphasised. It is *not guaranteed* and depends on the bonus performance of the company. If bonuses are better than have been allowed for in the package there will be a larger return. Usually this can be achieved even if the reversionary bonus is not greater, by the addition of the terminal bonus in the final year. However, if bonus rates fall and remain low for a long period, the return may not be large enough to repay the mortgage.

(c) **The situation on death is normally guaranteed**. The death benefit will be sufficient to repay the mortgage.

10.30 Unit-linked endowment policies

(a) Premiums buy units in a fund of the investor's choice. Units will be cancelled each month to buy the life cover. There is investment flexibility and funds can be switched.

(b) Units will be purchased at the offer price and sold at the bid price and there will be an annual management charge on the fund.

(c) The setting up costs will be covered by capital units or low allocations rates.

(d) Premium review dates are written into the contract. They occur every 5 years and at lesser periods close to maturity. This enables the investment situation to be reviewed.

(e) If the policy has been taken out in conjunction with a mortgage, the premiums may have to increase to ensure that the cover will be sufficient to repay the outstanding loan on the maturity of the loan.

10.31 Low start endowment

(a) This is a variation on the low cost theme and was introduced to help young 'first time house buyers'.

(b) The level of cover will be the same as for a low cost endowment but the premium starts at a lower level and increases by, say, 10% per annum for five years. It then remains constant for the remainder of the term. The eventual premium is higher than the level premium under a low cost endowment policy.

(c) The sum assured and benefits should be the same at maturity or on death under the low cost or the low start policy. The low start will, however, have cost more to achieve the same benefit.

10.32 Flexidowment

(a) These policies are designed specifically as savings contracts for the client who requires flexibility. The policy is written for a total term, to say age 65, with options to encash after 10 years, without penalty.

(b) The policies are normally written in segments to allow some to be encashed and some continued. This is an excellent type of policy for school fees planning.

10.33 Guaranteed income and growth bonds

(a) The guaranteed growth bond provides, as its name implies, a guaranteed growth on capital at the end of a fixed term, say five years.

(b) The guaranteed income bond offers a regular annual or monthly payment at a guaranteed rate for a fixed term. At the end of the term the original investment is returned.

(c) Some guaranteed growth and income bonds are written as single premium endowment policies. As such they are non-qualifying policies.

(d) The proceeds of a guaranteed income or growth bond could be subject to tax on encashment if the investor was a higher rate taxpayer. This would be calculated on the basis discussed earlier in this chapter (Paragraphs 8.9 and 8.11). A non-taxpayer or 10% taxpayer has no means of reclaiming tax.

10.34 Friendly society plans

(a) Friendly societies offer endowment policies with a difference because of the favourable tax treatment of their funds, which are tax-free.

(b) In the Finance Act 1995 the maximum premiums were increased to £25 per month or £270 per annum. Care must be taken to choose a friendly society with a good investment track record otherwise the tax advantage may be lost through poor performance.

(c) Friendly society products are usually offered on a with-profits or unit-linked basis.

Options

10.35 It is possible to write the following **options into an endowment policy**.

(a) **Extending** the term beyond 10 years, ie saving for a further 10 years.

(b) Adding **waiver of premium**. This option is useful if the policy is being used for house purchase purposes.

(c) Adding **critical illness**. This option is useful if the policy is being used for house purchase purposes.

Providers

10.36 **Insurance companies** are the providers of endowment policies. The secondhand market for such policies comprises approximately 20 firms.

Benefits

10.37 Provides a **tax free lump sum** at a known date in the future with the security of a lump sum on previous death.

Tax treatment

10.38 The **life fund** is subject to tax on interest and dividends received and to capital gains tax on investments. The **policyholder** (or the buyer of the policy, if it is sold secondhand) pays no tax on encashment so long as he has not broken the qualifying rules, eg by surrendering early.

Accessibility

10.39 It is a **contract for a fixed term**. It can be surrendered early but then there will be penalties and loss of qualifying status which could result in a tax charge for a higher rate taxpayer.

Penalties and charges

10.40 There will be **charges** on all endowment policies. The key features document for disclosure purposes makes it easier to see the extent of these, particularly on the with profit policies. (We have discussed the charging of unit-linked policies previously.)

Annuities

KEY TERM

An **annuity** is a contract whereby the insurance company agrees to pay to the investor a guaranteed income either for a specific period or for the rest of his or her life in return for a capital sum. The capital is non-returnable and hence the income paid is high.

10.41 The amount of income paid is based on the **investor's age**, ie the mortality factor and interest rates on long term gilts.

10.42 The **income payment frequency** is agreed between the insurance company and the investor at the outset. It can be annually, half yearly, quarterly or monthly. Obviously the greater the frequency the lower the income. Payments can be made in advance or in arrears. Say, a female client of 75 buying an annuity for a purchase price of £10,000 will receive an income of £1,366.80 per annum, if payments are made by monthly amounts or of £1,408.20 per annum, if the payments are made half-yearly.

10.43 Payments can be made with or without proportion. What does this mean? If a client has chosen '**with proportion**' and has an annuity payable half yearly in arrears, with payments on 15 December and 15 June and the annuitant dies on 15 March, then a payment of three months income will be made. If the scheme had been without proportion then no such payment would have been made.

10.44 Annuities can be on **one life or two**. If they are on two lives, the annuity will normally continue until the death of the second life. These annuities are known as 'last survivor annuities'.

Types of annuity

10.45 With an **immediate annuity** the purchase price is paid to the insurance company and the income commences *immediately* and is paid for the lifetime of the annuitant.

10.46 A **guaranteed annuity** works exactly the same as an immediate annuity but in this instance the annuitant selects a guaranteed period either 5 or 10 years. The annuity is paid for the annuitant's life, but in the event of early death within the guaranteed period, the income is paid for the balance of the term to the beneficiaries.

10.47 **Compulsory purchase or open market option annuities** are purchased with the proceeds of pension funds. The client will exercise an option to move a fund to a provider offering better annuity rates. Please note different taxation treatment applies (see tax treatment of annuities (c)). The fund arising from an occupational scheme or buy-out (S32) policy will purchase a compulsory purchase annuity. A fund arising from a retirement annuity or personal pension will purchase an open market option annuity.

10.48 With **deferred annuities,** a single payment or regular payments are made to an insurance company but payment of the income does not start for some months or years. This is very suitable for an investor funding for retirement or school fees.

10.49 The **annuity certain** or **deferred annuity certain** is often used for school fees purposes. The annuity is paid for a fixed period either immediately or after a deferred period, *irrespective* of the survival of the original annuitant.

Temporary annuity

10.50 In a **temporary annuity** a lump sum payment is made to the insurance company, and income commences immediately but is only paid for a limited period - say 5 years. Payments cease at the end of the fixed period or on earlier death.

Level annuity

10.51 A **level annuity,** of whatever type, provides a level income at all times. This of course does not keep pace with inflation.

10.52 With an **increasing or escalating annuity,** the annuitant selects a rate of increase and the income will rise each year by a set amount, say, 5% or 10% or even the RPI.

10.53 Some offices now offer an annuity where the 'performance' of the annuity is to some extent **linked either to a unit linked or with-profits fund** to give additional inflation proofing to the income.

Capital protected

10.54 One of the problems with annuities is that **if the annuitant dies early the capital is lost.** This can be overcome, to some extent, by buying a **capital protected annuity.** The workings are best explained by use of an example.

- An annuity is purchased for £10,000. The annual income or annuity is £1,000

- The annuitant dies after 6 years

- The total payments of the annuity have been only £6,000, so £4,000 is returned to the estate, (ie original investment less payments made).

If, however, the annuitant died in year 11 no payment would be made because the whole of the original purchase price would have been used up.

Home income plans

10.55 For many elderly people, income is low but their property is worth a substantial amount. If the client is aged over 65 this situation can sometimes be overcome by use of a **home income plan.**

10.56 In this instance, an **interest only mortgage** is raised on the property. The loan will be less than the value of the house, and 25% is a common limit. Although MIRAS was abolished from 6 April 2000, existing home income plans retain their tax relief if taken out before this date.

10.57 The capital then raised buys an annuity for life. 90% of the capital must be used for this purpose. The proceeds of the annuity are used to pay the interest on the loan and the balance provides an increased income for the retired person.

10.58 The schemes have **considerable disadvantages.** They work well only if the client is fairly old and, therefore, obtains a high annuity rate, or when annuity rates are high.

10.59 In the past in some schemes the interest was allowed to roll up. The providers of these policies now prevent this, as the result could be a debt greater than the value of the house!

10.60 Some schemes were devised which invested the money raised from the mortgage into an investment bond. Needless to say the performance was poor and the elderly person ended up with problems paying the mortgage, no income and loss of capital.

Providers

10.61 Annuities are provided by **insurance companies.**

113

Benefits

10.62 Annuities guarantee a **high level of income**.

Tax treatment

10.63 **Purchased life annuities** have a capital and interest element. The split is pre-agreed between the Revenue and the insurance company.

(a) The capital element is based on expectation of life tables and is tax free.
(b) The interest element is taxable (in the same manner as interest on a bank account).

This means that a non taxpayer can obtain a gross income from an annuity.

10.64 The tax treatment of the annuity is agreed between the insurance company and the Inland Revenue by completion of a PLA1 or R87 for a non taxpayer.

10.65 **Pension annuities.** The resulting payments from a company or personal pension are all taxed as earned income. There is no distinction between capital and income. This rule applies to open market options and compulsory purchase annuities.

Accessibility

10.66 **None**. Once the annuity is established there can be no return of capital!

Penalty and charges

10.67 The ultimate penalty is that the **investor cannot get his capital back**. Any **charges** the insurance company makes are taken into account when offering the annuity rate.

Back-to-back arrangements

10.68 Sometimes insurance companies package annuities and other qualifying policies or investments to provide clients with an income or growth investment funded from capital. These are known as **back-to-back arrangements**.

10.69 **Examples** of income/growth product packages are:

(a) 5 year temporary annuity and unit trust
(b) 5 year temporary annuity and personal equity plan/ISA
(c) 5 year temporary annuity and 5 year endowment

The original capital investment is split between the two investments.

10.70 If income is required, the annuity pays out the income and it is hoped that the growth on the investment will be sufficient to repay the original capital. **There is no guarantee.**

10.71 If growth is required, the income from the annuity is used to '**boost' the investment**.

10.72 Sometimes back-to-backs are used for **inheritance tax planning**. In this instance the combination of contracts is: **Immediate annuity** and **whole of life policy.**

The capital sum is split to purchase the annuity and pay the first premium under the whole of life policy.

Subsequent annuity payments are used to pay the premiums under the whole of life policy. The policy is written in trust so that on the death of the policyholder, the benefits pass to the beneficiaries free of inheritance tax.

11 GUARANTEED INCOME BONDS, GUARANTEED GROWTH BONDS AND GUARANTEED EQUITY BONDS

11.1 Guaranteed income bonds and guaranteed growth bonds are single premium insurance investments. The minimum investment is normally £5,000. The term of investment is usually one to five years.

11.2 With both types of product, the investor is guaranteed an amount of capital from the investment. The rate of return is guaranteed from the outset, and remains constant throughout the term of the investment.

   (a) With a growth bond, the interest is paid in one amount on maturity of the investment, ie at the end of the investment term.

   (b) With an income bond, the interest is paid at agreed intervals throughout the term of the investment, with capital repaid at the end of the investment term.

11.3 These products are provided by insurance companies. The income is therefore paid net of basic rate tax (22%). Higher rate taxpayers may therefore be liable for a further payment of tax at maturity. Non taxpayers cannot reclaim the tax.

11.4 Guaranteed equity bonds are similar in many respect to guaranteed growth bonds. A minimum amount of capital is guaranteed. In addition, the return on the investment is linked to the performance of a stock market index such as the FTSE 100. At the end of the term of the investment, the investor receives the minimum return plus a percentage of the growth in the stock market index over the period.

11.5 Guaranteed equity bonds might appeal to the investor who does not want to invest directly in equities and face the risk of poor equity performance, but who at the same time would like to benefit from any strong performance by equities. An investor in guaranteed equity bonds gets the benefits of both a guaranteed minimum return and an additional return if the stock market performs well.

12 INDIVIDUAL SAVINGS ACCOUNTS (ISAs)

> **KEY TERM**
>
> **ISAs (Individual Savings Accounts)** are packaged investments available from 6 April 1999. They consist of up to three components:
>
> (a) cash;
> (b) life insurance;
> (c) stocks and shares
>
> They are available to individuals who are over 18 and either UK resident or ordinarily resident. They are scheduled to be available for ten years, although a review will begin after seven years.

12.1 An individual can invest a **maximum** of £5,000 in a tax year, but £7,000 in the tax years 1999/2000 and 2000/2001. There are annual sub-limits for each component:

(a) Cash: £1,000 (£3,000 in 1999/2000 and 2000/2001)

(b) Life insurance: £1,000

(c) Stocks and shares: £5,000 (£7,000 in 1999/2000 and 2000/2001)

12.2 Each year, the individual can choose *either* a '**maxi ISA**' *or* a '**mini ISA**'. Once the individual has made their choice, they must stay with it for that year, although they may choose a difference type of ISA in a subsequent year.

Maxi ISA

12.3 With a '**maxi ISA**' all the money invested goes into one ISA. It can consist of:

(a) entirely stocks and shares (demutualisation shares are not allowed) - £7,000 in 1999/2000 and 2000/2001, £5,000 each year thereafter.

(b) stocks and shares *plus* either life insurance (£1,000 in any year) *or* cash (£3,000 in 1000/2000 and 2000/2001, £1,000 thereafter) *or* both, but always subject to the overall annual limit of £7,000/£5,000.

Each maxi ISA has one ISA manager.

Mini ISA

12.4 A '**mini ISA**' is restricted to any one of the three 'components' specified above: **cash; life insurance**; or **stocks and shares**. An individual can open up mini-ISAs with different ISA managers. The component and overall limits are the same as for maxi ISAs, except that a limit of £3,000 applies to a stocks and shares mini-ISA. The maximum an individual can invest in total overall is £5,000 in one tax year, or £7,000 in each of 1999/2000 and 2000/2001.

Investment and withdrawals

12.5 There is **no minimum investment level** other than that imposed by the provider. The provider may set a **minimum withdrawal level**, but this minimum must not be set above £10. Withdrawals can be made without loss of tax relief.

Permissible investments include the following.

Cash component:	Units in a money market fund
Stocks and shares component:	Shares traded on a main stock exchange (but not AIM shares)
	Gilts and corporate bonds with at least five years to redemption
	Securities and warrants units in a unit trust
	Cash for investment. The interest is not tax free.
	Warrants attached to shares from a public offer

CAT standards

12.6 Certain restrictions apply to each component part of an ISA. These restrictions are intended to provide uniformity of **charges, access and terms**: the initials of these three provide the title 'CAT standards'.

	Charges	**Access**	**Terms**
Cash	There should be no one-off or regular charges except for replacing lost documents.	Minimum transaction sizes must be no greater than £10, and withdrawals must be effected within 7 working days or less.	The interest rate should be no lower than 2% below base rate; upward interest rate changes must follow base rate changes within one calendar month; downward changes may be slower; no other conditions are allowed (an example being no limits on the frequency of withdrawals).
Life assurance	The annual charge must be no more than 3% a year of the value of the fund. There can be no other charges, eg. no separate charge for the guarantee on surrender values.	Minimum premiums can be no more than £250 lump sum pa, or £25 per month.	Surrender values should reflect the value of the underlying assets. After three years, surrender values should return at least the premium.
Stocks and shares	Annual charges can be no more than 1% of net asset value.	The minimum saving can be no more than £500 lump sum, or £50 per month.	The fund must be at least 50% invested in shares and securities listed on EU stock exchanges; units must be single priced at mid-market price; the investment risk must be highlighted in literature.

12.7 ISAs are **free from income tax and capital gains tax**. As with PEPs, the tax credit on dividends from UK equities, reduced to 10% from 6 April 1999, can be reclaimed. This will disappear from April 2004.

Question 9

John Harris arrives in your office and says he has heard about equity ISAs which he believes to have some tax advantages rather like a TESSA used to have. He would like to make an investment.

(a)   Is he right?
(b)   What particular points should you make when explaining an ISA to him?

Effect on TESSAs and PEPs

12.8   **No new TESSAs can begin after 5 April 1999**. Existing TESSAs can continue, and will have no effect on the ISA allowance. At maturity of a current TESSA, the proceeds can either be taken tax-free or the original capital can be transferred into the cash component of an ISA or a TESSA-only ISA. Such a transfer will not affect that year's ISA allowance.

12.9   **No new investment could be put into PEPs after 5 April 1999**, but existing PEPs can continue and will not affect the ISA allowance. They will therefore have no effect on ISAs,

nor will ISAs have any effect on PEPs, and PEPs can remain as a tax-advantaged investment in addition to any investment in ISAs.

Question 10

(a) Which is the most tax efficient investment for a basic rate taxpayer?

An ISA
A unit trust
A share
An investment trust

(b) What development made PEPs more attractive to cautious investors?

Chapter roundup

After studying this chapter, you should be aware of the three main categories of investment.

- Deposits

- Asset backed investments such as shares, unit and investment trusts.

- Insurance company products and packages, and their main features.

Quick quiz

Multiple choice

1   A client has £6,000 to invest for growth before the 5th April. He wants maximum security. Which of the following should he choose?

A   A TESSA
B   A PEP
C   A National Savings certificate
D   A unit trust, using an equity fund

2   What would be the *main* reason for a higher rate taxpayer to purchase a single premium bond?

A   the choice of funds
B   low charges
C   the 5% withdrawal facility
D   the minimal amount of life cover available

3   Which of the following investments would be most tax advantageous for an elderly woman taxpayer, aged 87, wanting an income producing asset?

A   Monthly income building society account
B   An immediate annuity
C   Guaranteed income bond
D   High income unit trust

4   A client is considering a regular savings plan for school fees. The fees are needed in 12 years time and he requires maximum security. Which choice should he make?

A   A flexidowment using a with profits fund
B   An ISA savings plan using a high income fund
C   A unit trust savings plan using an equity income fund
D   An investment trust savings plan using an international fund

5   A client wants to purchase an investment which will give him a tax free income. Should he choose:

    A   An ISA.

    B   A single premium bond using the 5% withdrawal facility.

    C   A national savings income bond.

    D   A national saving deposit account.

6   Which is the most suitable investment for a 17 year old?

    A   A national savings children's bonus bond

    B   A cash ISA

    C   A National Savings certificate

    D   An equity ISA

7   Which type of annuity is used as a back-to-back with an endowment policy?

    A   An immediate annuity

    B   A temporary annuity

    C   An annuity certain

    D   A reversionary annuity

8   Which of the following is *not* the name of a government security?

    A   War Loan

    B   Treasury Stock

    C   Index Linked gilt

    D   A debenture

9   A scrip issue is which of the following?

    A   The means of raising more capital, initially via the existing shareholders.

    B   The right to buy shares in the future at an agreed price.

    C   A paper transaction to increase the number of shares in the market.

    D   A new issue of shares.

In the following questions mark each option as TRUE or FALSE.

10   A client is confused about the relative merits of unit trusts and investment trusts.

    A   He prefers a unit trust because the manager must always buy back the units.

    B   The investment trust is likely to have lower charges.

    C   The unit trust will always give him a higher income than the investment trust.

    D   If the investment trust is at a premium it will be a 'good buy'.

11   A client considering a general savings plan, no particular aim in mind, makes these statements:

    A   A unit-linked endowment policy will give him access to a wide choice of funds.

    B   An ISA can be cashed in at any time.

    C   He can withdraw the whole of his tax free income from an existing TESSA at the same time as he saves.

    D   A unit trust savings plan will have lower charges than an endowment policy.

12   Consider the effect of changes in interest rates in connection with the following statements.

    A   The capital value of a gilt will look better if interest rates fall.

    B   A guaranteed income bond will be a good investment if there is an indication that interest rates will fall shortly.

    C   A fixed rate mortgage looks good if there is an indication that interest rates will fall shortly.

    D   Share prices should rise if interest rates fall.

13   If you were advising a client on the risk of certain investments, consider the following statements.

    A   A unit trust investing in the Far East will have a higher risk than a blue chip UK share.

    B   An ordinary blue chip share has a lower risk than a preference share.

    C   An investment in a managed fund of an insurance company will have a lower risk than a UK equity unit trust.

    D   A property fund has a higher risk than a fixed interest fund.

14   What does it mean if a unit trust is being sold at a 2% discount.

    A   The value of the trust is less than the value of the total units issued.
    B   The value of the trust is more than the value of the total units issued.
    C   The buying charge is reduced by 2%.
    D   There is no such thing.

15   Consider the tax implications of a number of different investments.

    A   A client will never have to pay capital gains tax on the proceeds of a unit trust.

    B   If an endowment policy is qualifying, the benefits on maturity will be tax free even if the investor is a higher rate taxpayer.

    C   A retired person may lose his age allowance in the year he cashes in a single premium bond, even if he is a basic rate taxpayer.

    D   If a client withdraws 5% of his original investment in a single premium bond, the amount will be paid without deduction of tax.

16   A back-to-back arrangement can be:

    A   A purchased life annuity and a whole of life policy.

    B   A means of providing a fund for inheritance tax.

    C   A means of providing a guaranteed income and always a guaranteed return of capital.

    D   A means of providing a guaranteed income and not necessarily a guaranteed return of capital.

17   What are the maximum amounts which can be invested in the following schemes?

    A   £5,000 per fiscal year in an equity ISA
    B   £9,000 as a total investment in an existing TESSA
    C   £10,000 in a national savings pensioners bond
    D   £10,000 as a reinvestment into the Index Linked National Savings Certificate

18   What are the advantages of buying a gilt through the Post Office?

    A   The ability to deal immediately
    B   Costs are cheaper
    C   Income paid monthly
    D   Tax free income

19   If you are an ordinary shareholder you have:

    A   the right to vote at all board meetings.

    B   the right to a dividend, if paid.

    C   the guarantee of recovering all your capital if the company goes into liquidation.

    D   the ability, sometimes, to buy the products of the company at a discount or receive vouchers.

The solutions to the questions in the quiz can be found at the end of this Study Text. Before checking your answers against those solutions, you should look back at this chapter and use the information in it to correct your answers.

Answers to questions

1   (a)   *National savings income bond*

   (i) Open to anyone.
   (ii) Variable rate.
   (iii) No fixed term.

  (b)   *Pensioners guaranteed bond*

   (i) Only open to those over 60.
   (ii) Fixed rate.
   (iii) Five year term.

2   (a)   National Savings certificates, a cash ISA or an existing TESSA.

  (b)   Bank or building society monthly interest account or a National Savings income bond or pensioners bond, if the client was over 60.

  (c)   National Savings accounts, ordinary and deposit income bond and pensioners bond.

3   (a)   £89.29
  (b)   £81.30

6   The main features of an investment trust are as follows.

  (a)   It is a company share.
  (b)   It must be bought and sold in the market.
  (c)   Additional funds can be raised by borrowing (known as gearing).

7   (a)   (i) *Unit trust*

    (1) Open ended investment. Manager can create units to meet demand
    (2) A trust
    (3) Manager must buy back the units
    (4) Price directly reflects the value of the underlying assets

   (ii) *Investment trust*

    (1) A closed fund, additional funds raised by borrowing (gearing)

    (2) A company share

    (3) Shares are bought and sold in the market

    (4) Price of share may not always reflect underlying value of trust, the price can be at a 'discount' or a 'premium'

  (b)   An investment trust

  (c)   A unit trust

9   (a)   Yes, to the extent that the return from the investment is currently tax free, but wrong for the following reasons.

   (i) An ISA has no restriction on access; an existing TESSA is a fixed term investment (5 years).

   (ii) An equity ISA is primarily an equity investment and carries a higher risk than a TESSA, which is a deposit-type investment.

  (b)   (i) The level of risk involved.

   (ii) That he should be considering investing for at least 5 years.

10   (a)   An ISA.

  (b)   The introduction in the Finance Act 1995 of the use of convertible and company bonds as an acceptable investment for PEPs.

Chapter 7

USE OF SAVINGS AND INVESTMENT PRODUCTS

Chapter topic list	Syllabus reference
1 Bank and building society accounts	B 3.1
2 Existing TESSAs	B 3.1
3 National Savings products	B 3.1
4 Shares	B 3.1
5 Gilts	B 3.1
6 Corporate bonds	B 3.1
7 Investment trusts	B 3.1
8 Unit trusts	B 3.1
9 Existing personal equity plans	B 3.1
10 Investment bonds	B 3.1
11 Maximum investment policies	B 3.1
12 Endowments	B 3.1
13 Annuities	B 3.1
14 Individual Savings Accounts	B 3.1

Introduction

In this chapter we learn how the products outlined in Chapter 6 can be used to satisfy client needs in particular circumstances. Let us look at the use of each type of product.

1   BANK AND BUILDING SOCIETY ACCOUNTS

1.1   All age groups need such accounts for an **emergency fund with easy access**. Such accounts are useful for short-term savings for a car or a holiday.

1.2   **Monthly income accounts** can be useful for the elderly. However the investor must be aware that interest rates are variable and the capital is not inflation proofed. Such accounts are useful for the low risk and cautious investor.

1.3   Suitable for investors who are **basic rate taxpayers** because the income is paid net. The accounts are administratively easy to handle.

1.4   **Non-taxpayers** can be paid interest from these accounts gross after completing a form R85.

2   EXISTING TESSAS

2.1   (a)   A **low risk deposit investment**.

(b)   **Tax-free returns** for basic and higher rate taxpayer, no particular use for non-taxpayers

(c)   If clients with cash holdings currently hold a TESSA they should maintain it, attempt to **fully fund** and then **transfer** to an ISA upon maturity.

3   NATIONAL SAVINGS PRODUCTS

3.1   **National Savings ordinary and investment accounts**

(a)   Interest rate is low, but the first £70 on the ordinary account is tax free. The interest rate on the investment account is attractive on low investments, under £500.

(b)   Interest is paid gross which is of interest to non taxpayers but only if the interest rate is competitive.

(c)   Reasonable access.

3.2   **Income bonds**

(a)   Useful for anyone wanting a regular monthly income. The interest rate is variable but usually competitive.

(b)   Interest is paid gross so useful for a non taxpayer.

(c)   The pensioner bond is aimed at retired people over age 60 wanting a **guaranteed income**.

3.3   **Capital bonds and certificates**

(a)   All the capital bonds and National Savings certificates are 5 year schemes.

(b)   The return on certificates is tax-free so they are of interest to basic and higher rate taxpayers.

The return on bonds is taxable.

(c)   These products are recommended for investors who want a low risk capital growth investment.

3.4   **Children s bonus bond.** Good investment for a child. This is tax free, even for parental gifts, but with a maximum limit of only £1,000 per issue.

4   SHARES

4.1   (a)   Shares are a **higher risk investment**.

(b)   Suitable for clients with a **large portfolio,** say, £40,000 or £50,000+.

(c)   Clients need an understanding of the **stock market** and the **risks** involved in equity investment.

(d)   Clients need **professional advice** from a stockbroker.

(e)   The less sophisticated investor, even with substantial capital to invest, may be better advised to enter the market via a **pooled investment** such as a unit or investment trust.

(f) **Higher rate taxpayers** should select growth stock, thus avoiding too much tax on dividends and by careful encashment and reinvestment minimise the effects of capital gains tax.

5 GILTS

5.1 (a) Gilts provide a **good spread within a large portfolio of investments**.

(b) Gilts are a **low risk investment**. Income is known and also the capital return, if the stock is held to redemption.

(c) Gilts are suitable for **higher rate taxpayers**. They should buy a low coupon gilt which should allow them to make a capital gain which will not be taxable (no CGT on gilts).

(d) At the other end of the spectrum, gilts are useful for **non-taxpayers** wanting a high income. The income, paid half yearly, will be received gross.

(e) A high coupon gilt may be useful for an **elderly person looking to achieve a high income** to pay nursing home fees without total loss of capital. Obviously he may suffer a small loss of capital if he buys the stock above par.

(f) Gilts can be used to **fund for a need at a specific date**, say school fees. A low coupon gilt may be useful in this instance.

6 CORPORATE BONDS

6.1 (a) The benefits of corporate bonds are similar to those of gilts.

(b) The investment risk is higher than with gilts, but corporate bonds offer a higher rate of interest.

(c) With the growth of the corporate bond market, bonds are easily bought and sold through a stockbroker.

7 INVESTMENT TRUSTS

7.1 (a) An investment trust is a pooled investment and is therefore ideal for the **less sophisticated investor** who wants exposure to the market without the high risk of buying individual shares.

(b) Charges may be **lower** than for unit trusts.

(c) Investment trusts can, hopefully, provide **capital gains** if shares can be purchased at a discount.

(d) The performance may be **volatile** because of the gearing.

(e) There may be a problem of **disposal** if no one wants to buy the shares.

8 UNIT TRUSTS

8.1 (a) **Slightly less risk than investment trusts**.

(b) A pooled investment which can be used to provide **income or growth,** or both.

(c) **Accessibility is good**. The managers must buy back the units.

(d) A unit trust is a **medium-term investment** therefore not necessarily suitable for the elderly, unless part of a large portfolio.

9 EXISTING PERSONAL EQUITY PLANS

9.1 If clients are willing to take the risk of the equity market either directly through shares or through pooled investments, such as unit trusts or investment trusts, it makes sense to **maintain existing PEPs** and build up a tax free fund.

(a) PEPs can be useful for providing a tax free income in retirement.

(b) PEPs are not for a fixed term. There is easy access.

(c) PEPs are very useful for higher rate taxpayers.

(d) PEPs should not be maintained just for tax purposes. The underlying fund should have potential for good performance and the charges should be reasonable. Otherwise the charges can offset the tax advantage.

(e) PEPs are of less use to basic rate taxpayers as such people are unlikely to be subject to capital gains tax. They only save a very small amount of income tax on dividends. Nevertheless it can be useful to build up a fund to provide tax free income in the future.

It must be remembered that PEPs are a risk investment.

10 INVESTMENT BONDS

10.1 (a) Investment bonds are useful for **higher rate taxpayers** because of the 5% withdrawal facility.

(b) Investment bonds are useful for **planning retirement** for a single or married person who is currently a higher rate taxpayer but will become a basic rate taxpayer by the time the proceeds are needed.

(c) An investment bond can prove to be a better investment for a higher rate taxpayer than direct shares. On direct shares he will pay 40% income tax whereas a life fund pays **only 20% tax**.

(d) The investment bond is an easy investment to operate for **elderly or unsophisticated investors**. There are no tax vouchers, warrants, scrip or rights issues to concern the client. All such matters are dealt with by the fund manager.

(e) The client has access to **managed funds** so they can leave the investment to professionals.

(f) Bonds are not so advantageous for a **basic rate taxpayer** who should receive a better deal, tax wise, from an investment in a unit trust or investment trust.

(g) The ability to **move funds** without charge is an advantage.

(h) The **5% withdrawal** does not reduce the age allowance for older investors. However, they may have a problem on encashment when their gain is not top sliced for the purpose of calculating whether they are entitled to an age allowance in that year.

11 MAXIMUM INVESTMENT POLICIES

11.1 (a) The policy provides a **tax free return** after a 10 year saving period.

(b) It is suitable for **higher rate taxpayers**. The life fund is taxed at a lower rate than the 40% charged on the proceeds of shares which could be an alternative investment.

BPP PUBLISHING

(c) **Basic rate taxpayers** would be better suited to a PEP/ISA, unit trust or investment trust savings plan.

12 ENDOWMENTS

Using endowments to repay a mortgage

12.1 (a) Endowments are used by many people to **pay back a mortgage**. Life cover and savings are then tied up in one plan.

(b) A full with-profits policy is available for the **risk adverse**, but this is very expensive.

(c) **Low cost policies** help to keep down the level of premium payments, but there is a risk that there will be insufficient capital to repay the mortgage at the end of the day.

(d) **Low start endowment policies** are very suitable for the first time buyer who has a financial problem which may ease in the future.

Using endowments as a savings vehicle

12.2 (a) **Flexidowment** is an excellent savings arrangement for those who are not sure when they may need their rainy day money. If it is unit-linked, encashment can occur when unit prices are high.

(b) Endowment policies are a **low risk investment** if the with-profits fund is used.

(c) **Unit linked endowments** are for the more risk conscious as the investor can choose the fund or funds which best suit his attitude to risk.

13 ANNUITIES

13.1 (a) Annuities are suitable for a **retired person** wishing to increase income.

(b) **Deferred annuities** are useful for **school fees planning**.

(c) Sometimes a **temporary annuity** is purchased alongside an endowment policy to provide income and return of capital at the end of, say, 5 or 10 years, see the section on back-to-backs (Chapter 6).

14 INDIVIDUAL SAVINGS ACCOUNTS

14.1 ISAs offer investors **tax free investment** in cash and equities either directly or through pooled investments and life insurance products. As a result they are appropriate for **all investors** who wish to invest in these investment categories.

14.2 As with PEPs and TESSAs, ISAs should not be maintained unless the underlying investment has potential for good performance and the charges are reasonable. The CAT scheme will enable investors to identify those providers who offer ISAs satisfying minimum standards on charges, access and terms.

Chapter roundup

- Having read this chapter you should have a good idea of the situations and the type of client who would wish to purchase both deposit and asset backed investments.

Quick quiz

Multiple choice questions

1   Who is most likely to purchase an immediate annuity?

A   A young person who is unemployed
B   A 35 year old planning retirement in 20 years time
C   A person wanting a short term high income
D   An elderly person wanting an improved income

2   Which of the following policies used to repay a mortgage of £40,000 would have the lowest initial monthly premium?

A   A low cost endowment, total cover £40,000
B   A with profits policy, sum assured £40,000.
C   A flexidowment, sum assured £40,000
D   A low start low cost endowment, total cover £40,000

In the following questions mark each option as TRUE or FALSE.

3   If a client invests in a single premium bond, when might a tax charge occur?

A   On death
B   On a partial surrender
C   On a full surrender
D   On taking an income of 5% of the purchase price in year 1

4   How is a compulsory purchase annuity taxed?

A   As earned income
B   As unearned income
C   Part as capital and part as interest
D   All as interest

The solutions to the questions in the quiz can be found at the end of this Study Text. Before checking your answers against those solutions, you should look back at this chapter and use the information in it to correct your answers.

Chapter 8

COMPARING SAVINGS AND INVESTMENT PRODUCTS AND PROVIDERS

Chapter topic list	Syllabus reference
1 Comparing different types of product	B 4.1
2 Comparing options	B 4.2
3 Different providers of the same product	B 4.3

Introduction

We have studied the various types of investment. Now we move on to decide which product is most suitable for the client's need and then which provider to choose.

1   COMPARING DIFFERENT TYPES OF PRODUCT

1.1   **Points to be considered** are as follows:

    (a)   Investment objective
    (b)   Surrender values
    (c)   Charging and commission structure
    (d)   Risk and accessibility
    (e)   Tax treatment

1.2   **Investment objectives**. The questions to ask are these:

    (a)   Does the client want a savings scheme?

    (b)   Does the client want to invest capital?

    (c)   Does the client want income?

    (d)   Does the client want capital growth?

    (e)   Does the client really want to save or invest? The question must be asked 'has he or she already satisfied all the protection needs?' For example, it is no good having a £50 a month savings scheme if the client has a family with no life assurance protection.

1.3   **Surrender values and penalties**

    (a)   Surrender values or penalties on leaving an investment early are very important.

    (b)   The adviser must attempt to establish the term of the investment required and the likelihood of early surrender.

(c) If it is the client's intention to commit himself to a long term investment, he must still have the early surrender penalties explained.

(d) The adviser in comparing investments must look at surrender values and, if he can find a similar product with a lower penalty on early surrender, this must be considered.

(e) The key features documents for life assurance products make it easier for the surrender values of these products to be identified.

(f) Looking at bank and building society accounts, the adviser must weigh up the rate of interest paid, the frequency, with the possible loss of interest on the early withdrawal from a 30, 60 or 90 day notice account.

(g) If the client is prepared to take risks, then shares, unit trusts or investment trusts have no surrender penalties as such. The client must remember that there will be transaction charges and also that, if he wants the money at a time when share prices have fallen, there could be a loss in the value of the shares or units.

1.4 Charging and commissions

(a) In order of cost of investment, starting with the cheapest, the investments we have considered can be listed as follows.

(i) Gilts
(ii) National Savings
(iii) Shares
(iv) Investment trust
(v) Bank and building society deposits
(vi) Annuities
(vii) Unit trusts
(viii) PEPs/ISAs
(ix) Investment bonds
(x) Maximum investment policies and endowments

It is difficult to say that this list is in the correct order. We know that the charges to buy a gilt are low, particularly if it is purchased through the Post Office and we know the stockbroker charges for the purchase of a share.

However, we do not know the charges within National Savings products, and the annuity. They are contained in the rate of interest offered to the investor. As far as the banks and building societies are concerned, again the charge is contained in the interest rate. We can obtain a rough idea by comparing the rate at which the building societies lend money and the rate they pay to the investor.

(b) The commissions paid to intermediaries, whether stockbrokers or IFAs, are clear on transactions of shares, gilts, investment and unit trusts because the amounts are shown on the contract note.

(c) Until January 1995 it was impossible for the investor in a life assurance product to know how much the intermediary was earning in commissions. With full disclosure and key feature documents, the commission is revealed and it is likely that insurance company charges will be forced down, as will commissions. There is a move for IFAs to take either level commissions or fees which should give the investor a better deal, certainly on early surrender.

BPP PUBLISHING

Question 1

(a) Which of the following investments has a low or nil surrender charge if encashed after a few months?

   (i)   Gilts
   (ii) Flexidowment
   (iii) Investment trust
   (iv) National savings children's bond

(b) Many investors say 'I would rather invest my money in the Building Society because they have no charges'. Is this statement correct and if not, why not?

1.5 Risk and accessibility

(a) In recommending an investment the adviser must be aware of the risk which the investor is prepared to run. The fact that the value of equities, whether direct or via unit trust and investments trusts, can fall must be clearly set out.

(b) The adviser must assess the amount of risk that the client can afford to take in relation to the money he has available. Therefore, if he only has £50 a month to save or £3,500 to invest, he must not be allowed to take the same level of risk as the man with £3,000 a month to invest or a capital sum of £150,000.

(c) The adviser should aim to suggest a well spread portfolio of the available assets in order to spread risk between types of investment and terms.

(d) As far as accessibility is concerned, the adviser must ascertain the client's need. If the money is required in 3 months time then it must not be tied up in any sort of contract with penalties. Alternatively, if the capital is not required, it should not be allowed to languish in a building society account with easy access.

(e) In all cases there must be an emergency fund with easy access. The amount of this emergency fund depends on the client's needs.

1.6 Tax treatment

(a) The tax treatment of the product is important. If the adviser is able to obtain a tax free return for a client who pays basic or higher rate tax this must be a goal.

(b) If a gilt can give a higher rate taxpayer a capital gains free return it merits consideration.

(c) If the client is a non taxpayer, an arrangement paying gross interest may be easier than having to fill out forms for the privilege of being paid gross. National Savings products may be the answer.

(d) A single premium bond or maximum investment policy will have tax advantages for the higher rate taxpayer.

1.7 The important factors in making a recommendation are all the points given above. None of these should be allowed to dominate. For example, there is no point in recommending a PEP/ISA on the tax advantage if the performance of the underlying fund is poor and the charges are high, or tying a client into an existing TESSA to get gross interest when he needs access to capital.

2   COMPARING OPTIONS

Available from the different providers of the same product type

2.1   **Bank and building society accounts and existing TESSAs**

Points to be considered:

(a)   interest rates;

(b)   minimum investments;

(c)   penalty periods (30, 60, 90 days);

(d)   the use of postal accounts (to some clients this would be an advantage, to others a disadvantage);

(e)   levels of investment at which interest rates increase is important;

(f)   penalties for moving funds - TESSA;

(g)   final loyalty bonus - TESSA.

2.2   **National Savings**

Points to be considered:

(a)   interest rates;

(b)   interest paid on early surrender;

(c)   reinvestment terms.

2.3   **Unit trusts and investment trusts**

Points to be considered:

(a)   availability of a new fund;

(b)   discount on purchase of units, eg 1% or 2%;

(c)   the ability to ISA a new fund;

(d)   availability of monthly savings plan and minimum premiums;

(e)   the availability of a particular fund such as a Tracker fund;

(f)   the past performance of funds;

(g)   the availability of specialist funds with good performance.

2.4   **PEPs/ISAs, shares and unit trusts, investment trusts**

Points to be considered:

(a)   charges;

(b)   exit penalties;

(c)   availability of special funds with good performance;

(d)   good choice of funds;

(e)   regular savings scheme and minimum contributions;

(f)   discount on unit price;

(g)   discretionary management;

(h)   single company ISA. Does the client have complete freedom of choice or only a choice from a menu of companies?

2.5 **Investment bonds**

Points to be considered:

(a) charges;

(b) any additional life cover available;

(c) special packaging of trust wordings etc for use for inheritance tax planning purposes;

(d) good fund choice;

(e) minimum contributions;

(f) unit allocations for larger investments;

(g) ability to top up amounts invested;

(h) reasonable charges for switching;

(i) good income facilities and method and frequency of payment. For example, the client may want a monthly payment of income. This is sometimes restricted unless the investment is substantial.

2.6 **Maximum investment policies and endowments**

Points to be considered:

(a) minimum premiums;
(b) charges;
(c) waiver of premium;
(d) choice of funds;
(e) segmentation;
(f) can critical illness cover be added?
(g) switching facilities.

2.7 **Annuities**

Points to be considered:

(a) competitive rates;

(b) guaranteed periods;

(c) payment methods;

(d) the availability of the type of annuity required. Some insurance companies do not offer all types of annuity;

(e) the availability of special rates for impaired lives or smokers.

3 **DIFFERENT PROVIDERS OF THE SAME PRODUCT**

3.1 You have now decided which product suits the client, so **which provider do you choose**? The three main considerations are:

(a) financial strength;
(b) service;
(c) past performance and investment choice;
(d) charges, access and terms.

3.2 Financial strength

(a) We have already considered the financial strength of the insurance companies in Chapter 4, Paragraph 3.2 *et seq*.

(b) However, when considering investments we are looking at other providers as well as insurance companies.

    (i) The government for National Savings and gilts - very sound!

    (ii) Banks and building societies are closely monitored.

    (iii) Unit trust managers are quite often owned by UK or international banking corporations. The adviser will be able to find out the total assets of such organisations fairly easily.

(c) In many cases it is worth remembering that the cautious investor will always feel happier with a household name and a big organisation. The more sophisticated will appreciate that it is often the smaller company and the niche player who can provide better returns, but at a higher risk.

3.3 Quality of service

The quality of service is important in all aspects of financial services. It is very important in the area of investment where the client needs to feel confident in the administration of the provider to whom he has often entrusted his life's savings. Incorrect documentation, or delays in investment, is not encouraging.

3.4 Investment choice and performance

(a) The adviser must keep up to date with the various funds available and their construction so that he can properly advise the client.

(b) Surveys will help to indicate past performance and current performance of funds. These can be found in *Money Marketing*, via the *Exchange*, *Money Management*, the financial pages of the national newspapers, *Investors Chronicle*, FT surveys etc. The Micropal service will allow the adviser to prepare comparisons of the performance of various funds in a graphic format.

(c) Meeting the fund managers and attending investment seminars will help to give the adviser knowledge of the current attitudes of a particular provider and his fund manager's approach to investment.

(d) Some fund managers pride themselves on stock selection, whereas others pride themselves on selecting the right asset or geographical spread.

(e) Past performance, as we all know, is not an indication of future performance and we have all seen the fund which was 'top of the pops' one year languishing at the bottom of the heap the following year (eg because it was a specialist technology fund or the like).

(f) It is more prudent to select a manager who offers consistent first or second quartile performance.

3.5 Charges, access and terms

These factors relate primarily to investment products. The Government's new CAT standards should facilitate comparison of providers.

Question 2

List the factors you would take into account when selecting a provider for the following investments

(a) A cash only ISA
(b) A unit trust

Chapter roundup

- This chapter has concentrated on how an adviser: selects the right product for the client, identifies the various options available and recommends a suitable company. This is a complex activity if carried out correctly.

Quick quiz

1   In selecting a provider for a cash ISA, which of the following would you consider to be the most important feature?

    A   Loyalty bonus at the end of 5 years
    B   An above average rate of interest, which should remain constant
    C   No charge on moving provider
    D   A local office for withdrawals

2   In selecting a suitable provider for an investment trust the adviser should do the following. (Mark each statement as True or False)

    A   Discover whether the trust is at a discount or a premium
    B   Ascertain if it is highly 'geared'
    C   Check surrender penalties
    D   Check on performance history

3   In selecting a suitable provider for a single premium bond which would be the most important feature?

    A   The ability to take a monthly income
    B   One free switch a year
    C   A good range of funds with consistent performance
    D   A special offer of an extra 1% allocation of units on investments over £25,000

The solutions to the questions in the quiz can be found at the end of this Study Text. Before checking your answers against those solutions, you should look back at this chapter and use the information in it to correct your answers.

Answers to questions

1   (a)   Gilts and an investment trust have no surrender penalty as such.

           The flexidowment would have a surrender charge.

           There would be no interest paid on the children's bond because it had been encashed within a year.

    (b)   Building societies, like all institutions, have administrative and management costs. These must be covered by charges. When they issue an interest rate they are willing to pay to an investor it is less than the interest they are charging the borrower. The difference between the two is their charge. This is being used to cover expenses in exactly the same way as unit trust companies and insurance companies charges cover their expenses.

2   (a)   Factors taken into account when selecting a cash only ISA

        (i)   The rate of interest being offered; is it fixed or variable?

        (ii)   Any penalties on switching

        (iii)   Any loyalty bonus

        (iv)   The financial strength of the bank or building society (which could be ascertained from their annual accounts)

        (v)   The service provided

    (b)   Factors taken into account when selecting a unit trust would be as follows.

        (i)   Investment managers experience and past performance.

        (ii)   The current portfolio construction.

        (iii)   Whether the fund has consistently good (first or second quartile, say) performance.

        (iv)   Fund charges, such as the amount of the annual management charge.

        (v)   The size of the funds under management of the unit trust house.

        (vi)   The quality of service.

Part C
Pensions

Chapter 9

PENSIONS IN THE FINANCIAL PLANNING CONTEXT

Chapter topic list	Syllabus reference
1　Evaluating a client's pension requirements	C 1.1
2　The factors upon which the pension requirements depend	C 1.2

Introduction

Students will be aware of the demographic changes in the population as we go into the next century. The result of the population growing older and living longer is a need for everyone to provide a sufficient income for their old age. The working population will be unable to contribute enough in terms of national insurance contributions to maintain the elderly by means of State benefits and therefore the need for proper pension advice and provision is of paramount importance.

1 EVALUATING A CLIENT'S PENSION REQUIREMENTS

1.1 The starting point for any pension evaluation is the **amount of income the client requires to live on in retirement**.

1.2 The answer the client gives **may be unachievable**. He may think he would like an income of two-thirds of his original earnings. The cost of this, particularly if the client is trying to achieve it himself without any help from an employer, may be prohibitive.

1.3 The client must be asked to sit down and work out his **expected income needs** in retirement. Most probably the mortgage will have been paid off. Perhaps the client will move to a smaller house which will involve lower outgoings.

2 THE FACTORS UPON WHICH THE PENSION REQUIREMENTS DEPEND

2.1 Having established how much pension the client would like to achieve, the adviser must then move on to establish, with the help of a **full fact find**, whether this is possible and **the means of achieving the client's aims**. It is sensible to plan towards a target pension of a % of final earnings and review the situation each year to ascertain the proximity to the target. In making his recommendations, the adviser will take into account a number of factors.

Previous and current pension arrangements

2.2 (a) **Checking on the client's existing pension arrangements** and his entitlement to the State pension is the first stage in the assessment process.

(b) It may be that the benefits from existing and previous pension schemes, together with the State benefits, will be **sufficient** and therefore there is no need for additional pension planning.

(c) The first step is to ascertain details of all previous pension schemes of the client, whether company schemes, retirement annuities (see Chapter 10) or personal pensions.

(d) If it is difficult to ascertain the information from the client, then the adviser must obtain his authority to write to the insurance companies concerned and the trustees of previous pension schemes, or even to trace old schemes through the Registrar of Pension Schemes.

(e) When all the information is received, it needs to be analysed to ascertain the total values of the schemes, in particular if there are any benefits on death or if the pensions increase up to retirement age and/or in retirement.

(f) The current pension scheme needs to be thoroughly researched. This can usually be done by means of the scheme booklet and the up-to date report and accounts of the scheme.

(g) It is important to ascertain whether the scheme is final salary or money purchase (see Chapter 10). Although the final salary scheme in most cases is superior to the money purchase scheme, nevertheless, if the client is a member for only a short time, the benefits will not be substantial.

(h) The adviser should aim to see if benefits increase in payment and if there are any plans to improve the benefits in the next few years.

(i) He should check the definition of final pensionable salary and whether the final benefits take into account the amounts received by the State. In both instances the final pension could be less than anticipated. If for example the final pensionable salary is based on basic pay rather than P60 earnings, say a salesman with high levels of commission or bonus could have a very reduced level of income in retirement.

(j) The adviser will also need to find out if there is an additional voluntary contribution scheme available and, if so, the basis and underlying investment performance.

2.3 The importance of this initial research and foundation work must be emphasised.

State pension

2.4 The State pension is in two sections.

(a) **Basic State pension**
(b) State Earnings Related Pension Scheme (**SERPS**)

Basic state pension

2.5 (a) Most clients will be entitled to a **basic State pension**. However the amount will depend on the amount of national insurance contributions paid. For the year 2000/01 the full pension for a single person who has made sufficient contributions is £3,510 per annum.

(b) Remember that many women will have had breaks in their working lives and as such will **not be entitled to a full pension in their own right**. They may have to rely on their husband's contributions. If they do this, their pension will be £2,100.80 per annum. Thus, a married couple's pension will be £5,610.80 or £7,520.00 per annum if they are both entitled to the full pension in their own right (unusual!).

(c) Also remember that some women have always paid a **reduced national insurance contribution**. This entitles them to a pension based only on the husband's contributions. (This option is no longer available). Full NI contributions must now be paid but those paying the married woman's rate may continue to do so).

(d) The Pensions Act 1995 introduced a **state pension age of 65** for men and women from 2020. This will be introduced over a ten year period, from 2010 for women born after 6 April 1955.

State earnings related pension scheme

2.6 (a) Only those who have been **employed** at some time will be entitled to this benefit. Those who have *always* been self employed will not.

(b) The State Earnings Related Pension Scheme commenced in 1978 and it is only **those retiring after 1998 who will receive the full benefit**.

(c) The benefits of the State Earnings Related Pension are based on **earnings between two bands**, the upper and lower earnings band (the upper earnings band being approximately 7 times greater than the lower) known as middle band earnings. For 2000/01 these earnings bands are:

   (i)   lower earnings limit £3,484 (£67 pw)
   (ii) upper earnings limit £27,820 (£535 pw)

(d) **Earnings above the upper earnings limit** will not be pensioned.

(e) For those retiring between 1998 and 2000, the DSS will revalue each of their band earnings in line with earnings inflation, take the best 20 years and then allocate a pension based on $1.25\% \times 20 = $ **25% of the inflation-proofed middle band earnings**.

(f) Those who have less than 20 years in the scheme, say 15, will simply have a calculation of $1.25\% \times 15 = $ **18.75% of the inflation proofed middle band earnings**.

(g) From the year 2010, the maximum calculation will be reduced to **20% of middle band earnings** of the average revalued middle band earnings throughout the member's whole working life. This will be particularly disadvantageous for those who have had working breaks to study or periods of self employment.

(h) The Pensions Act 1995 has introduced a new method of revaluing earnings which results in a **reduction in SERPS benefits** from April 2000.

(i) Clients may have **contracted out of the State Earnings Related Scheme** either by membership of a company pension scheme or an appropriate personal pension. This may have been for some, or all, of the potential years of membership of SERPS.

(j) In addition clients employed between 1961 and 1975 may be entitled to a very small state pension known as the **graduated scheme**.

(k) You will realise, having read the preceding paragraphs, that the state pension scheme benefits are **complex** and it would be very difficult for anyone to calculate correctly a client's benefit without help. Therefore, it is a worthwhile exercise for the adviser or the client to write to the Department of Social Security for an estimate of state pension entitlement, as this will include basic, graduated and SERPS benefits. Form BR19 is available from the DSS to allow this. Leaflet NP16 gives further details of state benefits.

(l) Refer to **Chapter 10** for additional information.

Question 1

Before proceeding, look back at FP1 and revise the notes on the state pension scheme, then answer the following questions.

(a) When was the State Earnings Related Scheme introduced?

(b) What will the calculation of SERPS be for a client who has been 'contracted in' throughout his working life, if he retires:

   (i)   in 2000?
   (ii) in 2013?

(c) Define middle band earnings.

(d) Do you think that state benefits in the future are likely to increase or reduce?

Age

2.7   The **age at which the client wishes to retire** is important. The adviser needs to ascertain if it is 65, 60 or earlier. The normal retirement age under the client's **contract of employment** is also important. Retirement planning should be fitted in around this.

2.8   The adviser should discover if the client wishes to **retire early** at say 50 or 55. Is this likely to be a reality or just a dream? The adviser will need to stress the expense of planning for early retirement. Advisers must be aware that the reverse can happen. Many directors of family companies have **no intention of retiring** and certainly will not hang up their boots until, say, age 70.

2.9   It is important to take into account the age of the **client's spouse or partner**. It is unlikely that one will wish to retire without the other, so the retirement planning must be dovetailed if possible. If the client is older than the spouse there may be a greater requirement to provide for adequate pensions for a widow or widower.

2.10 The **current age of the client** is also important. If he is young he has many years to achieve his objectives. The older the client, the fewer the years and the more expensive the exercise becomes. Many insurance companies provide leaflets emphasising the effect of 'delay' in pension planning.

Income

2.11 The client's **current level of income** is important. As with all other financial advice, the current income and outgoings must be analysed to ascertain the income available for investment into pensions. If this income is likely to increase on a regular basis, some form of indexing of premiums should take place.

2.12 In looking at the **client's outgoings,** it may be discovered that because of current commitments, such as school fees, he is unable to fund sufficient pension at the present time. It would then be useful to advise the client of how many years he can afford to delay if he wishes to achieve his aim, also the increased amounts which would then be involved to provide an adequate pension benefit.

2.13 If the client only has a small amount of spare income to commit to his financial needs, it is important that the **needs are prioritised**.

   (a) Cover for dependants.
   (b) Protection of income in the event of sickness.

(c)   Mortgage requirements.

(d)   Pension.

(e)   Savings.

(f)   Investment.

2.14   If the client is a director of his own company, then the discussion will centre around the amount which the **company can contribute** on his behalf; also the ability of the company to afford this from a cashflow point of view and to maintain the contribution level in the future. Often an adviser is called in when the company has had a good trading year. Before deciding on a level of contribution, it is important to ascertain whether this can be maintained in future, perhaps less profitable, years.

2.15   If an individual or a company has sufficient funds to contribute the next hurdle is the **Inland Revenue limits**. As the Inland Revenue gives tax relief to individuals and companies on contributions to pension schemes and the schemes themselves enjoy tax reliefs, the Revenue limits the amount of contributions which can be made. The maximum contributions must be checked. We will discuss maximum contributions later in Chapter 10.

Dependants

2.16   The **cost of dependants**, particularly children, can limit the amounts available to contribute to pension. It is also important to stress to clients that they must not, if at all possible, be **dependent on others for their pension provision**. Too often in the past, women in particular have taken the view that they did not have to fund for a pension in their own right because their spouse had made adequate provision. This is a fallacy. Changes in circumstances, such as a divorce, or death of the spouse can leave the client with no provision at all. The situation on divorce is changing. Pension benefits are now being taken into account in the settlement.

2.17   The client must ensure that in the event of his **death prior to retirement**, his spouse, partner or dependants are sufficiently covered. If life policies are not already in force this can be covered by pension life assurance and the return of the fund from the pension arrangement.

2.18   In designing the pension arrangements for a particular client care must be taken to ensure that any **dependants in retirement** will be properly covered, eg the spouse, partner or dependent children.

Question 2

The factors which effect a client's pension requirements can vary according to personal circumstances. Consider the following examples and prioritise the important factors in pension planning.

(a)   Andrew Johnson is aged 32, married with two young children. The children are being privately educated. Andrew belongs to his company pension scheme which will give him 35/60ths of his final earnings at age 65. He wishes to consider early retirement.

(b)   Terry Soanes is aged 50, he runs his own business as a self employed painter and decorator. To date he has only paid £50 per month into his pension arrangement. He can now afford £200 per month and single premium payments depending on profit.

(c)   John Jackson is aged 55 in a company pension scheme which he has only just joined. It will give him a pension of 10/80ths of his final earnings. He is concerned about providing sufficient pension for himself and his wife, who has never worked. He does have pensions from previous employment but does not know how much they are worth.

[]

Chapter roundup

- In this chapter we have highlighted the factors to be taken into account when evaluating a client's needs.

- The process is complicated, taking into account the state benefits, previous employers' schemes and the available income to fund pension benefits at the current time.

- The chapter emphasises the importance of targeting a pension benefit and keeping this under review.

Quick quiz

1   When evaluating a client's pension needs which of the following factors should be considered first?
   A   The size of the premium he will pay
   B   His disposable income
   C   His existing pension arrangements and the amount he will receive from the State
   D   His state of health

2   If a client has only a small amount of income to spend on savings and investment which of the following should be his most important consideration?
   A   Pension provision
   B   An ISA
   C   Adequate life cover for the family
   D   A Maximum Investment policy

3   Which of the following statements are True or False?
   A   A State pension is dependent upon a person's total National Insurance contribution history
   B   Women always rely on their husbands' National Insurance contributions to obtain a State pension
   C   If a client contracts out of the State pension he will receive no pension benefits from the state
   D   State pensions increase for the over 80s

4   In considering a client's previous pensions which of the following factors is most important?
   A   Only his existing personal pensions
   B   Only his existing retirement annuities
   C   His pension benefits from all sources
   D   Only his previous company pension schemes

The solutions to the questions in the quiz can be found at the end of this Study Text. Before checking your answers against those solutions, you should look back at this chapter and use the information in it to correct your answers.

Answers to questions

1   (a)   April 1978.

   (b)   (i)   25% × revalued middle band earnings for the best 20 years.
         (ii) 20% × revalued middle band earnings throughout whole working life.

   (c)   Earnings between the lower and upper earnings limit in a fiscal year.

   (d)   State pensions are likely to be reduced because of the increasing age of the population and the inability of the young to pay sufficient national insurance contributions to fund the pensions of the elderly.

2   (a)   (i)   Andrew Jackson has heavy financial commitments at present.
         (ii) His existing pension scheme is quite adequate.

(iii) He can afford to wait for a few years until his commitments reduce. He can then start funding Additional Voluntary Contributions.

(b) (i) Terry Soanes must fund his pension as quickly as possible, within Inland Revenue limits.

(ii) He must not rely heavily on the State. Because he is self employed, he will only be entitled to the basic State pension and not the earnings related pension.

(c) (i) John Jackson is in a company pension scheme but the benefits will only be small.

(ii) His previous pensions must be checked to calculate the total benefits available.

(iii) Particular emphasis must be laid on the widows pensions in all the schemes. At retirement it may be possible for John to sacrifice some pension in order to boost the widows pension if he is worried about this.

(iv) In these circumstances it would also be important to check the State benefits.

(v) If he has sufficient spare income, there is a good reason for funding additional voluntary contributions.

Chapter 10

KNOWLEDGE OF THE RANGE OF PENSION PRODUCTS

Chapter topic list	Syllabus reference
1 Clients' different needs	C 2
2 Occupational schemes	C 2.1
3 Personal pensions	C 2.2
4 Free standing additional voluntary contribution schemes	C 2.2
5 Retirement annuity	C 2.2
6 Section 32 buyout bonds	C 2.2
7 Proposed stakeholder pensions	C 2.2
8 Basic features of specialised schemes	C 2.3
9 Options available on leaving an occupational scheme	C 2.4

Introduction

We first discuss the providers, eligibility, contributions, benefits, options, tax treatment, statutory and pensions scheme office rules relating to: occupational pension schemes, occupational schemes which are contracted in or out, additional voluntary contributions and executive pension schemes.

Similarly, we cover the providers, eligibility, contributions, benefits, options, tax treatment, statutory and pension schemes office rules relating to: personal pension schemes, appropriate personal pension schemes, group personal pension schemes, pension term assurance, free standing additional voluntary contributions and retirement annuity contracts (s 226).

We then identify, the distinguishing features of: small self administered schemes, self invested personal pensions, funded unapproved retirement benefits schemes, simplified schemes.

Finally, we discuss, the options on leaving an occupational scheme.

The topic of pensions is a complex one because of the different type of schemes available to the employed and self employed. During the course of a client's life he can be in a number of different schemes and even change from being employed to self-employed and back again. A thorough knowledge of the range of pension products is therefore important.

1   CLIENTS' DIFFERENT NEEDS

1.1   Let us look at a few different situations.

(a)   Client A has **always been employed** and has the following sources of pension income:

(i)   basic State pension;

(ii)   some state earnings related pension scheme (SERPS) for the years he was fully in the State scheme;

(iii) some contracted out pension through an appropriate personal pension;

(iv) some pension from his company pension scheme.

(b) Client B is **self-employed**. His sources of pension income are:

(i) basic State pension;

(ii) retirement annuities;

(iii) personal pension.

(c) Client C. He is in his late 50s and is **currently self-employed**, although he has **previously been employed**. His sources of pension could be as complex, as follows:

(i) basic State pension relating to his entire working life;

(ii) state graduated pension;

(iii) some state earnings related pension scheme (SERPS) relating to the years when he was employed and contracted in;

(iv) some company pension benefits including contracted out benefits for a number of years;

(v) additional voluntary contributions relating to his company pension scheme;

(vi) personal pensions relating to his self employed years.

2 OCCUPATIONAL SCHEMES

> **KEY TERM**
>
> An **occupational scheme** is set up by an employer for his employees. The employer can be the government, eg the civil service, local authorities, large corporations or small family firms. Even a partnership or a sole trader can set up a scheme for its employees.

2.1 One of the greatest advantages of an occupational pension scheme is the **tax status** of the fund and the tax reliefs which are available on contributions and lump sum benefits. However in order to obtain the tax advantages, the scheme must be **exempt approved** and set up under an **irrevocable trust**. The trust and rules of the scheme must be approved by the **Pension Schemes Office**.

2.2 Let us look further at some of these expressions.

(a) **Irrevocable trust**. In order for the scheme to be approved it must be set up under an irrevocable trust. This means that the assets are not available to the employer's creditors in a liquidation.

(b) The **trust deed and rules**. These are complicated documents which take time to prepare and professional help has to be obtained. So, an interim deed is drawn up in order that the scheme can operate in the meantime.

(c) The **interim deed**

(i) The interim deed establishes the pension scheme and sets out how it will be administered.

(ii) Under the deed the employer appoints the initial trustees and gives them certain powers.

  (iii) The interim deed states that a **definitive deed** will be established within a specific period, usually 2 years.

 (d) **Exempt approved**. The trustees of a scheme will apply for exempt approval of their scheme for the following reasons.

  (i) Contributions paid by the employer can be treated as a business expense.

  (ii) Contributions paid by the employee can be eligible for tax relief.

  (iii) Contributions paid by the employer on behalf of the employee will not be treated as a benefit in kind.

  (iv) The pension fund investments will grow free of capital gains tax.

  (v) At retirement part of the benefit can be taken as a tax free lump sum.

 (e) Lump sum death benefits should be paid free of all tax and, in particular, inheritance tax so long as the trustees have discretion over the distribution of the benefits.

2.3 As well as exempt approved schemes, it is possible to find the following.

 (a) **Approved schemes**. These are schemes where employer contributions will not be taxed as benefit in kind, There are no other tax benefits.

 (b) **Unapproved pension schemes**. Following the Finance Act 1989 unlimited benefits can be given to an employee via an unapproved scheme. Under such an arrangement the investment income and capital gains arising in the fund are subject to tax. The taxation of contributions depend on whether it is funded or unfunded. Treated as a benefit in kind if funded and employer NICs are payable from April 1999.

Pension Schemes Office (PSO)

2.4 The **Pensions Schemes Office** is a department of the Inland Revenue which supervises occupational pension schemes. It does this through the issue of practice notes and guidance notes which lay down all the rules which must be followed if a Scheme is to be exempt approved and then maintain that status. Please note that the PSO has power to remove approval of a scheme.

Exam focus point
Do not confuse the PSO with the OPB (Occupational Pensions Board). The OPB was disbanded in April 1997 when the Pensions Act came into force, and replaced by the **Occupational Pensions Regulatory Authority** (OPRA).

Question 1
(a) Before moving on you should make sure that you understand the meanings of

  Interim deed
  Definitive deed
  Occupational pensions board
  Pension schemes office

(b) Llist the advantages of an exempt approved scheme.

The providers

Public sector schemes

2.5 Many people are covered by a **government or local authority pension scheme**, for example, civil servants, doctors, teachers, local authority workers, the police and the fire service. Some parts of the local authority workers are now coming under private schemes. As their departments go out to private tender, so too do their pension benefits.

2.6 Many of the public sector schemes will **not be set up under trust or be funded**. There is no need because they are backed by the government and the taxpayer.

Question 2

Do you understand the difference between funded and unfunded schemes? Give an example.

Private sector schemes

2.7 These are **schemes run by employers for their employees**.

 (a) When an employer establishes a pension trust and appoints trustees, the trustees must first decide how the scheme should be run and they will need advice on the following matters.

  (i) Administration
  (ii) Legal work and Inland Revenue approval
  (iii) Actuarial work
  (iv) Investment advice
  (v) Accountancy advice

 (b) The trustees have two choices:

  (i) to buy a package from an insurance company which includes all the services; or

  (ii) to establish a **self-administered scheme** where experts are appointed to deal with the individual matters. A self-administered scheme is more satisfactory for a large scheme and an insured scheme for the smaller group.

2.8 Whichever route the trustees decide to take, they will normally be assisted by a **professional pensions consultant** who will often be a director or employee of a specialist IFA employee benefits company, a firm of accountants or a firm of actuaries.

Product features: public sector

2.9 (a) Many of the **public sector schemes** are designed on the basis of the civil service scheme which provides 1/80th of final pensionable salary for each year of service up to a maximum of 40 years *plus* a tax free lump sum which can be up to 1.5 × final remuneration.

 (b) Pensions will be **increased by the retail prices index** between leaving service and normal retirement age and also in retirement.

 (c) Some schemes will be **non-contributory** (ie the members do not contribute).

 (d) The **early retirement pensions** due to ill health and redundancy are excellent.

 (e) Often there are **short-term service pensions** available.

(f)   Full value transfers to other similar schemes are available. This is known as the **transfer club.**

Question 3

All pension benefits under the statutory schemes are excellent. List the reasons why clients would be ill advised to transfer out of such a scheme into a personal pension. You may wish to defer doing this exercise until you have studied personal pensions (Section 4 of this chapter).

Private sector schemes

2.10   There are two types of private sector scheme. Their names are:

(a)   **final salary schemes,** also known as **defined benefit schemes;** or

(b)   **money purchase schemes,** also known as **defined contribution schemes.**

Final salary scheme

2.11   (a)   In this scheme the employee is promised a pension based on:

(i)   **years of service** in the scheme; and

(ii)   **salary close to retirement.**

The scheme will normally award him a fraction of final pensionable salary for every year in the scheme.

(b)   The fractions normally used are 1/80ths or 1/60ths of pensionable salary for each year of pensionable service. These fractions are often referred to as *accrual rates.*

For example, Fred Smith retires after 20 years in a scheme providing 1/60ths. His final pensionable salary is £10,000.

His pension will be 20/60 × £10,000 = £3,333.

(c)   One of the advantages of this type of scheme for the employee is that his pension is closely linked to his **income just prior to retirement.**

(d)   Another advantage is that the employee has a **guarantee** of the pension he will receive unless the employer changes the benefits.

(e)   The employer effectively has to write a blank cheque because he must contribute sufficient to the pension fund to ensure that the promised benefits can be paid out. The contribution is known as a **funding rate** and the actuary recommends this on a three yearly basis depending on the assets and liabilities of the scheme. In times of inflationary pay awards or poor investment performance, the funding levels can rise dramatically.

(f)   The employer can pay the total funding rate, if the scheme is non-contributory, or ask the employees to make a **contribution.** If the employees contribute, their payments will be a percentage of salary and will not normally increase if the funding rate rises. The employer will be responsible for picking up the difference.

For example, if the employee contribution is 5% of pensionable salaries and the funding rate is 12% of pensionable salaries, the employer pays 7% of pensionable salaries.

If at the next triennial valuation the funding rate rises to 15% of pensionable salaries, employees will still pay 5% of pensionable salaries but the employer will have to increase his contribution to 10% of pensionable salaries.

Question 4

Work out the pension for a man who has been in a 1/80ths scheme for 20 years on a final pensionable salary of £10,000.

Money purchase

2.12 (a) With **money purchase schemes** the employer decides an amount of contribution he is prepared to contribute to the scheme. This will normally be a percentage of salary and will automatically increase with salary rises.

(b) The employee may also be asked to contribute a **set percentage of salary**.

(c) The total contributions are invested and the final pension depends on the investment performance of the fund. **There is no guarantee** and it is less easy for the employee to predict his likely pension.

(d) The advantage of this scheme is that it is a **known cost** for the employer.

Common features of private schemes

2.13 The following are features of *both* final salary and money purchase schemes.

2.14 **Eligibility**

(a) The employer can decide which of his employees will be asked to join the scheme. He may decide on certain sections of the workforce, eg management only.

(b) The employer may give different levels of benefit to different grades of staff, eg 1/60th for management and 1/80th for works staff (provided there is no sex discrimination.)

(c) Normally the scheme will impose a lower and upper age joining limit, say age 18 - 60 or age 21 - 60. The reason for this is that young people often change jobs and at the older end, it is not worthwhile for an employee to be a member of a scheme for less than five years.

(d) A waiting period may also be imposed, say 1 or 2 years' service, or even as much as five years' service. This is done to reward long service and to cut out the administrative problems of transient employees joining and leaving in a short period.

(e) There are some restrictions that the employer can no longer impose. He must grant equal access to men and women under the terms of the Social Security Pensions Act 1975 and Sex Discrimination Act 1986. The Pension Act 1995 introduces an 'equal treatment' rule to all occupational pension schemes.

(f) The employer may have to offer membership to part-time employees if they would otherwise be barred from membership on the grounds of sex rather than their part-time status, for example if the full time work force was predominantly male and the part-timers all female.

(g) The employer can no longer make membership of the scheme compulsory or a condition of employment (the Social Security Act 1986). There is one exception: non-contributory schemes providing death in service benefits only can be compulsory. Not joining an employer's scheme is called opting out.

Question 5

See if you can put together an eligibility clause for a pension scheme using the points raised in the last section.

2.15 **Retirement age**

(a) Normally the retirement age under the pension scheme will be in line with the employee's contract of employment.

(b) Retirement ages will be between 60 and 75 with earlier retirement ages for certain occupations.

(c) Most schemes will allow employees to retire early on grounds of ill health without penalty.

(d) Early retirement for any other reason will normally be allowed with the trustees' approval, from age 50, but in this case an early retirement penalty will normally be applied.

(e) Following the case of *Barber v Guardian Royal Exchange 1990* taken to the European Court of Justice and the subsequent decisions in the *Ten Oever* and *Coloroll* cases, it is necessary for any new schemes to have the same retirement age for men and women.

(f) Existing schemes should by now have equalised retirement ages. *Equalisation* is only required for benefits accrued since 17 May 1990. If a scheme equalised pension ages after this date, then the benefits accrued for service in the interim period, ie the period between 17 May 1990 and the date of equalisation, must be levelled up to the more favoured sex.

Question 6

Although it is not essential for the examination, the student may like to read the details of the three very important cases, *Barber v Guardian Royal Exchange 1990*, *Ten Oever* and *Coloroll*.

2.16 **Contributions**

(a) The employer will decide whether the scheme is to be contributory or non-contributory.

(b) If the scheme is non-contributory the employer bears the total cost and if contributory the employee will make a contribution.

(c) The maximum contribution the employee can make in a fiscal year is 15% of gross remuneration (which can include benefits in kind).

(d) The employee contribution will normally be fixed at a percentage of pensionable salary.

(e) If the employer runs a money purchase scheme, his contribution will be a percentage of pensionable salary. However, if he is running a final salary scheme he must contribute the entire funding rate required less the employees' contribution.

(f) The definition of pensionable salary is important. In some cases this will be previous year's P60 earnings, in others it will simply be basic annual salary.

2.17 Benefits

(a) A pension scheme, whether money purchase or final salary, will normally provide the following benefits.

    (i) A pension payable throughout the lifetime of the employee but guaranteed to be paid for five years in any event.

    (ii) A pension payable to the spouse on the death of the employee in retirement. This pension may be 50% or 66.66% of the employee's pension.

    (iii) At retirement, part of the employee's pension can be commuted for a tax-free lump sum. If the employee elects this option it does not affect the level of the spouse's pension which continues to be a percentage of the uncommuted pension.

    (iv) Pensions must increase in payment (see Paragraph 2.35 on the Pensions Act).

(b) The basis of the pension will depend on the type of scheme. If it is a money purchase scheme, the pension will be based on the value of the fund at retirement date. If the basis is a final salary scheme, the benefits will depend on the accrual rate, whether it is, for example 1/45, 1/60 or 1/80 of final pensionable salary for each year of pensionable service.

Question 7

It may be useful to read through an example of how benefits at retirement can be taken.

Assumption

1/60ths Scheme, member has 20 years service and his final pensionable remuneration is £15,000. The scheme also provides a 50% spouse's death in retirement benefit.

At retirement he will have the following options.

Option 1

A full pension of 20/60 × £15,000 = £5,000 pa for the remainder of his life *plus* a spouse's pension of £2,500 pa payable from the date of his death.

or

Option 2

A tax free lump sum of 3 × 20/80 x £15,000 = £11,250 *and* a reduced pension of £5,000 - £11,250/9* = £3,750 per annum *plus* spouse's pension which remains the same at £2,500 per annum.

*The PSO publish a table of factors which are acceptable to them for commutation of pension, For a man of 65 they will accept that for every £9 of cash taken, £1 of pension is lost.

Now, if you are a member of a company final salary pension scheme, try and work out your potential benefits or if not, create an imaginary situation to ensure that you understand these calculations.

2.18 As previously mentioned the definition **of final pensionable salary** is important. Here are four examples of definitions which are acceptable to the Revenue.

(a) Basic pay in the year up to the date of retirement plus fluctuating payments (eg bonus and commissions and benefits in kind) averaged over the previous three years or more.

(b) Average of the total remuneration for any three consecutive years ending not earlier than ten years before the date of retirement.

(c)   Remuneration for any one year in the last five years prior to retirement.

(d)   Gross earnings in the last twelve months to retirement date.

2.19   Where the definition chosen is other than earnings in the last twelve months, the Revenue will allow each year's remuneration to be increased in line with the movement in the retail prices index up to the date of retirement. This is known as **dynamised final remuneration**.

2.20   The definition of final remuneration for controlling **directors** (ie those who singly or with their spouse, minor children and any trusts control 20% or more of the voting rights of a company) and those with final remuneration in excess of £100,000 must use the averaging definition because of potential abuse.

Question 8

Before proceeding, answer these questions.

(a)   Which definition of final pensionable salary would be allowed for a controlling director?

(b)   If you were a salesman on high levels of commission how would this be taken into account in a definition of final pensionable salary?

Which definition do you think would be most advantageous?

2.21   **Additional benefits**

Many schemes have additional benefits such as group life assurance schemes which provide lump sum and spouse's pensions in the event of an employee's death prior to retirement date. Others provide permanent health schemes which enable an employee to remain in service and continue as a member of the company pension scheme, despite a long term illness.

2.22   **Investment**

The pension premiums are invested by an insurance company or investment fund managers such as stockbrokers or merchant banks to create a fund from which benefits can be paid. Now let us look at the investment options available.

(a)   **Segregated fund.** This will be run by an investment manager for a self administered fund. The fund manager will select the day to day stocks and manage the portfolio and report to the trustees on performance, say every three months. The fund will normally be invested in a spread of equities, fixed interest and overseas holdings. Some large funds may have a property element. In some instances a specialised fund, such as USA or Far East would be used.

Some large schemes will have more than one fund manager and his performance will be compared to other pension funds using a statistics service such as CAPS.

(b)   If the trustees have bought an **insurance company package**, investment will be included. This can be in one of the following forms:

(i)   **Group deferred annuities.** In this case the insurance company guarantees the amount of pension at normal retirement date for a fixed premium. This can be with or without profits. The most common system would be with profits. The bonus each year would be added to the fund to build up sufficient reserve to meet the anticipated benefits. If performance was very good then it may be possible for the funding rate to reduce.

(ii) **Deposit administration**. This is a pooled investment where the premiums (net of expenses) of many schemes are accumulated in a pool to which interest is added and sometimes a bonus.

(iii) **Managed fund**. Investments into this fund participate with many other investors in the insurance company's managed pension fund. This will be a mixed fund of equities, fixed interest, sometimes property, overseas equities and bonds.

2.23 **Tax treatment**

Exempt approved status, (see Paragraph 2.2 (d)) will:

(a) obtain tax relief on employees' contributions;
(b) allow the employer's contributions to be treated as a business expense;
(c) allow employer's contributions for employees not to be treated as a benefit in kind;
(d) allow tax free cash at retirement;
(e) allow tax free lump sum on death.

Question 9

What is the difference between a money purchase and final salary scheme?

2.24 A scheme, whether money purchase or final salary, must comply with certain PSO rules concerning maximum benefits which are outlined below.

2.25 **The rules**. There are three regimes, depending on when an employee joined a scheme.

2.26 **Members of schemes who joined before 17 March 1987**

(a) *Pension at normal retirement date*

The normal maximum would be 2/3rds final remuneration after 40 years.

This pension can increase in line with the RPI.

Example

Employee with 40 years' service, final remuneration £20,000

Pension = 40/60ths × £20,000 = £13,333

(b) However, there are rules which allow a member to receive maximum benefits earlier. The maximum is 2/3rds of final remuneration after *10* years' service. This is known as *uplifted sixtieths*.

(c) If service is less than 10 years there is a sliding scale between 5 and 10 years.

These are the maximum benefits. The rules of a normal scheme will give a member with 10 years' service in a 60ths scheme only 10/60ths not 40/60ths.

(d) *Lump sum at normal retirement age*

The rule is 3n/80ths × final remuneration up to a maximum of 40 years where n = years of service.

Example

Employee with 40 years service and salary of £10,000

3 × 40/80 × £10,000 = £15,000

(e) However there are rules which allow an employee to obtain the maximum of 1.5 × final remuneration after *20* years' service.

155

If service is less than 20 years, then a special formula applies.

(f)   *Final remuneration* - no cash limit

(g)   *Employee contributions* - maximum 15% of total remuneration

(h)   *Early retirement* (not on grounds of ill health). There are two methods of calculating the maximum amount available, the better result can be utilised.

    (i)   *Method 1*

    1/60th of each year of actual service to date of early retirement subject to a maximum of 40 years × final pensionable remuneration at the date of early retirement.

    or

    (ii)   *Method 2*

    The use of the formula:

$$N/NS \times p$$

    where   N   = number of actual years of service subject to maximum of 40

    NS   = number of potential years of service subject to maximum of 40

    p   = the maximum approvable pension the member would have received if he had stayed in service to normal retirement age taking into account retained benefits

    The same method of calculation can be applied to the calculation of the tax free lump sum.

(i)   *Early retirement on grounds of ill health.* The pension can be equivalent to the maximum potential pension which could have been provided at normal retirement age together with the maximum tax free lump sum which could have been provided at the same time.

(j)   *Late retirement.* Members who continue in membership after normal retirement can continue to accrue benefits, if they have not achieved 40/60ths. If they have achieved 40/60ths by retirement date they can accrue a further 5 making up to 45/60ths.

(k)   *Death in service lump sum.* The maximum benefit is a lump sum equal to four times final remuneration plus the employee's contributions with interest.

(l)   *Death in service spouse's pension.* 2/3rds of the member's potential pension at normal retirement age is allowed. This pension can increase in line with the RPI. This will be 4/9ths plus dependants' pensions normally paid until age 18 or full time education is finished. The total of all these pensions must not exceed the member's potential total pension, ie 2/3rds of final remuneration.

(m)   *Death in retirement pension.* A pension equal to 2/3rds of the member's full (uncommuted) pension at retirement date increased in line with RPI plus dependants' pensions normally paid until age 18 or full time education is finished. The total of all these pensions must not exceed the member's potential total pension of 2/3rds of final remuneration.

(n)   *Leaving service benefits*

The following options are available.

(i) *Option 1*

If the member has belonged to the scheme for less than two years, he can have his contributions (but not the employer's) returned with a deduction of 20% tax.

(ii) *Option 2*

A deferred pension based on the ratio of actual to potential years of service and on the actual remuneration at the date of leaving.

All leavers since January 1986 have been entitled to an increase in their deferred pensions accrued since January 1985 by the smaller of the RPI or 5% pa (known as Statutory Revaluation).

For leavers since 1991 this increase applies to the total accrued pension for all service.

(iii) *Option 3*

A transfer value which can be taken to another occupational scheme, a personal pension or a s 32 buy out policy. AVCs will be included in this amount. If the scheme has been contracted out the Guaranteed Minimum Pension or protected rights will be kept separate in any transfers made so they can be separately identified by the new provider.

2.27 **Members of schemes established before 14 March 1989 who joined between 17 March 1987 and 31 May 1989**

(a) *Pension at normal retirement date.* The normal calculation is as previously shown, being 1/60th for each year of service up to a maximum of 40. This pension can increase in line with the RPI.

(b) For members of this regime the maximum 2/3rds final remuneration can be achieved after *20* years service. This is known as *accelerated accrual.*

(c) If service is less than 20 years the accrual rate can be 1/30th × final remuneration for each year of service.

(d) *Lump sum at normal retirement age.* The rule is 3n/80ths × final remuneration up to a maximum of 40 years service where n = years of service.

(e) Accelerated accrual can be used to increase the lump sum but only if it is also used to accelerate pension above the 1/60ths accrual rate and in the same proportion.

(f) For the high earner the total final remuneration which can be used for calculating the lump sum is £100,000.

Example

Employee with final earnings of £120,000 eligible for maximum lump sum commutation will only receive:

$1.5 \times £100,000 = £150,000$

(g) *Final remuneration.* No cash limit except on calculation of tax free lump sum.

(h) *Employee contributions.* Maximum 15% of total remuneration.

(i) *Death in service lump sum.* The maximum benefit is a lump sum equal to four times final remuneration plus employee's contributions with interest.

(j) *Death in service spouse's pension.* A 2/3rds member's potential pension at normal retirement age is allowed. This pension can increase in line with the RPI. This will be 4/9ths plus dependants' pensions normally paid until age 18 or full time education is finished. The total of all these pensions must not exceed the member's potential total pension, ie 2/3rds of final remuneration.

(k) *Death in retirement pension.* A pension equal to 2/3rds of the member's full (uncommuted) pension at retirement date increased in line with RPI plus dependants' pensions normally paid until age 18 or full time education is finished. The total of all these pensions must not exceed the member's potential total pension, ie 2/3rds of final remuneration.

(l) *Retained benefits.* These are benefits from other employers' schemes - these need to be taken into account when calculating maximum pension benefits but *not* the tax free lump sum.

(m) *Leaving service benefits.* The following options are available.

  (i) *Option 1*

    If the member has belonged to the scheme for less than 2 years he can have his contributions (but not the employer's) returned with a deduction of 20% tax.

  (ii) *Option 2*

    A deferred pension based on the ratio of actual to potential years of service and on the actual remuneration at the date of leaving.

    All leavers since January 1986 have been entitled to an increase in their deferred pensions accrued since January 1985 by the smaller of the RPI or 5% pa.

    For leavers since 1991, this increase applies to the total accrued pension for all service.

  (iii) *Option 3*

    A transfer value which can be taken to another occupational scheme, a personal pension or a s 32 buy out policy. AVCs will be included in this amount.

    If the scheme has been contracted out the GMP or protected rights will be kept separate in any transfers made so they can be separately identified by the new provider.

(n) *Early retirement* (not on grounds of ill health). There are two methods of calculating the maximum amount available. The more favourable one can be utilised.

  (i) *Method 1*

    1/60ths of each year of actual service to date of early retirement subject to maximum of 40 × final pensionable remuneration at date of early retirement.

  (ii) *Method 2*

    The use of the formula:

$$N/NS \times p$$

    where N = number of actual years of service subject to maximum of 40

      NS = number of potential years of service subject to maximum of 40

      p = the maximum approvable pension the member would have received if he had stayed in service to normal retirement age taking into account retained benefits

    The same method of calculation can be applied to the calculation of the tax free lump sum.

(o) *Early retirement on grounds of ill health.* The pension can be equivalent to the maximum potential pension which could have been provided at normal retirement age together

with the maximum tax free lump sum which could have been provided at the same time.

(p) *Late retirement.* Unlike members joining before 17 March 1987, members joining between 17 March 1987 and 31 May 1989 cannot earn extra 60ths on late retirement. They cannot exceed 1/30th for each year of service up to a maximum of 20/30ths.

2.28 Members of schemes established on or after 14 March 1989 and members of all schemes who joined on or after 1 June 1989 (or those who have opted to be subject to this regime)

(a) *Pension at normal retirement date.* Normal calculation as above: 1/60th for each year of service up to a maximum of 40 × final remuneration subject to *earnings cap* (see final remuneration below).

(b) The maximum pension of 2/3rds final remuneration can be earned after *20* years' service, known as *accelerated accrual.*

(c) If service is less than 20 years, 1/30th × final remuneration for each year of service is offered.

(d) *Lump sum at normal retirement age.* The rule is 3n/80ths × final remuneration subject to earnings cap (see final remuneration) up to a maximum of 40 years, where n = years of service.

(e) Accelerated accrual can be used to increase the *lump sum benefit* but only if it is also used to accelerate pension above the 1/60th accrual rate and in the same proportion.

(f) Another formula for calculating the lump sum benefit is available 2.25 × the uncommuted pension.

(g) *Final remuneration.* This is limited to an earnings cap of £91,800 (2000/01).

(h) *Employee contributions.* Maximum of 15% of capped remuneration.

Example

An employee earning £100,000 in 2000/01 can pay maximum total contributions to a company pension scheme of £13,770 (ie 15% of £91,800).

(i) *Death in service lump sum.* The maximum benefit is a lump sum equal to four times final remuneration plus employee's contributions with interest.

(j) *Death in service spouse's pension.* A 2/3rds member's potential pension at normal retirement age is allowed. This pension can increase in line with the RPI. This will be made up of 4/9ths plus dependants' pensions normally paid until age 18 or full time education is finished. The total of all these pensions must not exceed the member's potential total pension, ie 2/3rds of final remuneration.

(k) *Death in retirement pension.* A pension equal to 2/3rds of the member's full (uncommuted) pension at retirement date increased in line with RPI plus dependants' pensions normally paid until age 18 or full time education is finished. The total of all these pensions must not exceed the member's potential total pension, ie 2/3rds of final remuneration.

(l) *Retained benefits.* These are benefits from other employers' schemes and need to be taken into account when calculating maximum pension benefits, *not* the tax free lump sum.

No retained benefits need to be taken into account for members of a scheme joining on or after 31 August 1991 whose earnings are less than 25% of the earnings cap on joining. For example, when the earnings cap is £91,800, those with remuneration on joining of less than £22,950 pa will not need to take into account retained benefits.

(m) *Leaving service benefits.* The following options are available.

    (i)   *Option 1*

        If the member has belonged to the scheme for less than two years he can have his contributions returned, less tax at 20%.

    (ii)   *Option 2*

        A deferred pension based on 1/30 × final remuneration for each year of service subject to the maximum of 2/3rd final remuneration.

        All leavers since January 1986 have been entitled to an increase in their pensions accrued since January 1985 by the lower of the RPI or 5% pa.

        For leavers since 1991 this increase applies to the total accrued pension for all service.

    (iii)   *Option 3*

        A transfer value which can be taken to another occupational scheme, a personal pension or a s 32 buy out policy. AVCs will be included in this amount.

        If the scheme has been contracted out the GMP or protected rights will be kept separate in any transfers made so they can be separately identified by the new provider.

(n) *Early retirement (not on grounds of ill health).* A pension of 1/30 × final remuneration for each year of service subject to 2/3rds maximum on retirement at any time between 50 and 75. The tax free lump sum can be 2.25 × uncommuted pension.

(o) *Early retirement on grounds of ill health.* The pension can be equivalent to the maximum potential pension which could have been provided at normal retirement age together with the maximum tax free lump sum which could have been provided at the same time.

(p) *Late retirement.* Members cannot earn extra 60ths on late retirement. They cannot exceed more than 1/30th for each year of service up to a maximum of 20/30ths.

Question 10

(a) Calculate the maximum pension benefit which a man aged 20 who joined a 1/60ths scheme in 1990 could receive, if he remained in service until age 65 and his remuneration at retirement was £200,000. The scheme sets a normal retirement date of 65. Assume an earnings cap of £91,800.

(b) Calculate the maximum tax free lump sum he could receive.

(c) Make sure you know the definitions of the following.

    Retained benefits
    Accelerated accrual
    Uplifted sixtieths
    Earnings cap

2.29 Surplus

(a) In the past many pension schemes have been in surplus. This means their assets exceed their liabilities, primarily because of good investment returns.

(b) The Finance Act 1986 stated that any surplus of assets in excess of 5% had to be eliminated in one of the following ways.

(i)   Benefit improvement.

(ii)   A reduction in employer/employee contributions to eliminate the surplus over 5 years.

(iii) A payment from the scheme to the employer, with PSO approval, which would be taxed at 40%. The tax would be deducted by the scheme administrators and sent direct to the Revenue before the money was handed to the company.

(c) The refund to the company cannot be made until full *limited price indexation increases* (these are increases in line with RPI or 5% whichever is less) have been guaranteed to all pensions, ie in payment and deferred.

(d) Each scheme's surplus situation is checked by actuarial reports at least every five years.

Tax treatment of occupational schemes

2.30 (a) Employer's contributions are treated as a **business expense**.

(b) If a special contribution is made on or after 1 June 1996 into the fund, perhaps to pay for past service benefits, relief will be given in the year of payment up to a **maximum payment of £500,000.**

(c) Amounts will be spread as follows for tax relief purposes if they exceed the total of £500,000 and the employer's ordinary annual contribution:

£500,000 or over but less than £1,000,000	2 years
£1,000,000 or over but less than £2,000,000	3 years
£2,000,000 or over	4 years

(d) **Special contributions under £500,000** will need to be reported to the PSO unless the special contribution is equal to or less than the normal contributions made by the employer to the scheme *or* one half of the permitted maximum *or* is being used simply to provide cost of living increases for existing pensioners.

(e) Employee contributions up to **15% of their total remuneration** in a fiscal year are eligible for tax relief. The contributions are deducted from gross pay before calculation of tax.

Schemes contracted in or out of State Earnings Related Pension Scheme

2.31 (a) When a company pension scheme is established, the employer has a choice. He can give his employees **a benefit on top of all the state benefits,** in which case they will receive:

(i)   basic state pension;
(ii)   earnings related pension (SERPS);
(iii) company pension benefit.

(b) Alternatively he can provide the SERPS benefit within the company pension scheme. This is known as **contracting out** and for the years of membership of the scheme the employee will receive:

(i)   basic old age pension;
(ii)   company pension including SERPS.

(c) The **method of contracting out of an occupational scheme** depends on whether it is a final salary scheme or a money purchase scheme. We will look at each separately.

Question 11

Which situation provides the member with the overall better pension benefit, a 1/60th contracted in scheme or a 1/60th contracted out scheme?

Contracting out with a final salary scheme established prior to April 1997

2.32 (a) Both the employer and employee pay **lower national insurance contributions**. The employer's NI contribution is reduced by 3% of the employee's middle band earnings and the employee's NI contributions reduce by 1.6%. This will apply for a 5 year period ending 5 April 2002.

(b) Prior to April 1997 the employer ran a scheme which promised to provide a benefit at least equivalent to SERPS in terms of member's and spouse's pensions (this is known as a **guaranteed minimum pension** (GMP)). The spouse's pension had to be 50% of the member's GMP if the widow or widower had children or was aged over 45.

(c) The guaranteed minimum pensions both for the member and spouse must **increase in payment by 3%, or the RPI if less**. Benefits accruing after 5 April must increase by Limited Price Index at any time between age 60 and 75.

(d) The guaranteed minimum pensions can be paid.

(e) Guaranteed minimum pensions were **abolished for** service after 5 April 1997.

(f) If an employee **leaves a contracted out final salary scheme** his guaranteed minimum pension must be dealt with in one of the following ways.

(i) If he has less than two years service, he can be bought back into the State scheme by payment of a contributions equivalent premium (CEP), and he will then be treated as if he was never contracted out. The CEP is equivalent to the employer/employee NI rebates which have been given.

(ii) If the employee has been in service for a longer period he can transfer his GMP to another employer's scheme or a personal pension/buy out bond (s 32 bond).

(iii) If he preserves his pension in the scheme, the GMP has to be revalued up to state retirement date by one of the following methods.

(1) In line with *national average earning*. This is known as Section 21 orders. It is used by statutory schemes (also known as 148 orders).

(2) By a *fixed revaluation rate*, 7% for leavers after 5 April 1993 with a higher level for earlier leavers. In this case, if the increase in the national average earnings index is greater, the State makes up the balance. The revaluation rate reduced to 6.25% for leavers after 5 April 1997.

(3) A *limited revaluation*. In this case the benefit must be revalued by the national average earnings index or 5% whichever is the lower. Again if the national average earnings index is greater, the State makes up the difference. This option has not been available since 5 April 1997. (A limited revaluation premium was paid to the State to take on the liability.)

Contracting out with a money purchase scheme established prior to April 1997

2.33 (a) The employer guarantees to pay into a pension scheme his own and the employee's level rebate. These amounts then increase in value in line with investment returns and are known as **protected rights**. There is no guarantee of the value of the pension which

will be available at retirement. Further age related rebates are payable direct to the scheme by the Contributions Agency.

(b) The protected rights pensions **must not commence before age 60**. The pensions must increase by 3% or the RPI if less and a 50% spouse's pension must be paid if the widow or widower has children or is aged over 45. For protected rights built up after 5 April 1997 unmarried members have the option of taking an increased pension for this portion of the fund.

(c) It must be stressed that using this method there is no guarantee that the protected rights pension will be as great as SERPS or the GMP under a final salary scheme.

(d) Because this method does not guarantee a pension equivalent to SERPS and is dependent upon performance, the scheme will usually make provision for those under, say, 39 (females) and 47 (males) to contract out and those over that age to remain contracted into SERPS. The reason for this is that the rebates are not sufficiently large for those at the older ages to accumulate sufficient pension to compensate for the loss of the SERPS benefit.

(e) With effect from 2 July 1997 pension fund managers can **no longer reclaim the tax credits on dividends received from UK shares**. This will have the effect of reducing the investment returns of the fund. Therefore the feasibility of contracting out members of a money purchase scheme at any age must be re-considered.

Question 12

Before proceeding you must be able to identify the main difference between contracting out via a final salary scheme or a money purchase arrangement.

Summary of changes to contracting-out with effect from April 1997

2.34 (a) The **Pensions Act 1995** introduced changes to the methods of contracting-out for final salary money purchase and personal pension schemes. We will study each separately.

    (i)   *Final salary schemes*

        (1) Currently a contracted-out final salary scheme must provide a guaranteed minimum pension (GMP). From 6 April 1997, GMP accrual ceased.

        (2) Limited rate revaluation on GMPs will no longer be an option.

        (3) Final salary schemes will be able to contract out only if they pass a reference scheme test.

        (4) Contracted-out benefits accruing after April 1997 will increase by the Limited Price Index (LPI) rather than 3%.

        (5) The scheme's actuary must certify every three years that the scheme provides retirement pensions for members which considered as a whole are 'broadly equivalent' to or better than pensions under a reference scheme. The reference scheme benefits will be:

            • accrual rate - 1/80th

            • pensionable salary - 90% of band earnings

            • final pensionable salary - average of pensionable salary over last three tax years

            • Payable from age 65 for lifetime

- 50% spouse's benefit

(6) A flat rate rebate will apply to these schemes.

(ii) *Money purchase schemes*

(1) Age related rebates were introduced from April 1997.

(2) Reduced NICs are paid by the employer and employee. The employer makes equivalent contributions into the scheme with the employee portion receiving tax relief. The balance of the age related rebate will be paid by the DSS in arrears.

(iii) *Appropriate personal pensions*

(1) Age related rebates were introduced from April 1997.

(2) The rebates will continue to be paid into the scheme in arrears by the DSS. (Must contract out using form APP1. May contract back in using APP2.)

Additional voluntary contributions (AVC)

2.35 (a) It is now compulsory for companies to offer their employees the opportunity to invest **additional contributions** into their occupational pension scheme where there is one.

(b) Under the Revenue limits, an employee can invest up to **15% of his total remuneration** into an occupational pension scheme. Thus if he is already paying 5% of total remuneration to the scheme, he can pay a further 10% as an additional voluntary contribution.

(c) The amount of the contribution may be subject to **capped earnings** of £91,800 (2000/2001) depending on date of joining the scheme.

(d) Contributions obtain relief at the employee's **highest rate of tax**.

(e) Such contributions are deducted from pay before tax is calculated and can be **paid weekly, monthly or even by single payments**.

(f) Contributions can **be stopped at any time**.

(g) Contributions to AVC schemes can now only be used to buy **additional**:

(i) employee pension;
(ii) spouse's pension;
(iii) dependants' pension;
(iv) life assurance up to a total of $4 \times$ salary.

(h) If a member took out an AVC prior to 8 April 1987 he can take the benefits as a **tax free lump sum** subject to the overall limits on tax free lump sum payments for the whole scheme.

(i) It should be noted that often the definition of pensionable salary is **basic rather than total earnings,** which gives the member wider scope for AVC payments.

(j) It is important to ensure that by the use of an AVC the employee does not end up with an **overfunded pension** at retirement age. If this happened then the surplus AVC funds would have to be returned to the employee less tax at 32% (2000/2001). Higher rate tax payers would have an extra 16% tax to pay.

(k) Normally the employer runs a **separate AVC scheme** rather than investing the employee's own money in the main scheme.

(l) A large company may offer employees a **choice of AVC schemes,** maybe a managed fund and a building society scheme, so that employees can choose according to their risk profile.

The free standing AVC (FSAVC)

KEY TERM

Free standing AVCs were introduced in 1987. This is an additional voluntary contribution scheme which is run by an insurance company rather than the trustees of the employee's pension scheme.

2.36 (a) The free standing AVC is still part of the member's overall company pension scheme benefits but the **big advantage is the choice of investment.** The insurance company will offer the full range of unit-linked funds, equity, overseas equity, managed, international, property, specialist area funds such as America, Japan and the Pacific, as well as unitised with profits. The employee can select the fund into which his money is allocated and initiate switches between funds whenever he wishes.

(b) Contributions to the FSAVC can be on **a monthly or single premium basis** but the member can use only one provider per fiscal year.

(c) Contributions to the FSAVC can be paid **net of basic rate tax** but higher rate tax has to be reclaimed by use of a FSAVCC (a free standing AVC certificate).

(d) If the contribution to the FSAVC is **less than £2,400 per annum**, the insurance company need only minimal information regarding the main scheme. However, if the contribution is in excess of this amount, they will need full details of the main scheme to ensure that there is no overfunding. This is known as a headroom check.

(e) There are a number of individuals who are excluded from having an FSAVC

   (i) Members of simplified final salary schemes

   (ii) Members of s 590 Occupational Schemes (usually shareholder directors of investment companies)

   (iii) 20% directors (directors who alone or through associates own or control 20% or more of the ordinary share capital of a company)

(f) It **is** possible to use a Free Standing Additional Contribution plan to **contract out of SERPS,** in exactly the same way as an Appropriate Personal Pension. However, the employee rebate of National Insurance will not benefit from tax relief. It is preferable to recommend an Appropriate Personal Pension as a method of Contracting Out rather than using the FSAVC, as not only will tax relief be available but also the benefits from the APP would be payable **in addition** to the maximum benefits otherwise payable under the Occupational Scheme. This would not be the case with the FSAVC.

Question 13

(a) What is the maximum net payment that a scheme member could make to a FSAVC in 1999/00 assuming that his scheme was non-contributory and that his total remuneration was £100,000 pa.

(b) List the advantages and disadvantages of the company AVC and the FSAVC.

Tax treatment of AVCS and FSAVC

2.37 (a) As previously mentioned AVCs are deducted from gross pay and receive **instant tax relief.**

(b) FSAVCs can be paid net of basic rate tax and **higher rate relief claimed.**

(c) The underlying fund for an AVC or FSAVC suffers **no capital gains tax.**

(d) In the event of a member overfunding an AVC or FSAVC, the surplus funds would be paid to him net of 32% (2000/01) tax.

Executive pension schemes

2.38 **Features**

(a) Many directors of small to medium size family businesses are loath to become members of the main employee pension scheme because the disclosure rules will mean there is little confidentiality concerning their pension provision.

(b) They may also want a scheme with greater flexibility and investment choice.

(c) All these problems can be overcome by the use of an executive pension scheme. This is an individual pension arrangement for one person but it is governed by the same Inland Revenue rules as any other occupational scheme.

(d) Usually executive pension schemes are funded on a money purchase basis but with a view, if possible, to achieve a maximum funding.

(e) In the past, companies often put in high levels of regular and single premiums and if the employee then left service his benefits were overfunded. The Revenue has now brought in new limits which allow for a lower premium threshold increasing over the term of the contract.

(f) The executive pension will be offered by a range of insurance companies who will provide a full package of administration, legal and actuarial advice and a choice of investment funds. Some schemes will be set up as deferred annuities, others as pure endowments. It will be possible to include death in service benefits if required.

(g) In many instances the schemes will be non-contributory. However, if a director is about to receive a large bonus it may be sensible tax planning for him to forgo this in return for an additional contribution to his pension scheme, thus avoiding extra NI and taxation. This procedure is known as *salary sacrifice*. This, of course, would not be possible if the scheme were over-funded.

2.39 **Tax treatment**

(a) The employer contribution will be allowed as a business expense.

(b) If a large single payment is made, the tax relief may have to be spread as illustrated in this chapter at Paragraph 2.30(c).

(c) Employees' contributions will be allowable for tax relief at their highest rate and deducted from salary before calculation of tax. But care must be taken with directors with high levels of remuneration because of the earnings cap.

Pensions Act 1995

2.40 Here are the main provisions of the Act.

(a) **Member nominated trustees**

The members are given the right to nominate one-third of the trustees with a minimum of two (one if the membership is below 100).

(b) **The Occupational Pensions Regulatory Authority (OPRA)**

This is a new regulatory authority for occupational pension schemes. It will replace the OPB. OPRA has been given wide powers to monitor and intervene in the running of occupational schemes. It will be able to impose sanctions on trustees, employers and professional advisers.

(c) The pensions accruing after April 1997 from a final salary or money purchase scheme must be increased by a **limited price index** (LPI). This is an increase in line with the RPI up to a maximum of 5% per annum.

(d) A **minimum funding requirement** (MFR) will be imposed on final salary schemes. The scheme will be valued every three years and a contribution schedule drawn up and certified by the actuary to be sufficient to restore or maintain a 100% MFR for the next five years. Where a valuation indicates a funding level below 90%, the funding must be brought up to 90% within 12 months and a schedule of contributions must be agreed to bring the funding up to 100% within five years.

(e) New **winding up provisions** will apply to schemes subject to the MFR.

(f) Trustees will be required to maintain a **written statement of investment principles**.

(g) New rules have been introduced on **transfers**. Members who left the scheme before 1 January 1986 now have a right to a transfer value. New transfer value calculation standards will be introduced and the transfer value from a final salary scheme must be guaranteed for a period of three months.

(h) A scheme must have in place a **dispute resolution procedure** and information must be available to members.

(i) A new **pensions compensation board** is to be established to deal with pension scheme assets lost through theft or fraud. The scheme will be financed by a levy. Compensation will be made if the employer is insolvent. The maximum compensation will be sufficient to restore the assets to 90% of the liabilities.

3 PERSONAL PENSIONS

3.1 **Personal pensions** were introduced by the Social Security Act 1986 and became available from 1 July 1988. The aim was that all those not in company pension schemes could have their own fully portable pension arrangement designed on a money purchase basis.

Providers

3.2 In order to offer personal pension arrangements to the general public, the provider must have a scheme which is **approved by the PSO**. The following institutions are allowed to run these schemes.

(a) Insurance companies
(b) Friendly societies
(c) Unit trust companies
(d) Banks
(e) Building societies

Product features

3.3 **Eligibility**. The following category of person may effect a personal pension.

(a) Those in **non-pensionable employment** whether employee or director (except a controlling director of an investment company). This effectively means anyone who is not currently a member of a company pension scheme either because he has not been offered membership or he has refused.

(b) A self employed person taxed under Schedule D.

(c) A person who has more than one occupation, one of which is not pensionable, for example a National Health dentist who also undertakes private work.

(d) A person in a contracted in company pension scheme is allowed to take out a personal pension as a means of contracting out. This personal pension is known as an **appropriate personal pension** and only receives payment from the Contributions Agency in the form of rebates of national insurance contributions.

(e) A person in a company pension scheme may have a single premium personal pension as a vehicle for receiving a transfer payment.

(f) A person in a company pension scheme who is covered for death in service lump sum benefits only.

3.4 **Contributions**

(a) Contributions can be paid on a regular or single premium basis. Regular premiums are normally paid either monthly or annually.

(b) Most insurance companies will allow for premiums to be increased by a set annual percentage, the RPI, or average earnings index. Such inflation proofing of contributions is essential if a realistic level of pension is to be produced.

(c) If the policyholder cannot meet contributions in a particular year, they can usually be reduced to a minimum and if necessary a premium holiday can be arranged without penalty.

(d) The contributions which can be made depend on a person's age on 6 April each year.

(e) The maximum contribution is a percentage of net relevant earnings (NRE).

    (i) Net relevant earnings for the self employed means business profits reduced by allowable expenses and, if appropriate, capital allowances.

    (ii) Net relevant earnings for the employed means taxable remuneration, fees, bonus, benefits in kind, commissions.

The maximum percentages for 2000/01 are as follows:

Age at 6 April in year of assessment	*Maximum percentage of NRE*
	%
35 or less	17.5
36 – 45	20.0
46 – 50	25.0
51 - 55	30.0
56 – 60	35.0
61 or over	40.0

The earnings cap will apply to contributions to a personal pension.

(f) The maximum contributions can be paid by a self-employed person, an employee or an employer. If an employee and employer make contributions their total contributions cannot exceed the maximum allowed.

(g)   Up to 5% of the net relevant earnings can be used to provide a lump sum death benefit in the event of death before retirement.

Question 14

(a)   Work out the maximum personal pension contribution which an investor with a date of birth of 4 April 1943 can make in the tax year 2000/01 if her net relevant earnings are £10,000.

(b)   How much could she contribute if her net relevant earnings were £95,000?

Carry back and carry forward

3.5   Because personal pensions and, previously, retirement annuities (see Paragraph 5.1) were originally designed for the self employed, the Revenue recognised that a self-employed person often has an irregular income pattern and cannot necessarily contribute the maximum contributions to pension each year. Hence, they have instigated rules which allow the investor to make use of **unused reliefs from previous years**.

Carry back

> **KEY TERM**
>
> The exercise of **carry back** enables a contribution to be made in the current tax year but treated as if it were paid in the previous tax year.

3.6   (a)   If such a contribution is made, it will be based on the net relevant earnings for the previous tax year and allowable at the **tax rate for that year**. This can be a useful device if the investor's tax rate falls or if the Government reduces tax rates from one fiscal year to the next.

(b)   The contribution can be made **regardless of** whether any payment is being made for the current tax year.

(c)   If there are no net relevant earnings in the previous year the contribution can be carried back **one further year**.

Example

Self employed person aged 28

Tax year	Net relevant earnings	Contribution
2000/01	£20,000	£1,750 related to 1998/9
1999/00	nil	nil
1998/99	£10,000	nil

(d)   Contributions made by an employer **cannot be carried back**.

(e)   If an investor wishes to carry back a contribution he must make an election to the Inland Revenue by 31 January following the tax year in which the payment is made.

Carry forward of unused relief

> **KEY TERM**
>
> If **pension contributions** in any one tax year do not use up all the allowable tax reliefs, the balance can be **carried forward** as unused relief for up to 6 years.

3.7 (a) Before carry forward of unused relief can be exercised, the **maximum allowable contribution must be made for the current tax year**.

(b) If carry forward is utilised, the amounts carried forward must be calculated on the net relevant earnings of the policyholder **in that year** and his age on 6 April of that year.

(c) The **unused relief** for the earliest year must be used up first.

(d) The change in the earnings cap from year to year is relevant to the calculation of maximum amounts for a **high earner** making use of the carry forward provisions.

(e) **Carry back and carry forward can be utilised together**. If this is done, it is possible to carry forward for six years before the year of carry back.

(f) It is not possible by utilising carry back/carry forward to pay **more** in pension contributions in a tax year than the total net relevant earnings for that tax year.

3.8 **Retirement age**

(a) Benefits can be taken at any age between 50 and 75.

(b) There are special provisions for certain occupations. These people can take benefits prior to age 50.

(c) A policyholder does not have to retire in order to take the benefits. Many clients have a series of policies or break their policy down into segments which allows them to encash their pension benefits over a number of years.

(d) A new rule was introduced in the 1995 Finance Act which allows members of a tax approved personal pension scheme to defer purchasing an annuity at pension date. If they wish they can defer the purchase to age 75. In the meantime they will be able to take the tax free lump sum and withdraw amounts from their pension fund within a range of income agreed by the Government Actuary broadly equivalent to the annuity their fund would have provided. This is known as the draw-down facility.

3.9 **Benefits**

(a) *At retirement*

(i) At retirement if the draw-down facility is not utilised, the fund can be used to purchase a pension either from the host insurer or an alternative insurer if they offer more attractive terms. This is called an **open market option.**

(ii) The benefits which can be taken at retirement are:

(1) a full pension; or

(2) a tax free lump sum of 25% of the value of the fund (excluding any protected rights from contracting out) *plus* a reduced pension.

(iii) The pension purchased can be:

(1) level;

    (2)   escalating either by a set amount, or the RPI, or even linked to a with profits or unit-linked fund performance;

    (3)   on a joint life basis with a pension to the survivor of either:

          100%

          66.66%

          50%;

    (4)   guaranteed for 5 or 10 years;

    (5)   paid monthly, quarterly, half yearly or annually;

    (6)   with or without proportion at date of death.

(b) *Prior to retirement*

    (i)   Part of the contribution (up to 5% of net relevant earnings) can be used to purchase a lump sum death benefit payable on death prior to age 75.

    (ii)   In addition should the policyholder die prior to retirement there will be a return from the pension arrangement either:

        (1)   return of premiums paid with or without interest; or

        (2)   return of the value of the fund.

So long as the arrangement has been properly documented these benefits should pass to his family free of inheritance tax.

3.10 Options

(a) **Waiver of premium** can be added to the contract for a small extra premium. The policyholder buys this option to ensure that his premiums will be waived if he is unable to work through sickness or accident. In this case the premiums continue to be paid by the insurance company and benefit accrue.

(b) If the policyholder does select this option there will be an underwriting requirement even though the benefit is small.

3.11 Investments

(a) The policyholder normally has a choice of funds:

    (i)   traditional with-profits;

    (ii)   unitised with-profits;

    (iii)   managed;

    (iv)   international;

    (v)   property;

    (vi)   fixed interest;

    (vii) building society;

    (viii) specialised funds.

(b) There will be a facility to switch between funds. The first switch per annum will normally be free. Subsequent switches in a year will be charged at a nominal rate to cover administration.

(c) Some insurance companies now offer an automatic switching system. The young client starts in an equity fund. The client is automatically switched to, say, managed fund in early middle age and gradually to fixed interest by retirement date.

3.12 **Tax treatment**

(a) The personal pension fund, whoever the provider, is not subject to capital gains tax.

(b) The employee is eligible for tax relief at his highest rate. He pays premiums net of basic rate tax (22%) and the insurance company claim back the tax from the Revenue. The gross amount is invested.

(c) An employed person who is paying tax at only the lower rate of 10% can nevertheless pay his pension contribution net of tax at the basic rate of 22%.

(d) Policyholders who are employed and are also higher rate taxpayers will have to claim their higher rate tax relief from their Inspector of Taxes. Evidence is provided using a form PPCC (personal pension contribution certificate).

(e) If an employer makes a contribution he can claim this as a business expense.

(f) A self-employed person must pay his contributions gross and claim back all his tax relief through the use of the form PPCC.

Appropriate personal pension schemes

3.13 (a) Many people use personal pensions as a means of **contracting out** of the State Earnings Related Pension Scheme.

(b) They can do this by means of an **appropriate personal pension**. This scheme has been designed specifically to receive the rebate payments from the DSS. As well as being approved by the PSO it must also have a certificate from the Occupational Pensions Regulatory Authority (OPRA).

(c) The benefits secured are known as **protected rights**.

(d) Members of contracted in final salary or money purchase occupational pension schemes may use an appropriate personal pension **simply to contract out**.

(e) To contract out using an appropriate personal pension, the policyholder must complete a form **APP1**.

(f) If a person contracts out using an appropriate personal pension scheme, he and his employer will continue to pay **full national insurance contributions**.

At the end of the fiscal year, once the DSS have checked the member's NI contribution history, they will pass to the provider the policyholder's rebates for investment (usually September or October).

(g) From April 1997, the employer and employee **rebates are age related**.

(h) The policy provides pension benefits from age 60 to 75 and there must be **no cash payments**.

(i) The pensions, when paid, must **escalate** by 3% pa or the RPI, if less. The LPI applies for benefits accrued after 5 April 1997. There must be provision for a widow's or widower's pension in the event that on the policyholder's death there is a spouse over age 45 or with dependent children (a 'qualifying spouse'). The spouse's and dependant's pensions must be paid on death prior to or after retirement. For benefits accrued after 5 April 1997, unmarried persons have the option of selecting an increased pension.

(j) There is **no guarantee** under the appropriate pension that the benefits will equate to the SERPS relinquished through contracting out. The return is totally dependent upon performance.

(k) If the employee or the employer is making 'real contributions' to the scheme over and above the DSS rebates, then the protected rights must be **segregated** in the fund.

Group personal pension schemes

3.14 Many employers, particularly those with a mobile staff, have seen the wisdom of introducing a **group personal pension scheme** rather than an occupational scheme as a benefit for their staff.

Features

3.15 (a) Each individual has **his or her own policy** which is taken with the employee on leaving service.

(b) There may be some advantage given by the insurance company because of the **economies of scale** of dealing with a group of employees, for example a lower policy fee or higher unit allocations.

(c) The employer **may or may not contribute**.

(d) The employer has **complete flexibility** and can contribute different amounts for different employees.

(e) The employer will normally **deduct contributions** from payroll and hand over the total payments for the members to the insurance company.

(f) The employer enjoys **reduced administration costs** particularly with leavers.

(g) The employer who runs a group personal pension scheme can **avoid most of the legislative problems** of occupational pension schemes, in particular those concerning the disclosure of information to members.

(h) Each **individual** can decide whether he wishes to use the personal pension for contracting out purposes.

Question 15

What do you think are the benefits for an employer of running a group personal pension scheme?

Tax treatment

3.16 (a) The personal pension fund will pay **no capital gains tax**.

(b) If the employer pays contributions they will be treated as a **business expense**.

(c) Care must be taken because the **combined employer/employee contribution** must not exceed the maximum allowed for the employee's age and net relevant earnings in the year of payment.

(d) The employee will pay his contributions **net of 22% tax**. Therefore when the employer collects them, he will carry out his full pay roll operation and deduct the net premium from the final net pay.

Personal pension term assurance

3.17 (a) It is possible for the self-employed or any one eligible to contribute to a personal pension to use up to 5% of their net relevant earnings to fund **life assurance** (term assurance) which must cease by age 75.

   (b) This cover is particularly useful for the self-employed who may wish to use it for **partnership planning** or to provide life cover under a pension mortgage.

   (c) As well as level term assurance, some insurance companies will also write **mortgage protection and family income benefit policies** as pension term assurance with tax relief available on premium payment.

   (d) The term assurance can be **stand alone** or **attached to the pension policy**. It is often better to separate the pension and the life cover, choosing a good investment company for the pension and a company offering competitive term assurance rates for the life assurance.

   (e) If, however, the life assurance is combined with the pension contribution, many insurers allow the value of the fund to be **offset** against the total benefits required. Therefore as the value of the fund increases, the cost of the life cover decreases.

Tax situation

3.18 (a) The policyholder will be eligible for **tax relief at his highest rate**. The employed will be able to pay premiums **net of 22% tax**.

   (b) The self-employed must **pay premiums gross** and claim back the relief.

   (c) On payment of a claim, so long as there is a nominated beneficiary and the scheme has been properly documented, the benefits should be free of tax and pass to the family **free of inheritance tax**.

Question 16

A self-employed barrister can contribute 20% of his net relevant earnings to a personal pension. He decides to pay pension term assurance premiums of 2%. How much has he left to pay to his pension?

---

4 FREE STANDING ADDITIONAL VOLUNTARY CONTRIBUTION SCHEMES

4.1 We have already discussed this topic in relation to **company AVC schemes**.

4.2 We now highlight the features of the **Free Standing Additional Voluntary Contribution Scheme** (FSAVC).

   (a) It is an independent policy offered by an insurance company.

   (b) The policy is available to anyone who is currently a member of an occupational scheme, which can be a statutory or private scheme.

   (c) The following are not eligible for FSAVCs.

      (i) Controlling directors.
      (ii) Members of simplified final salary pensions schemes, see Paragraph 7.4.

   (d) It is a money purchase scheme similar to a personal pension. The policyholder has a wide choice of funds.

(e) The benefits can only be taken in the form of additional pension except in the case of serious ill health or if the pension is a trivial amount.

(f) The policyholder can only use one provider per fiscal year.

(g) Contributions can be paid by single premium or regular premium method.

(h) Premiums are paid net of basic rate (22%) tax and higher rate tax can be reclaimed through the use of a FSAVCC (Free Standing Additional Voluntary Contribution Certificate).

(i) If the employee contributes more than £2,400 in one year then the provider must refer back to the trustees of the main scheme for more information to satisfy themselves that there is no over funding. This is called a headroom check.

(j) Many employees use these schemes as a means of funding for early retirement. The FSAVC does not need to have the same retirement date as the main scheme so long as the main scheme has provision for early retirement.

(k) If an employee changes employer and joins a new company scheme, his FSAVC investment can continue with the same provider but the provider must segregate the benefits acquired under the different schemes for checking for over funding at the eventual retirement date.

(l) If an employee subsequently becomes self-employed, his FSAVC could be converted to a personal pension. A self-employed person with a personal pension can now convert this to a FSAVC if he subsequently becomes a member of a company pension scheme.

Tax treatment

4.3 (a) The FSAVC is a pension fund and pays **no capital gains tax**.

(b) The employee can pay contributions net of basic rate tax and **claims back higher rate tax** using a FSAVCC. (Look back if you need to see what this stands for.)

(c) If the eventual benefits under the FSAVC means that the employee's pension is overfunded he would have to suffer a return of contributions **net of tax** at 32% (2000/01) or 48% for higher rate taxpayers.

Question 17

Look back and revise the advantages and disadvantages of the FSAVC and the company AVC.

5 RETIREMENT ANNUITY

KEY TERM

Retirement annuities, (also known as RAPs), SERAs, (self employed retirement annuities) and s 226 policies were the forbearers of the personal pension. New retirement annuity policies ceased to be issued after 30th June 1988 but those policyholders who already had contracts could continue to make contributions.

5.1 **Providers**

    (a)   Insurance companies

    (b)   Friendly societies

5.2 **Type**. The policies were money purchase arrangements, with or without profits, or unit linked.

5.3 **Eligibility**

    (a)   The self employed

    (b)   Those in non-pensionable employment

    (c)   Those with two jobs, one of which qualified by being non-pensionable

5.4 **Contributions**

    (a)   Contributions can be paid to the insurance company as single or regular amounts.

    (b)   All contributions whether paid by the employed or the self-employed must be paid gross and tax relief claimed by use of a SEPC (Self employed premium certificate).

    (c)   No retirement annuity can be used for the purposes of contracting out.

    (d)   Up to 5% of the net relevant earnings can be used to purchase a s 226A term assurance.

    (e)   Contributions are linked to age and again are a percentage of net relevant earnings. The definition of net relevant earnings is the same as for a personal pension. Please refer to 3.4(e).

Schedule of maximum contributions

Age at 6 April in year of assessment	Percentage of NRE %
Up to age 35	17.5
35 - 50	17.5
51 - 55	20.0
56 - 60	22.5
61 +	27.5

    (f)   There is no earnings cap on contributions paid to a retirement annuity.

    (g)   It is possible to make contributions to both a personal pension and a retirement annuity. However, the contribution to the retirement annuity reduces the contribution available to be paid to the personal pension and in this instance the earnings cap does apply.

Example

    (i)   If a policyholder could invest £3,000 into a personal pension but has already paid £1,000 into a retirement annuity, his contribution to the personal pension must reduce to £2,000.

    (ii)   In the tax year 2000/01, if a policyholder aged 52 has net relevant earnings of £100,000 and contributes £20,000 to a retirement annuity, he can only pay another £7,540 to a personal pension, ie making a total of 30% of capped earnings of £91,800 which is the maximum percentage allowable for personal pensions at age 52.

Question 18

(a) Compare the contribution rate for a 44 year old to a retirement annuity and a personal pension.
(b) Compare the contribution rate for a 57 year old to a retirement annuity and a personal pension.
(c) Write out a full list of the differences between the personal pension and retirement annuity.

5.5 **Retirement age**

This can be between 60 and 75. Earlier retirement ages are possible for certain professions such as footballers.

5.6 **Benefits**

(a) At retirement age an open market option applies so the pension can be purchased either with the host company or another company which is offering a more competitive annuity.

(b) However, if the policyholder exercises the open market option unless he can transfer his fund to a company with whom he already holds a retirement annuity, his fund will pass into the new personal pension regime and he may be subject to a lower tax free cash sum (cash sum of 25% of the value of the fund under a personal pension and 3 × the residual pension for a retirement annuity).

(c) The pension in payment can be:

(i) level;
(ii) escalating;
(iii) joint pension with a spouse with or without reduction;
(iv) guaranteed for 5 or 10 years.

(d) If the policyholder does not want all pension, he can take a tax free lump sum and a reduced pension.

(e) The lump sum is calculated as three times the reduced pension. The reduced pension being calculated on an 'annually in arrears' annuity rate basis to give the highest cash figure.

(f) In times of high annuity rates, this calculation can give a higher tax free lump sum than a personal pension but in times of lower interest rates there has not been a significant amount of difference between the cash sums from a retirement annuity fund and a similar personal pension fund.

5.7 **Death in service benefits**

(a) Up to 5% of net relevant earnings can be applied to purchase life cover. This will normally be written under trust to enable the benefits to pass free of inheritance tax.

(b) The value of the pension will also be returned in the form of:

(i) return of premiums with or without interest; or
(ii) return of fund.

5.8 **Waiver of premium**

Waiver of premium benefits are available on regular premium retirement annuities to enable premium payment to continue during periods of incapacity.

5.9 **Tax treatment**

(a) The pension fund pays no capital gains tax.

(b) Both the employed and self-employed can receive tax relief at their highest rate on contributions paid.

(c) Both the employed and self-employed pay premiums gross and claim back tax from the Revenue.

Question 19

If an employed person was eligible to contribute 25% of his net relevant earnings of £20,000 to a personal pension but he also had a retirement annuity to which he contributed 17.5%, what actual payments would he make to the insurance company as single contributions?

6   SECTION 32 BUY-OUT BONDS

Introduction

6.1   The **Section 32 buy-out policy** was introduced as the first pension transfer product following the enactment of the Finance Act 1981. This enabled those leaving an Occupational Pension Scheme to transfer out their benefits even if they were not eligible to join their new employer's scheme. In 1988, personal pensions were introduced and used for transfers, and Buy-Out Bonds became less popular. However, they are still attractive, particularly for employees wishing to retain benefits controlled under occupational pension rules rather than personal pension rules. If a transfer includes a Guaranteed Minimum Pension (GMP) the guarantee can be preserved within the S32 buy-out policy.

6.2   **Providers**. Insurance companies. (Not *all* insurance companies market this product.)

6.3   **Eligibility**. Transfers from occupational schemes - both final salary and money purchase schemes.

6.4   **Contributions**. No further contributions can be made.

6.5   **Type**. The Scheme is a money purchase arrangement, with or without profits, or unit linked.

6.6   **Benefits**

(a) A tax-free lump sum and pension can be taken at any age between 50 and 75.

(b) On death prior to retirement a lump sum benefit can be paid of four times remuneration at date of leaving service. In addition members' contributions plus interest can be returned. If a surplus remains this can be used to buy a pension for a spouse or dependants.

(c) Pension draw down or phased retirement is not currently available.

6.7   **Retirement age**. Normal retirement age must be between 60 and 75.

6.8   **Tax treatment**

(a) The S32 Buy-Out Bond is a pension fund and pays no Capital Gains Tax.

(b) If the Scheme was overfunded, the surplus would be returned to the employer from whom the transfer had been received. Tax would be deducted from the amount returned.

6.9 **Statutory Pension Scheme Office Rules**

(a) The scheme is subject to Inland Revenue maximum benefits limits for Occupational Schemes.

(b) Maximum benefits are calculated on final remuneration and service with the transferring scheme.

(c) If the transfer value includes a Guaranteed Minimum Pension, it must be retained in this format. S32 Buy-Out policies cannot accept protected rights.

(d) It is possible to transfer from a S32 Buy-Out policy to a personal pension but not *vice versa*.

7 PROPOSED STAKEHOLDER PENSIONS

7.1 The UK government has expressed its intention of introducing stakeholder pension arrangements. The aim of stakeholder pensions will be to encourage low-to-middle income individuals (who are usually without access to an occupational pension scheme) to save for their retirement by means of a regulated pension scheme.

7.2 The government wishes to ensure that stakeholder pensions offer low charges, high flexibility and minimum regulatory requirements. Proposals announced in September 1999 included the following provisions.

(a) *Low charges*. Charges cannot exceed 1% per annum, and there must be no hidden charges.

(b) *High flexibility*. The minimum contribution will be £10 per annum. Contributions to existing pension schemes can continue alongside payments to stakeholder pensions. If contributions are less than £3,600 per annum, they can be made regardless of the earnings position of the individual (stakeholder), thereby allowing the unemployed, housepersons and those taking a sabbatical to contribute.

(c) *Minimum regulatory requirements*. Questions will be asked about the individual's earnings only if annual contributions exceed £3,600.

7.3 Stakeholder pensions will affect financial planning in two important ways.

(a) If contributions are less than £3,600, stakeholder pensions will effectively be an addition to the range of tax-efficient investment schemes that are available.

(b) They could have a significant effect on personal pension schemes, because the flexibility and low cost of stakeholder pensions will make them attractive. Personal pension schemes will have to prove themselves to have superior investment features, to compensate for the comparative 'weaknesses' of their current format.

8 BASIC FEATURES OF SPECIALISED SCHEMES

Small self administered schemes (SSAS)

8.1 (a) Small self administered schemes are regulated by the **Retirement Benefit Schemes** (restriction on discretion to approve) (Small self administered schemes regulations) 1991.

(b) Under these regulations a SSAS is defined as a scheme which is **not invested solely in insurance policies** and which has fewer than 12 members, at least one of whom is related to another member of the scheme or a trustee of the scheme or to a member or a person connected to that member who has been a controlling director of the company at any time during the preceding 10 years.

(c) It is a condition of approval of a SSAS that a **pensioneer trustee** must be appointed. This person is approved by the Inland Revenue to act in such a capacity and has the responsibility of running the scheme in accordance with the Revenue rules. The pensioneer trustee may not also be a scheme member.

(d) The **funding** of a SSAS is closely monitored and actuarial reports are required every three years.

(e) A SSAS has certain **advantages for small companies,** eg:

   (i) loans can be made to the company, 25% of the assets of the fund for the first two years (excluding transfers in) and 50% thereafter;

   (ii) the fund can be used to purchase property and the trustees have power to borrow to finance such a purchase.

(f) Normally SSAS schemes are run by a **firm of actuaries or pension consultants** who provide actuarial and administrative services plus the services of an investment manager.

(g) In some instances part of the funds can be invested in insurance polices, in which case the insurance company may undertake the actuarial and administrative services for a fee. Such a scheme is known as a **hybrid SSAS**.

(h) A SSAS may invest in any of the following investments

   • Cash
   • Stocks and shares in listed companies
   • Unlisted companies, with restrictions
   • Loans to the principal employer
   • Commercial property
   • Unit and Investment Trusts
   • Financial and commodity futures
   • Traded options
   • Insurers investment funds

(i) A SSAS is prohibited from investing in:

   • Personal chattels, eg wines, stamps, paintings

   • Residential property (except if part of a business and for use by a non-connected person)

   • A loan to the employer company to help prevent insolvency

   • A loan on non-commercial terms ie not at a commercial rate of interest (this is generally considered to be 3% above the current bank base rate)

   • Loans to scheme members are prohibited and also to any 'connected person' ie relatives and business associates, or to a company where the member is a 20% controlling director

   • Shares or other assets owned by the scheme member or a connected person in the last three years

Self invested personal pensions (SIPPs)

8.2 (a) It is possible for a personal pension to be invested in assets other than insurance policies. The **permitted investments** are:

    (i)   commercial property;

    (ii)   listed and unlisted securities;

    (iii) overseas securities;

    (iv) unit trusts;

    (v)   investment trust;

    (vi) deposits;

    (vii) units in insurance company pension unitised funds.

    (b) The features and benefits of a SIPP are exactly the same as a normal personal pension, the only difference is the **investment philosophy**.

    (c) An **investment manager** will be appointed to manage the fund's investments.

    (d) These schemes will be of interest to **the wealthy client** who wants control over his pension investment and already has a stockbroker or other fund manager.

    (e) Such a scheme is also useful for any self-employed person or group of self-employed persons who wish to **purchase commercial property**. Partnerships of professionals such as solicitors or accountants could make use of such a scheme.

    (f) If commercial property is being purchased it is possible for further funds to be raised by means of a **loan**.

    (g) The schemes can be run by **insurance companies, actuaries or pension consultants**. Fees will normally be charged for the operation of such a scheme.

Funded unapproved retirement benefit schemes (FURBS)

8.3 (a) Because of the introduction of the earnings cap, there was a need to provide the highly paid with additional pension benefits by some other method than the approved pension arrangement. The legislation allowed for additional pension benefits to be provided by **unapproved schemes**. These can be funded or unfunded.

    (b) If the schemes are **funded**, the employer's contributions can be treated as a business expense.

    (c) The pension fund will however pay **income and corporation tax**.

    (d) The employee will **not receive relief** on his contributions and will be taxed on his employer's contributions as a benefit in kind.

    (e) The schemes normally provide a **tax free lump sum at retirement**. The size of this can be unlimited.

    (f) **Death benefits** can also be provided under a FURBS and, with care, inheritance tax on the payment can be avoided.

    (g) It should be noted that this is a very **complex area of financial planning**.

9 OPTIONS AVAILABLE ON LEAVING AN OCCUPATIONAL SCHEME

9.1 **Option 1.** If the member has been a member of a scheme for less than two years, a refund of his contributions is given, less tax at 20%.

9.2   **Option 2.** If the member has been a member of the scheme for longer than two years, a preserved pension must be provided which must be indexed up to retirement age by 5% or the RPI, if less.

9.3   **Option 3.** If the member has been in the scheme for longer than two years he can take a **transfer to another occupational scheme,** a section 32 transfer scheme or a personal pension. AVCs will be included in this amount.

9.4   If the scheme has been **contracted out,** the GMP or protected rights will be kept separate in any transfers made so they can be separately identified by the new provider.

Chapter roundup

- This chapter has looked at the full range of pension schemes.

- We have looked at the difference between the statutory and private pension arrangement.

- We have considered the different type of private pension scheme: final salary or money purchase arrangements.

- We have studied the three Inland Revenue regimes noting in particular the maximum benefits allowed under each.

- We have explored how clients can make their own personal pension provision through the medium of personal pensions, free standing AVCs or retirement annuities.

- Finally, we have explored the more specialist schemes available, the self administered arrangement for both the company director and the self employed and how to provide benefits for those who earn above the earnings cap by means of a FURBS.

Quick quiz

Multiple choice

1   How much can a male aged 52 with net relevant earnings of £25,000 contribute to a retirement annuity contract?

   A   £7,500
   B   £5,000
   C   £3,750
   D   £4,375

2   On leaving service and the company pension scheme which of the following statements is correct?

   A   If you leave with under 5 years pensionable service you can have your contributions back.

   B   If you leave with under 5 years pensionable service you can have your contributions back less 20% tax.

   C   If you leave with under 2 years pensionable service, you can have your contributions back.

   D   If you leave with under 2 years pensionable service you can have your contributions back less 20% tax.

3 In defining total pensionable earnings for pension scheme purposes, you can take into account

    A   only basic pay
    B   basic pay plus commission and overtime
    C   basic pay plus commission and overtime and benefits in kind
    D   basic pay plus commission and overtime, dividends and benefits in kind

4 At retirement from an occupational pension scheme, a member has the choice of a pension of £10,000 or a tax free lump sum of £27,000 and a reduced pension of £7,000. If he selects the reduced pension, and he dies leaving a widow what is the maximum pension she can receive?

    A   £3,500
    B   £4,666
    C   £6,666
    D   £5,000

5 If an employee retires on a final pensionable salary of £70,000 and has been a member of a 1/60ths scheme for 10 years, what will his pension be?

    A   £46,666 per annum
    B   £8,750 per annum
    C   £11,666 per annum
    D   £12,800 per annum

6 What is the maximum contribution based on total pensionable salary that an employee aged 57 can make to a company pension scheme, is it:

    A   17.5%
    B   35%
    C   15%
    D   22.5%

In the following questions, mark each option as TRUE or FALSE

7 Which of the following people may be members of a public sector pension scheme?

    A   Civil servants
    B   Nurses
    C   Doctors' receptionists
    D   Teachers

8 The features of a public sector scheme are as follows:

    A   The pension is index linked in payment
    B   It is a defined contribution scheme
    C   The members belong to a transfer club
    D   The members can take 25% of their fund as tax free cash

9 A defined contribution occupational pension scheme

    A   Gives a pension based on salary close to retirement date
    B   Gives a tax free cash sum at retirement based on service
    C   Gives a maximum pension of 2/3rd final salary
    D   Can give a pension which increases in payment

10 An approved pension scheme must be the following:

    A   A condition of employment
    B   Open to all employees in a particular category
    C   Open equally to men and women
    D   Open to employees immediately they join service

11 If a pension scheme is exempt approved

    A   A tax free cash benefit can be taken at retirement
    B   The employer can treat contributions as a business expense for tax purposes
    C   The employees will receive tax relief on their contributions
    D   A pension paid to a spouse will be treated as tax free income

BPP PUBLISHING

12 If an occupational pension scheme is more than 5% in surplus

    A   The employer must carry out benefit improvements

    B   The employer and employee can take a premium holiday over 10 years

    C   A payment of the surplus can be made back to the employer tax free

    D   Before a surplus can be repaid full limited price increases must be made to both deferred and pensions in payment

13 Considering contracting out,

    A   Protected rights give equivalent benefits to SERPS
    B   By 2001, SERPS will have been operating for 23 years
    C   Age related rebates will be introduced in 1997
    D   If you contract out using a personal pension, you must complete a form APP1

14 Which of the following are features of a Section 226 pension policy?

    A   Retirement age can be between 50 - 75
    B   The policyholder does not need to retire to take benefits
    C   The policy cannot be used for contracting out
    D   If the member is employed he can pay contributions net of tax at 22%

The solutions to the questions in the quiz can be found at the end of this Study Text. Before checking your answers against those solutions, you should look back at this chapter and use the information in it to correct your answers.

Answers to questions

2   A funded scheme is one where an employer puts aside money which is invested to provide pension benefits in the future. An unfunded scheme is one where the employer collects in contributions and immediately pays out benefits using the same money, 'a hand to mouth' operation. The state pension provision is unfunded.

3   The main reasons are these.

    (a)   They are moving from a final salary scheme which offers a guarantee to a personal pension scheme, the benefits from which depend totally on fund performance.

    (b)   Pensions are index linked in deferment and retirement.

4    $20/80 \times £10,000 = £2,500$

5   The wording can be of your own choice but it could read:

    'The XYZ pension scheme is open to all employees, male and female, whether full or part time who have completed 24 months service as at 1 January in any year and are aged over 21 and under 60 on the date of entry into the scheme.'

8   (a)   The definition of final pensionable salary allowed for a controlling director will be the average of the best three years pensionable salary in the last 10 years preceding retirement.

    (b)   For a salesman, the best definition would be 'P60 earnings for the previous fiscal year' because this would take into account commission and bonus. However some employers have a definition of basic pay which is not advantageous for salesmen.

    In some cases an allowance is made for the state pension as a deduction from the calculation of pensionable salary.

    If a scheme has a retirement age of 60 it may provide a *bridging pension*, that is a higher pension until the male employee reaches state pension age of 65. At which point the state pension will commence and the additional private pension cease.

9   A member of a final salary scheme will be promised a pension such as 1/80ths or 1/60ths of his final remuneration close to retirement.

   The member of a money purchase scheme has no such promise, there will simply be a fund of money available for the purchase of benefits.

   Both types of scheme will be subject to all the maximum benefit rules listed in the text (Paragraph 2.20 onwards).

10   (a)   A pension of £61,200 assuming the cap of £91,800 (40/60 × earnings cap).
    (b)   Tax free lump sum £91,800 × 3 × 40/80 = £137,700 (3n/80 × earnings cap).

11   The contracted in scheme provides the better benefits because the employee will receive basic state pension, earnings related state pension *and* the company scheme. In the contracted out scheme the employee will receive only the basic old age pension and his company pension will include his SERPS benefit.

12   Contracting out via a final salary scheme provides a guaranteed minimum pension equivalent to SERPS.

   Contracting out via a money purchase scheme provides no similar guarantees, the protected rights are totally dependent upon performance.

13   (a)   £10,740 (15% of £91,800, net of 22% tax)

    (b)   *The company AVC*

       This will have lower charges.

       Contributions will be paid from gross salary giving higher rate taxpayers instant full tax relief.

       The FSAVC

       Will have higher charges

       Premiums will be paid net of basic rate tax but the higher rate will have to be claimed back from the Revenue.

       The FSAVC has greater fund choice.

       The FSAVC investment can remain with the same insurance company even if there is a change of main scheme.

14   (a)   £3,500 (£10,000 × 35%)
    (b)   £32,130 (£91,800 × 35%)

15   The main advantage is the ease of administration. There is also no commitment to contribute. No disclosure requirements. Ease of administration when a member leaves service.

16   18%.

18   (a)   RAP = 17.5% PP = 20%

    (b)   RAP = 22.5% PP = 35%

    (c)   *Personal pension*

       (i)   Can be used for contracting out
       (ii)   Employers can contribute
       (iii)   Retirement ages 50 - 75
       (iv)   The employed can pay contributions net of 23% tax
       (v)   Tax free cash at retirement equal to 25% of the fund value
       (vi)   Contribution limits different
       (vii)   Earnings cap applies

       Retirement annuity

       (i)   Cannot be used for contracting out
       (ii)   Employer cannot contribute
       (iii)   Retirement ages 60 - 75
       (iv)   Both the employed and self employed pay gross contributions

        (v)   Tax free cash 3 × residue pension

        (vi)   Contribution limits different

        (vii)   Earnings cap does not apply

19   £1,500 to personal pension (gross) but he would pay £1,170(net of 22% tax)

       £3,500 to the retirement annuity (gross)

Chapter 11

USE OF PENSION PRODUCTS

Chapter topic list	Syllabus reference
1 Use of basic pension schemes	C 3.1
2 Use of specialised schemes	C 3.1

Introduction

We will now consider the circumstances in which the products defined in Chapter 10 can be used to satisfy client needs.

All pension arrangements have the obvious advantage that they provide a useful way for both the employed and the self-employed to save for retirement with significant tax incentives. We will consider each type of arrangement and how it can best be used.

1   USE OF BASIC PENSION SCHEMES

Occupational pension schemes

1.1   (a)   Joining a company pension scheme **cannot be made a condition of the contract of employment**. However the offer of an occupational pension scheme is a considerable advantage for an employed person.

(b)   There would have to be an extraordinary reason for an employee not to join a company pension scheme because of the incentive of the **employer's contribution**.

(c)   In addition the offer of, particularly, a **final salary pension scheme** is of great benefit to an employed person. It takes from his shoulders much of the burden of saving for his own retirement.

(d)   Occupational schemes will provide a pension which will **escalate** in whole or part in payment either by a fixed amount or by the increase in the Retail Price Index. An inflation proofed retirement income is obviously advantageous.

(e)   Occupational schemes have a further advantage that frequently they provide substantial amounts of **life assurance cover** which obviates the need for further family protection.

Additional voluntary contribution schemes (AVC)

1.2   (a)   The reason for paying extra contributions would be to **provide additional pension at retirement age**. Even if a client is in a final salary pension scheme he needs to be a member for 30 or 40 years to provide a reasonable level of pension. So, there is a great need to 'top up'.

BPP
PUBLISHING

(b) Another reason for employed clients to use an AVC is to provide **extra benefits in the event that they wish to retire early**. Many schemes have a substantial penalty for early retirement (other than on the grounds of ill health). The benefits accumulated under the AVC schemes can help to alleviate this penalty.

(c) Some company pension schemes only provide, say, a 50% **spouse's pension** and the client may wish to provide a higher pension for a partner in which case an AVC could be utilised.

(d) The vast majority of clients in a company pension scheme will never succeed in securing a full **40 years service**. Paying AVCs is an excellent savings medium because of the tax relief which is unavailable with alternative savings methods.

(e) If employees invest via the in-house AVC scheme there will normally be **no extra charges involved** (see also paragraph 1.3 below on FSAVCs).

(f) It is a **flexible means of saving** because contributions can be varied from year to year.

Free standing AVC (FSAVC)

1.3 (a) Employees may wish to join a FSAVC scheme because it provides a **better investment choice** than is offered by the company AVC. Company schemes are quite often restricted to either with profits or building society investment.

(b) The employee may like the idea of **spreading the risk** by investing in another insurance company.

(c) The employee may not wish his employer to know he is making substantial AVC contributions. There is an element of **confidentiality** with a FSAVC, perhaps more perceived than real. The provider has to tell the trustees of the main scheme of the FSAVC contribution but there is no requirement to reveal the actual amount.

(d) Some clients may wish to use the provision of a FSAVC to buy **additional life assurance and claim full tax relief**. If, for example, the main scheme provided 2 × salary life cover, a further 2 × salary life cover could be purchased via the FSAVC.

Executive pension schemes

1.4 (a) The main use of the executive pension scheme is to allow company directors to have pension arrangements which are separate from their main employee benefit scheme. In this way they can **keep their financial affairs confidential**.

(b) Having a separate scheme allows the directors or key employees to have **different benefits** from those provided in the main scheme (often known as a top-up or top-hat scheme).

(c) An executive scheme will no doubt give the director a **greater investment choice** than the employees' scheme.

(d) An executive pension can be a very **tax efficient way** of rewarding an executive or director. If a contribution is made into a pension arrangement on his behalf rather than given to him as, say, increased pay, then there will be a personal saving in tax and national insurance contributions. Such a contribution also means a national insurance saving for the employer.

(e) Although we tend to think of these schemes in terms of directors and key employees there is another very important use and that is for the **very low earner**. A professional person may employ his or her spouse to carry out certain work and pay them just below the threshold for national insurance purposes. However, it is possible to pension these earnings. In this case a 'mini company pension scheme' or executive scheme is set up with, say, the doctor or barrister as the 'employer' and the spouse as the employee. The premiums paid for such a scheme will be treated as a business expense.

Personal pensions

1.5 (a) As we have seen in the previous chapters the main purpose of the personal pension is to give those who are **not in a company pension scheme** the opportunity to make pension provision for themselves.

(b) This is the only means of pension provision for the **self-employed**. In their case it is absolutely vital as they have no 'employer' to care for them and they will have a very limited state pension. You will recall that they will not be entitled to SERPS (State Earnings Related Pension Scheme).

(c) The ability to save into these schemes by monthly or single premium contributions makes them **flexible**. They are particularly attractive to the self employed who may not know from one year to the next the amount of their profit and therefore the amount of spare cash available for investment.

(d) A personal pension is useful for the **itinerant employee**, perhaps someone in the computer or advertising world, who is highly paid but very mobile. He can effectively carry his pension on his back and hopefully persuade employers to make contributions to his scheme as part of his remuneration package.

(e) These schemes will be useful for a client who specifically wants to **retire early** at, say, 50 or, perhaps, work fewer hours in early retirement. A company pension has to be drawn on retirement, a personal pension does not! So, a client can continue to work full-time or part-time and take some benefits from a personal pension scheme.

(f) Clients who have more than one job must consider pensioning the **non-pensionable employment** with a personal pension. Any occasional earnings can be pensioned and it must not be overlooked that the employed person can deduct 22% tax from the contribution even if he is a non-taxpayer.

(g) Mortgages will be discussed in Chapter 14 but it must be remembered that some clients will wish to use a **personal pension as part of their mortgage arrangement**. The tax free lump sum from the pension, at normal retirement date, will be used to pay off the mortgage.

(h) In financial planning, the **income of the spouse** is often overlooked. If a wife or husband is not the main breadwinner and works, say, part-time, it is still worth pensioning these earnings to give both partners an income in retirement. A husband and wife both with a pension and remaining within the basic rate tax band is preferable to a husband with a large pension taking him into higher rate tax bracket and a wife with no pension income.

Pension term assurance

1.6 (a) Up to 5% of net relevant earnings can be used to purchase **term assurance** upon which tax relief at the client's highest rate can be claimed.

(b) Obviously this is a very important way of keeping costs down on the purchase of protection life assurance and can be used by **both the employed or self employed**. The employed can effect such a policy if they are not in an occupational pension scheme. (If they are, then they should be able to use AVC life cover: see paragraph 1.3 above.)

(c) Some insurance companies will write **pension level term, family income** or even a **mortgage protection policy**. In this way it is possible to cover all the protection needs with tax relief on the premiums. The only problem is that overall the client is reducing the maximum amount which can be placed in a pension arrangement each year.

(d) **Pension life assurance can be 'stand alone'.** It does not have to come from the same provider as the pension and in fact the pension term assurance could be taken out even if the client had made *no* pension provision.

Appropriate personal pensions

1.7 (a) These will be used mainly by **employed persons who are not in a company pension scheme**. This will be their only means of contracting out of the state earnings related pension scheme.

(b) With effect from April 1997, **age-related rebates** have been introduced for those contracting out. As we have seen earlier, changes in legislation mean that it is now impossible for pension fund managers to reclaim the tax credits from dividends. Both of these facts make it unlikely that any investor will produce a higher return by contracting out other than via a final salary occupational scheme. Some insurance companies have positively advised against any policyholder contracting out via an appropriate personal pension, whatever their age.

(c) A person in a contracted-in company pension scheme is allowed to use an appropriate personal pension for the purpose of **contracting out only**.

Group personal pensions

1.8 (a) This is a method used by employers to provide a 'modified' pension scheme for their employees. It is simply a **collection of personal pensions** with a centralised premium collection service.

(b) From the employee's point of view it may have the advantage that the **employer will contribute** and also that there may be **additional premium allocations** available because of the group arrangement.

Retirement annuities

1.9 (a) These are the **predecessor of the personal pension** held by both the employed and self-employed. No new policies have been issued since 30 June 1988.

(b) Many clients still own these policies and **continue to make contributions**. The advantage is that the tax free lump sum under the schemes may be greater, but not necessarily, depending on interest rates at retirement date.

(c) A particular advantage of these schemes is that they are not subject to the **earnings cap** and can therefore be useful to a high earner.

(d) It is possible for a client to contribute to **both a personal pension and a retirement annuity,** but the retirement annuity contribution must be deducted from the maximum allowed under the personal pension.

(e) At some ages the percentage of net relevant earnings allowed as a premium under a retirement annuity is **lower** than the personal pension.

S32 buyout bonds

1.10 The principal benefit of a s32 policy is that the client is able to retain benefits under the occupational pension rules rather than the personal pension, the chief benefit being maintenance of guarantees.

Question 1

What sort of clients would find the following arrangements of particular advantage?

(a) A retirement annuity
(b) Pension term assurance
(c) FSAVC term assurance
(d) AVC

---

2 USE OF SPECIALISED SCHEMES

2.1 Now we will look at how specialised **schemes can be used to satisfy clients' needs**.

Small self administered schemes (SSAS)

2.2 (a) These schemes can be used by the directors of small family businesses to save tax by **making pension contributions rather than having large taxable profits**.

(b) It gives the directors the chance to build up a **very flexible pension arrangement** with the opportunity for the company to borrow back cash from the pension scheme for business purposes, if necessary.

(c) The small self administered scheme allows a **wide range of investments** within the pension fund. The directors can employ a fund manager to manage the investment of these monies.

(d) Perhaps the most valuable advantage of the SSAS is the ability of the pension fund to **purchase property** which in turn can be leased back to the company for its office or industrial use. There is even the facility for the trustees to borrow funds to facilitate this action.

(e) It enables a director to **fund for retirement** and keep control of the assets in his pension fund without locking away monies with insurance companies.

Self invested personal pensions (SIPP)

2.3 (a) These schemes provide similar facilities for the self employed to those enjoyed by the employed through use of a SSAS. However, they are not quite so useful because of the restriction on amounts of premium which can be invested in personal pensions. Thus, it takes longer to build up a sizeable fund for **diverse investment**.

(b) The self invested personal pension gives, say, a partnership, the opportunity of **purchasing a property** (as long as it is not owned by the pension member and it is a commercial, not a residential, property).

(c) The SIPP is an ideal vehicle for the **sophisticated investor** who wants the tax advantage of personal pensions but not the restrictions of insurance company investment. He can select his own fund manager to run his pension portfolio. Such a manager may be instructed by the client to invest in shares which have a much higher risk than would normally be encountered in a package insurance product.

Funded unapproved retirement benefit schemes (FURB)

2.4   (a)   This is of prime use for the **high earner**.

     (b)   Such a scheme will be offered to a key executive when his **earnings exceed the earnings cap** and he has already been credited with maximum benefits under an approved company pension scheme.

Simplified schemes

2.5   The idea behind these schemes was to provide 'streamlined' pension schemes with minimum administration, and virtually instant Revenue approval. However they have not been a great success, probably because the **group personal pension now offers an excellent alternative which is much more flexible.**

Question 2

Before moving on, please go back to Chapter 10 and ensure that you know the meaning and uses of:

(a)   the SSAS
(b)   the SIPP
(c)   a FURB

Chapter roundup

- This chapter has reviewed the use of the various pension products for the employed and self-employed and also the use of the more specialised vehicles such as the SSAS and the SIPP.

Quick quiz

1 Identify which of the following statements is true or false.

A The percentage of net relevant earnings contribution which can be paid to a personal pension is always greater than that payable to a retirement annuity

B The employed pay their contributions to a retirement annuity net of 23% tax

C The tax free lump sum is always greater under a retirement annuity than a personal pension

D In no circumstances can a member of a company pension scheme take out a personal pension

2 Which of the following statements is true and which is false?

A A member of a company pension scheme can contribute more to a FSAVC than to an AVC

B If you are eligible, you do not need to have a personal pension in order to take out pension term assurance

C The benefits of a free standing AVC can be transferred to a personal pension

D You can contribute to more than one FSAVC in one financial year

3 A company director is considering setting up a pension arrangement for himself. Which are of the following arrangements will give him, greatest flexibility of investment?

A A personal pension
B AVCs
C A small self administered scheme
D A funded unapproved retirement benefit scheme

The solutions to the questions in the quiz can be found at the end of this Study Text. Before checking your answers against those solutions, you should look back at this chapter and use the information in it to correct your answers.

Answers to questions

1 (a) A client whose earnings exceeds the earnings cap.

(b) A self employed person seeking family protection life cover, or an employed person if he is not in a company pension scheme.

(c) An employed person who is a member of a company pension scheme but wants to buy additional life cover with tax relief.

(d) A member of a company pension scheme who wants to make provision for additional retirement pension.

Chapter 12

COMPARING PENSION PRODUCTS AND PROVIDERS

Chapter topic list	Syllabus reference
1 Comparing different types of product	C 4.1
2 Comparing the options available from different providers of the same product type	C 4.2
3 Comparing different providers of a particular product	C 4.3

Introduction

The question explored in this chapter is which pension arrangement to recommend to the client. Having decided on the arrangement, which options are available from different providers and finally which provider to use.

Let us start by looking at which type of arrangement to recommend.

1 COMPARING DIFFERENT TYPES OF PRODUCT

Eligibility

1.1 (a) The choice of pension policy is restricted by **eligibility**. For example a self employed person has no choice: he can only effect a personal pension.

(b) The only other choice a self-employed person *may* have is if he has an **existing retirement annuity**. In this instance he needs advice as to which contract to use to advantage and, if both, in what proportions.

(c) Similarly an **employed person who does not have a generous employer** offering a pension scheme has no choice. He must select a personal pension.

(d) If the employee is offered membership of a company scheme, then there is a decision to be made: does he join or take out a personal pension? He cannot have both. On the whole, unless he envisages a great deal of mobility, **the choice must be to join the company scheme** and take advantage of the employer's contributions. If the employee wants to make contributions he can do this by means of an AVC or FSAVC.

(e) The decision made by the employee as to whether to join an occupational scheme must be influenced by the **type of scheme** offered. At one end of the scale it could be a final salary scheme offering excellent benefits, at the other end a money purchase scheme with low contribution levels and investing in an insurance company pension fund which has shown poor results.

(f) The employee may have another problem. If he has recently left pensionable employment, he may need to decide whether or not to **take a transfer of his benefits**

to a new scheme. In making this decision he will need professional advice to ensure that the benefits are properly compared. In some instances, for example, going from a statutory scheme to a money purchase arrangement, the best advice will normally be to leave the benefits with the original scheme.

(g) Some people have **earnings from a number of sources** so they may be eligible to join a company pension scheme *and* effect a personal pension.

(h) A **director or highly paid executive** may have a different dilemma. Should he join the company pension scheme, or set up his own executive pension, or even go down the road of a small self administered pension scheme? The latter option may be more expensive but it would provide him with the facility to invest in property and have more control over the investment of his pension fund. The SSAS has the further advantage of allowing the trustees to lend pension fund monies to the company for specific uses.

(i) The employed will also be faced with a decision regarding **contracting out**. If the scheme they join is contracted out, the decision is removed but if it is not, they must decide whether to contract out based on age and remuneration.

(j) A highly paid executive may find that because of the size of his remuneration the **whole of his earnings cannot be pensioned** and there is then a case for an unapproved scheme to be considered.

Minimum contribution levels

1.2 (a) It is important that a client can **sustain his level of pension payments** and so it would be unwise to persuade the client to enter into a contract with a high minimum premium.

(b) The choice of company selected may be restricted by **minimum contribution levels** whether single or monthly.

(c) The minimum contributions for **increases in payment** are important, so too is the minimum to which premiums can be reduced in a time of financial crisis.

Charging and commission structure

1.3 (a) If a client is fortunate enough to belong to a **final salary company pension scheme**, it is likely that the administration charges will be met by the employer and that the employee's contribution will not be subject to charge.

(b) However if the client takes out his own personal pension this will be subject to **charges**. If the policy is a traditional with profits arrangement these will be less easy to understand but must now be shown on a key features document.

(c) If the policy is **unit-linked**, then the charges could be as follows:

(i) A monthly policy fee of, say, £2.50.
(ii) Bid/offer spread of 5% on the purchase of each month's units.
(iii) An annual management charge on the fund of, say, 0.875%

In addition the insurance company will have to pay its upfront charges by the issue of two types of unit, capital and accumulation, or a reduction in allocation of units in the early months, eg a 45 year old paying £50 per month until age 65 may have 67.5% of his contributions used to buy units for the first 18 months of the contract, followed by 99% for the next 42 months and from year 6 onwards 100%.

(d) The method of **funding the up front charge** is particularly important for pension contracts. It is often better to have the charges taken out in the early years because this leads to penalty free early retirement.

(e) The **level of monthly charge** is also important. For the client paying a low premium it can in many cases invalidate the contract. This can happen with contracted out only personal pensions (appropriate personal pensions) where the client's earnings are low.

(f) It must be remembered that if a client effects a **free standing AVC** this will have a charging structure similar to that described above, whereas if he pays contributions into the company AVC scheme there will most probably be no charges.

Commission

1.4 Since the onset of **disclosure of commissions** most insurance companies offer a menu of commissions so that the adviser can choose how much commission to take and possibly how much to reinvest back into the contract for the client's benefit.

Question 1

If students have access to the information, they may find it a useful exercise to obtain a number of quotations for a personal pension assuming different rates of commission to see the effect on the reduction in yield.

Transfer values

1.5 (a) When a member leaves a company pension scheme he is given a **number of options** (see Chapter 10). One of these options will be to take a transfer value to another company pension scheme or personal pension.

(b) The **transfer value** will have been calculated in a number of different ways.

(i) If it is a final salary scheme, the transfer value will be worked out by the actuary and will be the cost of providing the member's current preserved benefit.

(ii) If it is a money purchase scheme, it may be the value of the member's fund, comprising his and the employer's contributions *plus* interest or growth *less* a penalty for moving the money. For a unit-linked policy this will be the current value of the units *less* a discontinuance penalty.

(iii) If the scheme is a traditional with profits or non profit scheme, the actuary will calculate a surrender value.

(c) If the employee wishes to take the transfer value to a new company pension scheme his adviser must **compare the benefits of the two schemes** because it may well be that the transfer value will not purchase equal benefits in the new scheme. In such circumstances it would be preferable to leave the pension with the original company pension scheme as a paid-up or deferred pension.

(d) The adviser should undertake a **full comparison of the two schemes** and compare such items as follows.

(i) **Type of scheme**, ie is the client going from a final salary scheme to another final salary scheme, or from a final salary to a money purchase scheme, or from one money purchase scheme to another?

(ii) If he is going from one final salary scheme to another, then it is important to compare the **accrual rate**. If the move is from 1/60th to 1/60th, this is fine, but it may not be so advantageous if it is from 1/60th to 1/80th.

(iii) If the transfer is to a final salary scheme the member will normally receive **additional years' service** in the new scheme. Calculations will have to be done, assuming various hypothetical salary increases, to see if the years of added service are attractive.

(iv) On the whole, it is a good idea to transfer into a final salary scheme, as the reason for changing jobs is usually to receive a higher salary and a final salary scheme, as we know, links service and salary, so the added year of service will count at an enhanced salary.

(e) **Example**

Tom Stride stays in a final salary scheme offering 1/80th for each year of service. His years of service to retirement date are 20 and his final pensionable salary £20,000 - the pension he will receive is £5,000 pa.

However let us assume he changed jobs after 8 years and was offered 5 years added service for his transfer from his original scheme. In his new employment his earnings increase sharply so that at retirement age his pensionable salary is £50,000. In this instance he will only have 17 years pensionable service but because of his increased remuneration, his pension will be £10,625 per annum.

(i) If a client is moving from one money purchase scheme to another then the adviser should look carefully at the investment performance of both funds.

(ii) Usually it would *not* be considered good advice to move from a final salary scheme which is giving a guaranteed return to a money purchase scheme which is only giving a return based on performance.

(iii) The adviser should also compare the following.

(1) Increases in pension payment: are these fixed or discretionary?
(2) Level of spouses' and dependants' pensions
(3) Death in service benefits
(4) Tax free lump sums at retirement
(5) Provision for early retirement

(f) The member may indicate that he wishes to **transfer from an occupational scheme to a personal pension**. He may make this choice, if he is going to work for a new employer who has no pension scheme or if he is becoming self employed. If the client indicates that he wishes to make this choice, the adviser must look at the benefits of both scheme in great detail and carry out a full analysis. The personal pension may look attractive on projected growth rates but that is all they are, they rely totally on *performance*, whereas the scheme from which he is transferring may be a final salary arrangement with guaranteed pension benefits. The adviser must consider all the points in (e) (iii) above.

(g) Care should also be taken if a client wants to **transfer from a contracted out final salary scheme to a personal pension**. In this case he must give up the guaranteed minimum pension, which equates to SERPS for a protected rights pension which is totally reliant on performance.

(h) Sometimes a client with a personal pension may wish to **transfer to an alternative provider because of the poor performance of the original policy**. This may not be a good idea if the original provider applies too high a penalty. If this is the case, the new

BPP PUBLISHING

provider will have to achieve outstanding performance to leave the client better off. Account must also be taken of the setting up costs and charges of the new policy.

(i) In some circumstances clients may wish to **transfer from retirement annuities to personal pensions**. This often happens if they wish to retire before age 60 (the minimum retirement age for a retirement annuity). If a penalty is imposed this may be acceptable if it achieves the overall aim.

Question 2

The ability to be able to compare the benefits of various pension scheme types in the context of transfers is very important, so before proceeding re-read transfer values.

Benefits payable

1.6 (a) It is important that a pension scheme provides **the benefits the client really requires**.

(b) The disadvantage of company pension schemes is that they are designed for the **whole of the workforce** and not tailored for individual needs. For example an occupational scheme may provide a spouse's pension, which is not of much use to the unmarried employee, or if the scheme provides a pension for a spouse, what about the employee with a partner, perhaps of the same sex. How can such a partner be catered for?

(c) The member of a company pension scheme may want **greater death in service** benefits than those being provided by the scheme. This can usually be resolved by paying AVC contributions, either to the company scheme or a FSAVC.

(d) For the employee who wants to provide a **greater spouse's pension**, it is usually possible for him to give up some of his own pension at retirement to allow for a greater pension to continue to his wife.

(e) The AVC facility can also be used by the employee in a company pension scheme who is **not in the scheme long enough** to build up sufficient pension benefits.

(f) Another problem with the occupational scheme is that the **employer selects the underlying investment medium** for the main scheme and often the AVC arrangement. This may well be a very conservative investment such as 'with profits'. If this is a money purchase scheme it can have a restricting effect on the employee's overall return. The answer to this dilemma is to effect a FSAVC with another insurance company and use a variety of funds to spread the risk.

(g) The personal pension allows the client **total flexibility**. He simply builds up a fund and chooses his benefits at retirement. At that stage he can have a pension payable to a spouse at whatever level and pensions increasing, level or index linked. If there is a need for life assurance this can also be added to the overall package.

(h) In conclusion, the great drawback to the company pension scheme is that the **employer is dictating the design of the employee's retirement package** and there is little room for choice. The personal pension gives plenty of choice but the employee misses out on the employer's contribution, and potentially charges are higher. For the employee who is offered a company pension scheme, the obvious answer must be to join the scheme and then make maximum use of AVCs to buy additional life cover and pay extra pension contributions into a fund of the client's choice.

Tax treatment

1.7   (a)   When comparing pension schemes with other types of product, **from a tax point of view**:

(i)   pension premiums obtain tax relief at the client's highest level of tax;

(ii)   the investment is in a fund which pays no capital gains tax;

(iii) there is the opportunity for some payment to be made in the form of a tax free lump sum.

No other investment offers all these facilities.

(b)   However, there are a number of **disadvantages to a pension as an investment**:

(i)   the benefits cannot be withdrawn until pension age;

(ii)   the pension is taxed as earned income in retirement;

(iii) only part of the benefit can be taken as cash.

(c)   Although pension provision should be number one priority, for the client with plenty of money there may be scope for an **ISA** to run alongside the pension to provide tax free capital or income on a more flexible basis.

(d)   At retirement, if a client requires the total benefit of his pension arrangement in the form of a pension, it may still be advantageous for him to take the tax free lump sum and buy a **purchased life annuity** rather than have all the pension as an earned income. The reason for this is that the purchased life annuity has a capital element which is not taxed, so the overall effect should be lower taxation or a higher net income.

(e)   Pension schemes are a **tax-efficient vehicle for companies**. If they are running a company pension scheme for employees, they can claim the payments as a business expense, and it will save on national insurance if they can pay money into a pension scheme instead of giving employees a pay rise.

(f)   Establishing a **directors' pension scheme**, and particularly a **small self administered pension**, can have considerable tax advantages, as well as the tax relief on the contributions. The trustees of the scheme can purchase property which in turn can be leased back to the company. The company then pays rent (claimed as a business expense) into its own pension fund which rolls up tax free. When the property is eventually sold, there will be no capital gains tax to pay because it is held within a pension fund.

Question 3

Revise the features of an existing TESSA and an equity ISA (see Chapter 6) and compare with a personal pension (see Chapter 9). List the features.

Waiver of contribution

1.8   This is a **useful option** to include in a personal pension contract, retirement annuity or executive pension. In deciding on the contract the adviser should take into account:

(a)   charges for the benefit;

(b)   term of deferment, usually 26 weeks;

(c)   definition of disability;

(d)   underwriting considerations.

2 COMPARING THE OPTIONS AVAILABLE FROM DIFFERENT PROVIDERS OF THE SAME PRODUCT TYPE

Exam focus point

The following remarks relate to individual pension arrangements rather than company schemes.

2.1 **Price**. This may be a consideration if a client is effecting pension life assurance or FSAVC life assurance.

2.2 **Charges**. These are particularly important if the client wants flexibility over retirement dates. Upfront charges normally mean a penalty free early retirement benefit.

2.3 **Premium holidays**. The extent of the premium holiday must be investigated. This option is particularly important for women who may have time off to raise a family.

2.4 **Investment options**. A range of risk rated funds is essential and good switching options are important. Many offices now offer an automatic system of gradually switching client's investments from equities to fixed interest over a period leading up to retirement.

2.5 As far as group schemes are concerned options such as a **continuation option on life assurance when a member leaves service** (rare nowadays) would be useful. So too would be a high level of free cover on the group life assurance.

3 COMPARING DIFFERENT PROVIDERS OF A PARTICULAR PRODUCT

3.1 The factors are the same as for all other products.

   (a) **Financial strength** of the provider
   (b) **Quality of service**
   (c) **Investment choice and performance**

Financial strength of the provider

3.2 We have seen in previous chapters the importance of the **financial strength** of the insurance companies.

3.3 It is of particular importance when selecting a **provider for a pension policy or group scheme**. If an adviser is recommending a 10 year savings plan or 5 year guaranteed income bond, this is not a long investment term, but a pension policy may run for 30 or 40 years. It is therefore very important that the adviser can feel confident that the insurance company has sufficient financial strength so that it will still be there to pay out!

Question 4

Re-read the section on free asset values (Chapter 4).

Quality of service

3.4 (a) Of all the areas of advice, **service** on pension schemes is of paramount importance.

   (b) It is important that **benefit statements** are prepared correctly and promptly.

(c) It is vital that employees approaching retirement are **given their options well in advance** so that they can make their decision and that, having made the decision, the cheque for the tax free lump sum is available for the retirement party on the day they leave, not two weeks later!

(d) Many schemes include a **death in service benefit**. When a member dies, it is important that the claim is dealt with sympathetically and swiftly.

(e) **Collection of premiums**, particularly under group schemes, has caused many headaches in the past and it is important that the insurance company provides a good level of service in this area.

Investment choice and performance

3.5 (a) Pensions are long term investments and therefore it is important that **consistent performance can be achieved over longer terms**.

(b) **Past performance statistics** are available for both personal pensions and occupational schemes. *Money Management* and *Pensions Management* produce half yearly surveys and large occupational schemes performance can be compared by using statistics provided by CAPS and Wood McKenzie.

(c) The provider must offer a **good range of funds**, risk graded and with easy switching facilities.

Chapter roundup

- This chapter highlights the pension choices available and by explaining the features helps the decision process.

- Having made the correct decision the chapter helps the student to understand the options available under contracts offered by different providers.

- We have also covered the vital decision of which company to use, based on financial strength, investment choice and performance and the very important feature of quality of service.

Quick quiz

1   Identify which of the following statements is true and which false.

   A   A self-employed person is eligible to contribute to a Free Standing AVC

   B   A person in non-pensionable employment is eligible to contribute to a Free Standing AVC

   C   A self-employed person is eligible for SERPS

   D   A member of a contracted in money purchase occupational scheme can effect an appropriate personal pension to contract out of SERPS

2   Which of the following matters would an adviser take into account when advising whether a client should transfer benefits from a previous company pension scheme to his new occupational scheme. (Identify which is true and which is false.)

   A   The type of scheme provided by the new company
   B   The history of the existing scheme; has it increased pensions in payment?
   C   Whether the client is a smoker
   D   The client's marital status

3   Consider the following statements as they relate to pension arrangements. (Identify which is true and which is false.)

   A   Tax-free lump sums are available
   B   The pension when paid is tax-free
   C   The fund has tax advantages
   D   Contributions are eligible for tax relief

The solutions to the questions in the quiz can be found at the end of this Study Text. Before checking your answers against those solutions, you should look back at this chapter and use the information in it to correct your answers.

Answers to questions

3   (a)   Features of an existing TESSA

          (i)   Five year scheme
          (ii)   Deposit scheme
          (iii)   Gross interest paid
          (iv)   Total contribution over 5 years £9,000 per person

     (b)   Features of an equity ISA

          (i)   No fixed term
          (ii)   Single equities or unit trusts
          (iii)   Investment rolls up free of income and capital gains tax
          (iv)   Total contribution per person per annum £5,000

     (c)   Features of a personal pension

          (i)   No benefit until retirement age
          (ii)   Choice of investment funds, with profits or unit linked
          (iii)   Investment rolls up free of capital gains tax
          (iv)   Contributions eligible for tax relief at client's highest tax rate
          (v)   Maximum contribution based on a percentage of net relevant earnings subject to an earnings cap

Part D
Mortgages

Chapter 13

ARRANGING A MORTGAGE

Chapter topic list	Syllabus reference
1 The factors which determine the client's borrowing capacity	D 1.1
2 Other costs associated with arranging a mortgage	D 1.2

Introduction

Many clients' decision-making powers are swayed when in the process of buying a house. They must have the house at any cost and they do not think logically about how much they can borrow and the possible costs involved. It is the adviser's role to provide sensible and logical advice to these clients in this bewildering time.

First, we will look at the factors which determine how much they can borrow

1 THE FACTORS WHICH DETERMINE THE CLIENT'S BORROWING CAPACITY

1.1 The factors determining a **client's borrowing capacity** are:

   (a) Income
   (b) Liabilities
   (c) Amount of deposit
   (d) Credit history
   (e) Employment status

Income

1.2   (a) The question of the **amount of the client's income** is a vital consideration in determining how much loan a lender will be willing to offer. The lender must be assured of the client's ability to make the mortgage payments not just for the first few months but for the term of the mortgage.

     (b) Most lenders will consider a loan based on a **multiple of the borrower's earnings**:

        (i)   if they are single it may be 3 times earnings;

        (ii)   if they are borrowing jointly with another person, 3 times one earner plus 1 times the second or 2.5 × joint earnings is a common formula.

     Thus, it can make a difference which lender one chooses, if different lenders are willing to consider different multiples. At the time of writing, some lenders will offer multiples of 4 or even 5.

     (c) Let's look at an **example**.

A couple, wanting to buy a house, have the following income: Tim £30,000, Jane £15,000.

Which multiple would be most advantageous?

If it is 3 × one partner's earnings, *plus* 1 × the other's earnings, they could borrow £90,000 + £15,000 = £105,000.

If it is 2.5 × joint earnings, they could borrow 2.5 × £45,000 = £112,500.

(d) The **method the lender uses to calculate the earnings** is also important. Most lenders will take into account all guaranteed income. However, commissions, overtime, bonus etc are more difficult to deal with. If a consistent pattern of these earnings can be established over, say, three years then they may be taken into account in full but, mostly they will only be partially taken into account.

(e) Sometimes, clients have other forms of income, such as **rental income** or **investment income**. In this instance the lender would need full details and would wish to see a consistent flow of income or rent if he were to use this in calculating the amount to be lent.

(f) If the client is **self-employed**, the lender will need to see at least three years' accounts. Sometimes if the client has only recently become self-employed a letter from the accountant will be required, together with some income projections.

(g) In the case of an employed person, the lender will need proof of income by the supply of **pay slips** etc.

Question 1

In order to understand the method of calculating maximum borrowings, the student should work out a few examples, perhaps using his own salary.

Liabilities

1.3 (a) A client may have a high level of income but this is of little use if he has **existing liabilities** which will mean that he has insufficient income left to make the mortgage payments.

(b) The lender will want details of any other mortgages or debts, such as **credit cards, hire purchase arrangements, bank loans, overdraft facilities, maintenance** or **court orders**.

(c) It is important that the adviser gives his client **sound advice**. The result of a thorough factfind should reveal how much is *really* available to pay a mortgage. The client should not exceed this, however much he wants a particular property. In the long term the client must be able to afford the mortgage payments.

Employment status

1.4 (a) In deciding whether they are prepared to lend, the bank or building society will take note of the client's **employment status**. As already mentioned, if the client is self-employed the lender will want to see three years' accounts.

(b) If the client is employed, the bank or building society will always seek a **reference from his employer** as to reliability and to check employment details.

(c) If the employed person has only recently joined a new firm, the bank or building society will refer to the **previous employer**.

(d) If the client has moved jobs frequently the building society may not be interested in lending to him/her as the lender needs to be assured of the client's **ability to maintain payments**. An inconsistent work pattern may prove that this will not be the case.

Credit history

1.5 (a) The client's ability to make the mortgage payments is of paramount importance and the lender has to check to ensure that the client does not have a **history of bad debts**.

(b) If at all possible the client will be **interviewed by the lender** and in conversation much can be discovered about attitudes to money, debt and so on.

(c) A **reference** will be taken from an existing lender, if there is one, or from previous landlords, in which case sight of the rent book may be required.

(d) The lender will normally check the client's **credit rating** through a credit bureau, in particular to ensure that there are no County Court Judgments or other arrears.

(e) If it were discovered that the potential borrower was an **undischarged bankrupt** then no borrowing would be possible.

Amount of deposit

1.6 (a) Although it is possible sometimes to find **100% mortgages**, they have become almost a thing of the past.

(b) Most borrowers will need to put down a **deposit of between 5% and 10%** of the purchase price.

(c) The **larger the deposit** the greater the choice of lender and type of interest scheme available.

(d) A reasonable level of deposit tends to **keep down the mortgage payments**.

(e) From the lender's point of view a reasonable deposit shows a **commitment** to the house buying exercise.

(f) If the borrower can put down a deposit in excess of **25% of the purchase price**, then there will be no requirement for an **indemnity guarantee payment** (see Paragraph 2.5 below) and this will help to keep down costs.

Question 2

Before proceeding, list the most important items a lender must check before considering a loan to a client.

---

2 OTHER COSTS ASSOCIATED WITH ARRANGING A MORTGAGE

2.1 Many clients are unaware of the **additional costs** involved in arranging a mortgage and the fact that they will need spare cash to meet these charges. The charges are:

(a) arrangement fee;
(b) legal fees;
(c) stamp duty;

     (d) indemnity guarantee premium;

     (e) survey fee.

Arrangement fee

2.2   (a) Some advisers, particularly mortgage brokers, will ask for an **arrangement fee** to cover the cost of their work in finding a suitable lender for the client.

     (b) In addition, the bank or building society may demand a **non-refundable arrangement fee**. This is to cover their initial work and to discourage timewasters. A fee of, say, £250 to arrange a fixed interest mortgage is not uncommon.

Legal fees

2.3   (a) The client will need to appoint a solicitor to carry out the **conveyancing** of the property and deal with the legal requirements of the mortgage.

     (b) If the client has a house to sell and another to buy the solicitor will be required to deal with **both transactions** on his behalf.

     (c) Most solicitors will now give an indication of their **fee** to the client before the work commences.

     (d) There are **licensed conveyancers** who may offer a conveyance service cheaper than a solicitor. However clients must remember that the legal aspects of purchasing a house are complex and if something goes wrong it can be a costly business.

     (e) The solicitor's charges will cover:

        (i)   **local searches** to make sure that there are no building plans for the area of the house, for example, the erection of a factory or motorway in close proximity;

        (ii)   **land registry fee**;

        (iii) **stamp duty if applicable**;

        (iv) costs of **telegraphic transfer of the funds** on the day of the completion.

Stamp duty

2.4   (a) Stamp duty is charged at 1% on properties purchased for £60,001 - £250,000.

     (b) With effect from 28 March 2000, the stamp duty on properties purchased for £250,001 - £500,000 is 3%, and for properties purchased for an amount in excess of £500,000, the stamp duty is 4%.

     (c) Sometimes the price of a property can be kept just below the thresholds of £250,000 and £500,000 by asking the purchaser to pay for carpets, curtains and fittings separately.

Indemnity guarantee premium

2.5   The general requirement for borrowers to pay an **indemnity guarantee premium** for advances in excess of 75% of the property value has now been withdrawn for commercial reasons. Lenders will only insist on such a premium if the borrower is considered to be a very high risk.

Survey fee

2.6 (a) Under the terms of the Building Societies Act 1986, the building society must arrange for a **report and valuation** before making an advance.

(b) It is obviously sensible that all lenders should have sight of a **survey** to satisfy themselves about the property which they are taking as security for their loan.

(c) The borrower will have to pay for the **basic survey report**. The aim of this report is to satisfy the building society that the property offers reasonable security for the amount lent, ie that the valuation is reasonable.

(d) From the **borrower's** point of view there are three surveys available.

    (i) **Basic building society valuation**. The aim of this report is for the building society to satisfy itself about the market value of the house. The building society will have a scale charge for this valuation.

    (ii) **Report and valuation**. This takes the valuation a stage further and reports on the state of the property from the point of view of any need of for repairs and comment on the structure. The cost of such a survey would be between £250 and £400.

    (iii) **Structural survey**. This takes the valuation still further by adding a full survey on the structure of the property. The fee will be greater again and the borrower will be able to ask the surveyor to comment on certain features, such as the state of the roof or possibility of subsidence in the area.

(e) The value to the building society of this independent valuation is that it will reveal any **major structural defects** which could effect their ability to sell the property in the event of the borrower defaulting on payment.

(f) They are relying on a professional to give an **unbiased valuation** of the property. The surveyor will have a duty of care to be exercised in the performance of this duty.

(g) The professional valuer or surveyor may discover **tenants** or **potential neighbourhood problems** which the building society staff cannot ascertain without inspecting the property directly.

(h) The building society will have a **panel of surveyors** from whom they select to carry out this work.

Question 3

List the reasons why you think a prospective buyer may be prepared to pay the fee for a full structural survey.

Chapter roundup

- In this chapter we have explored the early stages of taking out a mortgage, the basis upon which a lender is prepared to make an advance and the initial expenses which the borrower will incur.

Quick quiz

1   To which of the following people is a building society *least* likely to lend?

   A   A self-employed window cleaner
   B   A salesman who earns mainly commission
   C   A self-employed accountant
   D   An employed person who has had 5 jobs in 4 years

2   What indemnity guarantee premium would have to be paid (assuming a rate of 8%) on a loan of £82,000, on a purchase price of £85,000?

   A   £1,640
   B   £1,460
   C   £510
   D   £240

3   A and B are jointly applying for a mortgage, A earns £30,000, B earns £12,500. They have a choice of building societies offering different multiple of salaries. Which should they choose?

   A   The society offering 3 × the highest salary
   B   The society offering 2.5 × the joint salaries
   C   The society offering 2.5 × the higher salary + 1 × the lower

Answer the following questions as TRUE or FALSE

4   In calculating income for the purposes of lending, a building society:

   A   Only takes into account basic pay
   B   Takes into account basic pay plus some proportion of commission or bonus
   C   Will not take into account investment income
   D   Will not take into account income from an occupational pension scheme

5   Which of the following costs would be incurred by a person taking out a mortgage of £30,000 on a property valued at £59,500?

   A   Legal fees
   B   Indemnity guarantee premium
   C   Stamp duty
   D   Survey fee

The solutions to the questions in the quiz can be found at the end of this Study Text. Before checking your answers against those solutions, you should look back at this chapter and use the information in it to correct your answers.

Answer to questions

2   The lender must consider:
   (a)   employment status;
   (b)   income;
   (c)   previous credit history;
   (d)   other liabilities.

3   The purchaser may require a full structural survey for the following reasons:

   (a)   Age of the property
   (b)   Concern about part of the structure, roof, construction of walls
   (c)   If the house had been left for many years without maintenance
   (d)   If there was a history of subsidence or say flooding in the area

Chapter 14

KNOWLEDGE OF THE RANGE OF MORTGAGE PRODUCTS

Chapter topic list	Syllabus reference
1 The types of mortgage	D 2.1
2 The interest options for mortgages	D 2.2
3 Methods of repaying an interest only mortgage	D 2.3
4 Flexible mortgages	D 2.4
5 Cashback mortgages	D 2.4
6 The use of ancillary products in connection with mortgages	D 2.5

Introduction

In this chapter we are looking at the two methods of repaying a mortgage, capital and interest and interest only. Then, the various interest options. How the client may fund to repay the capital if they have selected the interest only mortgage and finally some of the ancillary products which are used to protect the mortgage payments in the event of death, redundancy or sickness.

The information in this chapter is mainly concerned with the repayment of mortgages on *residential* property.

1   THE TYPES OF MORTGAGE

The providers

1.1   (a)   Before looking at mortgages and the options available, it is important to know something about the **lending sources**. They are as follows.

(i)   Banks

(ii)   Building societies

(iii)   Insurance companies

(iv)   Mortgage corporations, for example one which specialises in lending to farmers, the Agricultural Mortgage Corporation

(v)   Credit companies - who mainly lend on unsecured loans

(b)   Students sometimes become confused about the role of the lender and the insurance company in the mortgage process. The two are quite distinct.

(i)   The lender, bank or building society **advances the money** and each month he is repaid either a repayment (capital and interest) or an interest amount.

BPP PUBLISHING

(ii) At the same time if there is a **policy**, either a mortgage repayment policy, endowment policy or pension policy, being used in connection with the mortgage, monthly payments are being made to the insurance company.

The mortgage choice

1.2 There are broadly two types of mortgage.

(a) Capital and interest (the **repayment mortgage**)
(b) **Interest only**

It is possible to **combine the two types of mortgage**. For example, a borrower might borrow £70,000 on a repayment basis plus £30,000 on an interest-only basis.

Capital and interest (the repayment mortgage)

1.3 (a) In this instance a loan is made for a fixed term, say, 25 years and the borrower repays on a monthly basis. **Each monthly payment is made up of both capital and interest.**

(b) In the early years the monthly repayment pays more interest and the **capital reduces slowly**. As the mortgage becomes more mature each payment pays off more capital and the interest part is smaller. Therefore, when the borrower receives his annual statement, in the early years there is very little reduction in the loan outstanding but as the years go by the capital begins to reduce substantially.

(c) If there are **changes in the interest rate**, the monthly payments will be increased or reduced to reflect this.

(d) The **repayment method is very flexible**. If, say, interest rates fall, a borrower could keep the monthly payments unchanged and so redeem the mortgage quicker.

(e) Conversely, if interest rates increase the borrower may be able to keep payments at the same level and **extend the term of the loan**.

(f) If a borrower runs into **financial problems** the arrangement is flexible and the lender may be prepared to rearrange payments at least on a temporary basis.

(g) **Advantages of a repayment mortgage**

To the borrower

(i) He has the guarantee that his mortgage will be repaid at the end of the term.

(ii) Many borrowers like the satisfaction of seeing the capital outstanding reduce each year.

(iii) Consequently the borrower likes the feeling that he holds a bigger equity stake in his home each year.

(iv) The arrangement is flexible and can easily be rearranged to reduce payments in time of financial hardship.

To the lender

(i) He has the satisfaction that the borrower is paying back capital, so the lender has a security against the loan which is increasing in value.

(ii) The bank or building society has the opportunity to relend the capital repaid to a new borrower.

(h) **Disadvantages of a repayment mortgage**

To the borrower

(i) There is no cash sum available when the mortgage is repaid.

(ii) As only interest is repaid in the early years, if the borrower moves frequently he can find himself with a constant 25 year mortgage which may not be paid off until retirement age, whereas an interest-only mortgage may have been paid off sooner.

Interest only mortgage

1.4 (a) In this case **the capital remains outstanding** until the end of the mortgage term and the borrower pays only interest.

(b) The borrower must have some **method of repaying the capital** at the end of the term. Traditionally this was done by use of an endowment or low cost endowment policy. However over more recent years, the tax free lump sums from pension products have been used or the returns from personal equity plans and, in the future, ISAs.

(c) In the past the bank or building society lending its money would insist on the endowment policy being **assigned** as collateral in the event of default of payment. This happens less and less and it is the borrower's responsibility to maintain an investment scheme which will provide sufficient funds to repay the mortgage. It could be anything, not necessarily the types of product listed above. If a client were interested in antiques or vintage cars he could earmark one of these items to repay his mortgage. However it would not be very sensible because of the potential volatility in value. In some cases the lender will require confirmation of the method used.

Question 1

Before moving on the student should recap on the main features of repayment and interest only mortgages. Remember:

(a) with a repayment mortgage, the capital outstanding is reducing;

(b) with an interest only mortgage, the full capital amount is outstanding until repayment.

---

2 THE INTEREST OPTIONS FOR MORTGAGES

Fixed rate mortgage

2.1 (a) The borrower is offered a **fixed rate of interest for a fixed term**.

(b) This rate is **guaranteed** and remains unaltered despite changes in overall interest rates. It can work to the borrower's advantage or disadvantage.

(c) The **length of the fixed rate** is agreed at outset between the lender and borrower. It could be anything between a few months and five years.

(d) Usually the lenders **do not offer long-term fixed rates,** if they feel interest rates will rise.

(e) The scheme has the particular advantage that the borrower knows his **exact mortgage outlay for a fixed term** and is not going to be subjected to a sudden shock of increased payment following an interest rate rise.

(f) At the end of the fixed period the rate **usually reverts to the then current variable lending rate**.

Variable rate mortgage

2.2 (a) With this type of mortgage, the rate of interest required by the lender will **vary from time to time in line with overall interest rates**.

(b) From the borrower's point of view his monthly repayment can **vary up or down** depending on interest rates. Obviously it can be to his advantage if interest rates fall and conversely if they rise.

(c) Many lenders only modify the payments on an **annual basis**.

Capped and collared mortgages

2.3 (a) In this instance the borrower is charged the current interest rate, say, 8.0% but is given a **guarantee** that the rate will never rise above, say, 10.0%. This is known as the cap.

(b) Conversely, the interest rate paid by the borrower **will not be allowed to fall** below 7.5% (the collar) even if overall rates fall beneath this.

Discounted mortgage

2.4 (a) Lenders offer a **discounted rate of interest** for a short period usually a maximum of 12 months, eg 3.75% discount for 12 months.

(b) The discounted rate is usually only offered to **first time buyers**.

(c) At the end of the discounted period the rate of interest **reverts** to the current variable rate being charged to borrowers.

Low start mortgage

2.5 (a) This is a **repayment mortgage** with a difference. In the initial period which may be two years, **only interest is paid to the building society**.

(b) In year three, the full repayment mortgage starts on the total loan and **payments will be more expensive**.

Deferred interest mortgage

2.6 (a) In this case the borrower pays **only part of the interest for a period**.

(b) At the end of the period the full mortgage starts and the loan has been increased by the **deferred and unpaid interest**.

Question 2

Having studied the interest options available, which type of interest option do you think would be suitable for:

(a) a young married couple who want a known budget of mortgage costs?

(b) a professional person who knows he will be receiving an increased salary in 18 months time and desperately wants to take out the maximum mortgage available to him at the present time?

(c)   a middle aged couple who have moved house and want as competitive a deal as possible but think interest rates may rise?

---

3   METHODS OF REPAYING AN INTEREST ONLY MORTGAGE

The endowment mortgage

3.1   Features

(a)   As we have seen from 1.2 above an interest only mortgage has to be repaid in full at the end of the term. A client can take out an endowment for a similar term to repay the loan.

For example, assume a client has taken out a loan of £40,000 for 25 years. The client will take out a 25 year endowment policy with a sum assured of £40,000 to repay the outstanding loan in 25 years time.

(b)   In the example shown above there is bound to be sufficient capital to repay the loan because the guaranteed sum assured is equal to the loan. In some cases, as we will see, the client may try to save money by taking out reduced cover, in which case he may not have sufficient at the end of the term to repay the mortgage. It is important that clients understand the risks involved.

(c)   The death cover under the endowment policy, whatever type, must always be sufficient to repay the loan.

Types of endowment

3.2   (a)   **Non-profit endowment**. This policy will have a guaranteed sum assured sufficient to repay the outstanding loan on death or survival (see example in Paragraph 3.1(a)).

(b)   **With-profits endowment**

(i)   In this case, the borrower will take out an endowment policy for the same term as the loan and a sum assured equal to the value of the loan.

(ii)   Reversionary bonus and, hopefully, terminal bonus will be added to the sum assured so that at maturity there should be a surplus over the amount required to repay the mortgage. This amount will be returned to the borrower by the building society as a tax free cash sum.

(iii)   In the event of death the sum assured will be sufficient to repay the outstanding loan plus a surplus depending on bonus performance.

(c)   **Low cost endowment**

(i)   The low cost endowment was introduced in an attempt to keep down the cost of repayment of the outstanding loan.

(ii)   The policy is a combination of a traditional with profits endowment policy and reducing term assurance (see Chapter 6).

(iii)   The policy is effected for total cover equal to the loan outstanding. The cover is then split between an endowment policy and a reducing term assurance. A conservative level of bonus is assumed and the term assurance reduces each year by this amount. If the endowment sum assured has risen at the same rate then the total amount of cover required will be maintained.

(iv)   If bonus rates fall there is no guarantee that the return under this policy will be sufficient to repay the mortgage.

(v)   If the reversionary bonuses are better than predicted then there should be a tax free surplus. Similarly a terminal or vesting bonus payment could lead to a surplus cash sum.

(vi)   There is always a guaranteed level of death benefit equal to the outstanding loan.

(d)   **Unit-linked endowment**

(i)   This policy is effected for the same term as the mortgage.

(ii)   This policy provides a guaranteed death return equal to the outstanding loan.

(iii)   Premiums are used to buy units in a chosen fund and units are then cancelled to purchase the life cover.

(iv)   The maturity value is dependent upon the performance of the units and therefore there is no guarantee that there will be sufficient to repay the loan.

(e)   **Costs and fees**

(i)   The borrower will have the normal fees:

    (1)   arrangement fee, if appropriate;
    (2)   survey fee;
    (3)   legal fees;
    (4)   indemnity guarantee premium;
    (5)   stamp duty, if appropriate.

(ii)   The lender may charge extra interest, say 0.25% for an endowment mortgage or an additional arrangement fee, but this is now unusual.

(iii)   The borrower will suffer the normal setting up charges on the endowment policies whether traditional with profits or unit-linked.

Question 3

Go back to Chapter 6 and revise the section on charges on savings policies. Make sure you know the different charges made on the unit-linked policy and how the actuary calculates the with profits premium to take into account the charges.

Conditions and penalties

3.3   (a)   The lender will probably require the endowment policy to be **assigned** to them, although this does not always happen.

(b)   The building society may only accept the endowment policies of **certain insurance companies on their panel**.

(c)   The building society will require that in calculating the level of cover required to repay the loan, the insurance company should only **assume a growth rate of, say, 7.5%**, and, in the case of a traditional with profits low cost endowment policy that they assume 80% of the current reversionary bonus and take no account of terminal or vesting bonus.

(d)   In the event that the borrower **defaults on payment**, the building society, after a period of non-payment, may be forced to sell the property to recoup its loan. In the event of such a forced sale the amount raised is often below the current market value of the property and the borrower may find himself in a position where the sale proceeds do not fully repay the loan.

(e) In the situation outlined above, the building society would have a **lien on the endowment policy** and could surrender it to help to repay the debt.

(f) Obviously if the endowment is surrendered in the early years, there will be **little or no surrender value**.

Tax treatment

3.4 (a) Until 2000/2001 tax relief was available on the interest payable on the first £30,000 of a qualifying mortgage under a system called **MIRAS (Mortgage Interest Relief at Source)**. MIRAS relief was abolished from April 2000.

(b) A qualifying mortgage has to satisfy three conditions.

   (i) The interest must be **relevant loan interest,** that is interest which applies to a loan or the purchase of land, the main residence , a caravan or houseboat in the United Kingdom or Northern Ireland.

   (ii) It must be to a **qualifying borrower.**

   (iii) It must be advanced by a **qualifying lender,** a category which includes building societies, local authorities and life assurance companies authorised to carry on long term business. Most banks are also authorised lenders.

(c) Under the MIRAS system the borrower made his interest payment to the lender **net of the tax relief** (relief was 10% at the time of its abolition) and the building society recovered this amount from the Inland Revenue.

(d) From August 1988 to its abolition in April 2000, MIRAS tax relief was limited to loans of **£30,000 per property**. Prior to that date joint borrowers could effectively obtain MIRAS on a total of £60,000 borrowing.

(e) Despite separate taxation, **husbands and wives** were entitled to MIRAS (up to 6 April 2000) on only one amount of £30,000, but they could decide how to split the relief between them to maximum tax advantage.

(f) As stated earlier, MIRAS tax relief was abolished for 2000/01 onwards.

(g) Turning to the endowment policy being used to repay the mortgage, this is a **normal qualifying policy** and so long as it runs for 75% of its term or ten years, the proceeds will be tax free. No life assurance tax relief will be available unless the policy was taken out prior to 13 March 1984.

Pension mortgages

Features

3.5 (a) Normally a borrower will use a **personal pension to repay his mortgage** and the remarks made in this section will be based on the use of a personal pension.

(b) However if it is acceptable to the building society, **the tax free lump sum from an occupational scheme** *could* be used if it were sufficient to repay the loan.

(c) In the case of the personal pension, **25% of the value of the fund** at retirement age can be taken as a tax free lump sum and it is this sum which must be used to repay the mortgage.

(d) Once again, the bank or building society will expect the insurance company to assume **modest growth in the value of units,** say 7.5% and take into account, say only 80% of the reversionary bonus on a traditional with profits contract and no terminal or vesting bonus.

(e)   At retirement, if bonuses have been better than expected there should be a **surplus** of the tax free cash which remains the property of the borrower. In addition, he has of course, funded a pension.

(f)   The restriction is that the borrower has used part of his pension contribution to pay for his mortgage and as a result has **limited the amount of pension he can fund**.

(g)   The **youngest age** that benefits can be taken from a personal pension (except in the case of approved occupations) is 50 and therefore the mortgage must run to that age so that the capital is available at the right time to repay the mortgage.

(h)   It must be pointed out that despite tax relief on the payments the cost of the pension to repay the mortgage will undoubtedly be **more expensive** than the endowment method.

(i)   **Level term assurance** for a sum assured equal to the amount of the loan and for the same term must run alongside the pension policy to provide a benefit in the event of the borrower's death. It would make sense for this to be taken out as pension term assurance and tax relief obtained on the premiums paid.

Costs and fees

3.6   (a)   The borrower will pay the **normal fees**.

(i)   Arrangement fee, if appropriate
(ii)   Survey fee
(iii)   Legal fees
(iv)   Indemnity guarantee premium
(v)   Stamp duty, if appropriate

(b)   As mentioned above the **actual costs** of a pension mortgage will be much greater than an endowment.

(c)   The pension policy will bear the **normal charges**. If it is unit-linked, there will be up front charges, bid offer spread, and annual management charges.

Conditions and penalties

3.7   (a)   The pension policy is, by law, a non-assignable contract and as such **cannot be assigned to the building society**. However, assignment of the term assurance policy may be required.

(b)   In the event that the borrower defaults on payment, the building society after a period of non-payment may be forced to **sell the property to recoup their loan**. In the event of such a forced sale the amount raised is often below the current market value of the property and the borrower may find himself in a position where the sale proceeds do not fully repay the loan.

(c)   The **pension contract cannot be encashed until age 50** and so cannot provide any funds to help in a default situation if the borrower is younger than 50 at the time.

(d)   There may be **penalties** imposed by the building society in the future if the borrower wants to change to repayment or an endowment method because he is no longer eligible to continue a personal pension policy, ie he has joined a company pension scheme or he does not have sufficient net relevant earnings to sustain the pension payments.

(e) If the pension policy becomes **paid up** because the borrower becomes ineligible to continue to make the contributions, there may be penalties imposed.

Tax treatment

3.8 (a) Up to 5 April 2000, **MIRAS** applied to the payment of interest as outlined in Paragraph 3.4 above. MIRAS relief was abolished from April 2000.

(b) The premiums paid to the pension arrangement are of course eligible for **full tax relief**. If the borrower is employed he will be able to pay his contributions net of basic rate tax and claim back any higher rate relief from the Revenue.

(c) The contributions paid to the scheme are invested in a **fund with tax advantages**.

(d) The cash taken from the fund to repay the mortgage is of course **tax free**.

Individual savings account and personal equity plan mortgages (ISA/PEP mortgages)

Features

3.9 (a) This is just another method of **accumulating capital** to pay back an interest only mortgage.

(b) Although the **charges are lower** and the scheme is more **flexible** there are **greater risks** with a PEP/ISA mortgage The accumulation of the capital to repay the mortgage is totally dependent on the performance of the fund or funds chosen.

(c) The client could make his ISA/PEP contributions on a **monthly basis** or by **annual or single payments**.

(d) The ISA/PEP has **no fixed term** so if the investment is sufficiently good the outstanding capital may be repaid early.

(e) If the plan has a period of **excellent performance**, it may be in the borrower's best interest to cream off some profit and repay part of the outstanding capital.

(f) The building society will insist on **level term assurance** with a sum assured equivalent to the outstanding loan to cover the life or lives of the borrower. This can be pension term assurance if the borrower is eligible.

Question 4

Before proceeding further, re-read Chapter 6 on the subject of ISAs so that you understand fully this type of investment.

Costs and fees

3.10 (a) The borrower will pay the **normal fees**.

    (i) Arrangement fee if appropriate
    (ii) Survey fee
    (iii) Legal fees
    (iv) Indemnity guarantee premium
    (v) Stamp duty if appropriate

(b) The costs of the ISA/PEP will be **lower** than either the pension or the endowment method. The initial charge will probably be 5% - 6% and the annual management charge 1% - 2%.

Conditions and penalties

3.11 (a) The individual savings account and personal equity plan **cannot be assigned** to the building society but assignment of the term assurance will be required.

(b) In the event that the borrower defaults, the building society, after a period of non payment, may be forced to **sell the property** to recoup their loan. In the event of such a forced sale the amount raised is often below the current market value of the property and the borrower may find himself in a position where the sale proceeds do not fully repay the loan. The ISA/PEP could then be encashed to help the situation.

Tax treatment

3.12 (a) **MIRAS** applied up to April 2000 to the payment of interest as outlined above in Paragraph 3.4. MIRAS relief was abolished in April 2000.

(b) The payments made to the ISA/PEP will accumulate in a **tax free fund**.

(c) The proceeds of the ISA/PEP will be **free of income and capital gains tax**.

Question 5

(a) Compare the costs of a personal pension and an ISA.

(b) What do you consider to be:

(i) the advantages and disadvantages of a personal pension as a means of repaying an interest only mortgage?

(ii) the advantages and disadvantages of an ISA as a means of repaying an interest only mortgage?

4 FLEXIBLE MORTGAGES

4.1 Flexible mortgages are repayment mortgages provided by banks and building societies, that offer some flexibility of arrangement to the borrower. The flexibility arises from the following features.

(a) *Irregular payments facility.* The borrower can make payments in irregular amounts, rather than paying a constant amount each month. The irregular payments can be underpayments (ie less than the regular monthly amount), overpayments or payment holidays. However, underpayments and payment holidays are restricted by the amount of overpayments the borrower has previously made.

(b) *Additional borrowing facilities.* Flexible mortgages include a facility to increase the amount borrowed. Additional borrowing facilities are agreed in advance up to a maximum loan-to-value (LTV) ratio, typically 75% to 80%.

4.2 A further key feature of flexible mortgages is the calculation of interest on the outstanding loan. Interest is calculated on a daily basis. Borrowers will therefore obtain an immediate benefit from any overpayments they make.

Costs and conditions

4.3 As a result of competition in the mortgage 'market', most lenders offer flexible mortgages with no early redemption fees or charges.

Tax treatment

4.4 In common with other mortgages, flexible mortgages were subject to MIRAS relief up to 5th April 2000. MIRAS relief has now been abolished.

5 CASHBACK MORTGAGES

5.1 Cashback mortgages are a marketing device used to attract new mortgage business or to retain current mortgage business in cases where the borrower is moving home. Existing borrowers who are not moving home are normally prohibited from re-mortgaging with a cashback mortgage facility.

5.2 A 'cash back' is a cash discount to the borrower on completion of the loan agreement. The amount of cash paid back varies with the lender and the loan. The higher the loan, the larger the cashback will be. Similarly, higher cashbacks are usually given where the amount paid by the borrower towards the purchase price is a higher percentage of the property value.

5.3 A cashback is typically several hundred pounds, but can be well over £1,000. The money can be used by the borrower towards covering the costs of buying the property and moving into it.

5.4 The lender recovers the cost of the cashback through the interest rate structure applied to the mortgage.

Costs and conditions

5.5 There are normally no arrangement fees or revaluation fees associated with cashback mortgages. however, early redemption charges are payable if the mortgage is repaid within a minimum period, typically three to five years. The redemption charge is usually a given number of months of interest charges on the amount of the loan repaid.

Tax treatment

5.6 In common with other mortgages, flexible mortgages were subject to MIRAS relief up to 5 April 2000. MIRAS relief has now been abolished. The cash back itself is tax free.

6 THE USE OF ANCILLARY PRODUCTS IN CONNECTION WITH MORTGAGES

Mortgage protection

6.1 (a) If a client has a capital and interest mortgage, he needs life assurance to cover the outstanding debt at any one time. This is amply solved by a **mortgage protection policy**.

(b) This policy has a **reducing sum assured**, the reduction being in line with the repayment of capital under the mortgage.

(c) There may be an option to **increase cover** without further medical evidence if the client moves house and needs a larger mortgage.

Redundancy protection

6.2   (a)   We have already studied this type of cover in Chapter 2.

       (b)   Re-read the section and note that the aim of such a policy is to provide an income to pay the mortgage for a period of up to **two years in the event of redundancy**.

Sickness and accident

6.3   (a)   We have considered these policies in detail in Chapter 2. Re-read this section and note that the aim of these policies is to provide an **income in the event of sickness or accident**.

       (b)   The policies only pay out for a **maximum of two years**.

       (c)   A more satisfactory answer is a **Permanent Health policy** but this is more expensive.

Critical illness

6.4   (a)   This type of cover has already been described in Chapter 2.

       (b)   This policy pays out a lump sum on diagnosis of a specified medical conditions. The lump sum benefits are not taxable. A policy could therefore be arranged to provide mortgage protection, so that the lump sum payable is sufficient to repay the outstanding mortgage in the event of critical illness of the policy holder.

       (c)   Critical illness policies can be 'stand alone' or added to a life policy. If added to a life policy, the policy will not pay out on death if a claim has previously been made for critical illness.

       (d)   The definition of 'critical illness' can vary between different policies, although there is a 'core' of critical illnesses common to most policies.

Chapter roundup

- Having studied this chapter, the student should be able to distinguish between the various methods of repaying a mortgage and outline the advantages and disadvantages of each.

- The schemes discussed are capital and interest and interest only. In the latter case we looked at the various types of endowment, the personal pension and the PEP as a means of repaying the outstanding capital.

Quick quiz

1   Which of the following mortgage repayment methods has the lowest risk?

     A   Endowment
     B   Capital and interest
     C   Pension
     D   Equity ISA

2   If you wanted to be sure of your mortgage payments for a specific period, which of the following types of interest would you want:

     A   Variable
     B   Capped
     C   Fixed
     D   Collared

3   Who is most likely to obtain a discounted mortgage?

  A   Someone who only wants to borrow a small percentage of the value of the property.
  B   A first time buyer.
  C   Someone with an endowment mortgage.
  D   A self-employed person with three years' excellent accounts.

4   If a client who is a non-taxpayer has a gross interest only mortgage payment of £80.00 per month for her mortgage (£12,000) what net amount will she pay from 6 April 1999?

  A   £80.00 because she cannot claim any tax relief
  B   £60.00
  C   £64.00
  D   £72.00

In the following questions mark each option as TRUE or FALSE.

5   A unit-linked endowment mortgage:

  A   Repays the whole mortgage on death.
  B   Guarantees to repay the mortgage at the end of the term.
  C   Always gives a better return if the premiums are invested in a high risk fund.
  D   Can include waiver of premium.

6   A personal pension mortgage is suitable for:

  A   An accountant who is one of the partners in a large firm
  B   A company director who is a member of an executive pension scheme
  C   An employee who is a member of a contracted in money purchase scheme
  D   An employee who is a member of a contracted out money purchase scheme

7   A self-employed person should protect his pension mortgage with:

  A   A redundancy payment policy
  B   Permanent health insurance
  C   A mortgage protection policy
  D   Waiver of premium

8   The building society will have the following attitude to the repayment of a mortgage.

  A   They will only repossess the property if it is a repayment mortgage.

  B   If the mortgage is being repaid by a personal pension they will require the policy assigned to them.

  C   If the mortgage is being repaid by an endowment policy they will wish to restrict the amount of bonus which can be taken into account when calculating the estimated maturity value.

  D   They prefer endowment mortgages because they can see the amount of the outstanding capital reducing.

The solutions to the questions in the quiz can be found at the end of this Study Text. Before checking your answers against those solutions, you should look back at this chapter and use the information in it to correct your answers.

Answer to questions

2   (a)   A fixed interest mortgage.

    (b)   Deferred interest mortgage or low start.

    (c)   A capped mortgage, because they will have a competitive rate now and the assurance that the rate cannot rise above the cap.

BPP PUBLISHING

5   (a)

	Personal pension plan	Equity ISA
Initial charges	Low allocation or initial units	Low
Bid offer spread	5%	5% - 6%
Annual management charge	1%	1% - 2%
Policy fee	£2.00 per month	Nil

(b)   (i)   The advantages of a personal pension are:

(1)   tax relief on premiums;

(2)   investment in a fund with tax advantages.

The disadvantages of a personal pension are:

(1)   more expensive than an endowment;

(2)   not very flexible, may have to change method of paying mortgage if the client becomes ineligible to pay the premium;

(3)   part of the maximum pension contribution is being used to fund the mortgage so there may only be a low level of pension after the mortgage has been repaid.

(ii)   The advantages of an equity ISA:

(1)   low charges;

(2)   tax free roll up of investment;

(3)   greater flexibility, for example, it will be easier to pay off the mortgage earlier.

Disadvantages of an equity ISA to repay a mortgage are:

(1)   high risk;

(2)   if the client is using the majority of his ISA annual exemption to pay his mortgage, then this is not available for other investment.

Chapter 15

USE OF MORTGAGE PRODUCTS

Chapter topic list	Syllabus reference
1 Type of mortgage	D 3.1
2 Which interest option?	D 3.1
3 The choice of endowment, pension or ISA	D 3.1
4 Affordability of ancillary products	D 3.1

Introduction

This chapter identifies the circumstances in which the various mortgage products can be used to satisfy client needs.

When a client needs mortgage advice, the first decision which must be reached is the type of mortgage most suitable to his needs and then the method of repayment. We will now consider both these aspects.

1   TYPE OF MORTGAGE

1.1   The two main types of mortgage under consideration are:

(a)   **repayment** (capital and interest);
(b)   **interest only**.

Factors to be taken into consideration

1.2   The adviser will need to undertake a **full factfind** and discuss with the clients the following factors.

(a)   Cost
(b)   Portability
(c)   Change in circumstances
(d)   Flexibility
(e)   Attitude

EXAMPLE 1

1.3   Peter and Sarah Thomas have just married. This is their first mortgage and they are concerned about their ability to meet their commitments.

SOLUTION

1.4   In their case, the **repayment mortgage** may be the best route because of **cost and flexibility**.

BPP
PUBLISHING

The cost is likely to be lower than the low cost endowment and should they have problems meeting their mortgage repayments in the future, the building society will find it easier to help them with a repayment than an interest only mortgage. Payments can be rescheduled.

EXAMPLE 2

1.5 Simon and Miranda are in their early thirties. Previously they have worked abroad, now they are back permanently in the UK. Simon expects to be moved frequently as he receives promotions. They wish to discuss the method of repaying a mortgage.

SOLUTION

1.6 In this case an **interest only mortgage** using an endowment policy may be the answer on the grounds of **portability**. Each time they move house they can simply take out another interest only mortgage, keep the original endowment and top this up as appropriate. They could even top up with an ISA if they wanted to spread the risk.

EXAMPLE 3

1.7 Paul is a young surveyor, unmarried and taking out his first mortgage. He says he is not sure of his work pattern in the future. He may work abroad or even live in rented accommodation from time to time.

SOLUTION

1.8 A repayment mortgage may be the answer because of potential **change in circumstances**. If he takes out an interest only mortgage with perhaps an endowment policy, *and* he moves on after a few years the surrender value from an endowment policy will be small or non-existent and neither has he repaid any capital; a bad deal!

EXAMPLE 4

1.9 Susan is 28, an unmarried accountant in a stable job. She is buying her first flat.

SOLUTION

1.10 A repayment mortgage. This may seem an odd recommendation, because financially she can afford an interest only plus endowment or ISA mortgage. The problem in this case is *attitude*. Susan has read a number of articles stating that the returns from endowment policies may not be sufficient to repay a mortgage and she is not prepared to take the risk of an ISA mortgage. She prefers the idea of the security of the repayment mortgage and seeing her debt reduce.

2 WHICH INTEREST OPTION?

Fixed rate mortgage

2.1 (a) These are best suited to **first time buyers** who need the security of knowing the amount of their monthly payments.

(b) The more mature borrower may be interested in such a 'deal' if he is of the opinion that interest rates are **likely to rise in the future**.

      (c)   They are useful for **anyone who finds budgeting difficult**.

Variable rate

2.2   (a)   The vast majority of mortgages are based on the **variable rate** and this allows the borrower to benefit from interest rate falls as well as rises.

      (b)   If the borrower has a repayment mortgage and the rise is too dramatic, he can possibly **extend the term of his loan**.

Low start mortgage

2.3   (a)   This is useful for **first time buyers** because it gives them a breathing space to buy furniture etc for their home before the payments rise.

      (b)   The adviser must, however, be confident that the **borrowers can afford the payments once they rise**.

Capped and collared mortgage

2.4   (a)   The capped mortgage will be of particular interest to **the borrower who thinks interest rates are set to rise**.

      (b)   If it is also collared, the borrower must be made aware of the fact that should rates fall below the collar, he will be paying **more than the 'going rate'**.

Deferred interest mortgage

2.5   (a)   This is suitable for a client who can **definitely see that his income is going to increase in the future**.

      (b)   This type of mortgage then lets him borrow the maximum but **defer the full payments until he is in a financial position to bear the cost**.

      (c)   However the client must be made aware of the fact that this method means that the **outstanding loan will increase**. This could be a problem in a time of poor property prices when the loan outstanding could be higher than the value of the house.

Discounted mortgages

2.6   (a)   Again this is a device particularly aimed at the **first time buyer**.

      (b)   It allows them a **breathing space** to buy furniture etc.

      (c)   There is **no increase in the capital outstanding** and the client must be aware that when the discount finishes, they will pay the variable rate.

Question 1

Before proceeding, see if you can answer the following questions.

(a)   Which interest option is best suited to the first time buyer?

(b)   Which interest option is best suited to the client who thinks interest rates are going to rise?

(c)   Which interest option is best suited to a client who is stretched to pay the mortgage but there is a guarantee of an improvement in financial circumstances in say two years time.

3 THE CHOICE OF ENDOWMENT, PENSION OR ISA

3.1 (a) If an interest only mortgage has been selected, then the borrower must decide **how he will repay the capital at the end of the term**.

 (b) The **main considerations** are:

 (i) cost;
 (ii) attitude to risk;
 (iii) term of the loan;
 (iv) age of the borrower;
 (v) portability;
 (vi) tax considerations.

 We will look at these in turn.

Cost

3.2 The following should be considered.

 (a) **Endowment**

 (i) A full endowment is the most expensive method
 (ii) A low cost or low start will help to keep costs down

 (b) **Pension**. The cost here could be higher even than the full endowment because only 25% of the value of the fund is being used to repay the mortgage, the rest is to provide pension. In considering the cost, the client needs to add together what he is prepared to pay for pension *and* mortgage. There will also be the additional cost of term assurance.

 However for a higher rate taxpayer, the combined cost of pension and mortgage repayment net of 40% tax may be attractive.

 (c) **ISA (or existing PEP)**. The cost of an ISA will most probably be somewhere between the endowment and pension if the borrower is giving himself a 'cushion' for times of bad performance. He must also consider that if he picks a poor investment, it may be necessary to increase payments to ensure that there is sufficient to repay the loan. This could also happen with the endowment and pension method but it is unlikely to be so dramatic because the investment of these contracts should be more conservative. The borrower will also be called upon to pay for life assurance, if he selects this repayment method.

Attitude to risk

3.3 The main concern of the borrower is normally to have sufficient to repay the loan at the end of the term. Some will be prepared to take more risks than others. We will now look at the **risk aspect** of each product.

Endowment

3.4 (a) A **full endowment** presents no risk because the sum assured is equal to the loan even before any addition of bonus.

 (b) In the same way a **non profit endowment**, although a poor return financially, is totally guaranteed.

(c) A **low cost endowment** offers no guarantee and the borrower is dependent upon bonus performance. However, there is some security in the fact that reversionary bonuses once added cannot be taken away.

(d) The **low start policy** has a similar investment arrangement to the low cost endowment.

(e) **Unit linked endowment.** In this case there is a higher risk because the premiums are invested in an asset backed fund, the value of which can fall as well as rise. If the client is invested in an equity fund close to the maturity of the policy and repayment of the loan, the benefits could be inadequate.

Pension

3.5 (a) The investment situation is similar to that described for an endowment policy. If the client has selected **with profits** there is a reasonable level of security because once bonuses are added they cannot be taken away.

(b) If the investor has selected a **unit linked** fund there is a **greater risk**.

(c) With this method the investor is taking a risk with **both his mortgage repayment method and his pension**.

ISA/PEP

3.6 This is the method in which there is the **most risk** because the value of these schemes can go down as well as up.

Term of the loan, age of the borrower

3.7 The **age of the borrower** is significant, as is the **term of the loan**. Let us have a look at a few examples.

EXAMPLE 1

3.8 John is aged 59 and wants a short-term mortgage to age 65.

An endowment policy would be inappropriate on two counts.

(a) It would need to run for 10 years to be a qualifying policy.
(b) The endowment policy would be very expensive.

EXAMPLE 2

3.9 Nigel, a newly qualified dentist, aged 25, wants a pension mortgage for 25 years but does not envisage wanting his pension until age 60.

As he is unable to take the tax free cash to repay the mortgage without taking the pension, this means that he will have to consider a 35 year mortgage or change his mind and take out an endowment or ISA mortgage.

Portability

3.10 (a) The **pension is the least portable** method because if the client changes status and is no longer eligible to contribute to the pension, (eg if he joins an employer's pension scheme,) then the pension will have to be made paid up.

BPP PUBLISHING

(b) The **ISA/PEP mortgage can lack portability.** If a client moves house and wants to change lender, the new lender may not be happy about the risk of the ISA/PEP particularly if the investment return to date has been poor.

(c) **Endowments are the most portable,** because the client can move house, take out a new mortgage and continue the endowment policy, just topping up if more cover is needed.

Tax considerations

3.11 (a) The **pension policy has tax relief** on contributions.

(b) ISA/PEP arrangements have the advantage of a **tax-free fund** for investment growth. This is no longer the case for pension funds where the manager can no longer reclaim tax on UK dividend payments.

(c) All three schemes offer **tax-free cash at maturity.**

Question 2

Rate an endowment, a personal pension and an equity ISA as a means of repaying an interest only mortgage in a category 1 - 3 (1 = excellent, 2 = good, 3 = poor) on the following matters.

(a) Risk
(b) Tax considerations
(c) Portability

4 AFFORDABILITY OF ANCILLARY PRODUCTS

4.1 It is important that the client **protects his mortgage payments** in the event that he cannot work through redundancy or sickness. The cost of this cover should be taken into consideration by the adviser when deciding on the level of mortgage the client can afford.

4.2 **Mortgage protection policy.** This is cheap and essential for the client who has selected the capital and interest method of repaying the mortgage.

4.3 **Redundancy protection** is vital for the employed.

4.4 **Sickness and accident cover.** Although the short term accident policies have their limitations, nevertheless they can be very helpful in providing an income to pay the mortgage for at least a two year period. The real answer is Permanent Health insurance but this is much more expensive.

Chapter roundup

- In this chapter we have identified the type of client who will find a repayment or interest only mortgage fits his needs, the interest options available and the most advantageous method of repaying the interest only mortgage.

- If there is sufficient income available, it is vital to protect the mortgage payments by use of redundancy and sickness type cover

Quick quiz

1   Which is likely to be the most expensive way of repaying a 10 year interest only mortgage for a man of 45?

   A   A personal pension
   B   A unit trust savings plan
   C   An equity ISA
   D   A low cost endowment

In the following questions, mark each option as TRUE of FALSE

2   A deferred interest mortgage is:

   A   A mortgage where at the end of the deferred period the outstanding loan has increased
   B   Suitable for someone who expects a promotion at work in 12 months time
   C   Suitable for someone who has insufficient income to substantiate their borrowing
   D   Will cost less than a variable interest loan

3   A risk averse client should choose which of the following methods of repaying a mortgage.

   A   A capital and interest mortgage
   B   An ISA mortgage
   C   A full endowment policy
   D   A unit linked retirement annuity

The solutions to the questions in the quiz can be found at the end of this Study Text. Before checking your answers against those solutions, you should look back at this chapter and use the information in it to correct your answers.

Answers to questions

1   (a)   Discounted mortgage or fixed interest.
    (b)   Fixed interest.
    (c)   Deferred interest mortgage.

2   (a)   Risk 1 = low, 2 = medium, 3 = high.

         With profits endowment = low = 1.

         Low cost endowment = medium = 2 (because return may not be sufficient to repay loan).

         Unit-linked endowment = high = 3 (use of unit linked funds increases the risk).

         With profits pension = medium = 2 (because bonus rate may be insufficient to realise a large enough cash sum to pay back the loan).

         Unit-linked pension = high = 3 (use of unit linked funds increases the risk).

         ISA = high = 3 (equity investment).

    (b)   Tax considerations

         Pension = 1 = tax relief and tax free fund.
         ISA = 2 = tax free fund.
         Endowment = 3 = no tax considerations.

    (c)   Portability

         Endowment = 1 = can be transferred from each mortgage without loss.
         ISA = 1 = can be transferred from each mortgage without loss.
         Pension = 3 = problems, if client changes status and is no longer able to make contributions

Chapter 16

COMPARING MORTGAGE PRODUCTS AND PROVIDERS

Chapter topic list	Syllabus reference
1 Comparing different types of mortgages	D 4.1
2 Comparing different providers of a particular mortgage	D 4.2

Introduction

Having decided on the mortgage most suited to his client, the adviser must now select a bank, building society or other lender.

1 COMPARING DIFFERENT TYPES OF MORTGAGES

1.1 The **factors** are:

(a) redemption penalties;
(b) flexibility of repayment term;
(c) arrangement fees;
(d) overall APR.

Redemption penalties

1.2 (a) In the past most building societies required a **redemption fee** if the borrower repaid the loan before the expiry of the term. This is now rare with variable interest mortgages.

(b) Redemption fees do, however, apply if the borrower has been given some **advantageous treatment** as in the case of:

(i) fixed rate loan;
(ii) capped loan;
(iii) deferred interest loan.

In these cases if the loan is repaid early then the building society will make a once off charge. This is usually related to a loss of so many months' interest payments, for example three months interest. In the case of a long-term fixed interest loan the redemption fee could be as high as seven months' interest.

(c) If a borrower has a fixed interest mortgage and has to re-arrange the mortgage because of a **house move** during the term, so long as he remains with the original lender there should be no redemption penalty imposed.

Flexibility of repayment term

1.3   (a)   As we have seen earlier in these chapters, one of the advantages of the capital and interest repayment method is the ability to **restructure payments** and, if necessary, **extend the term of the loan**.

(b)   It is, therefore, important that the adviser ascertains that this flexibility is available. He will need to know if there is a term beyond which the lender will not extend the term and also whether they will be willing to extend it **beyond retirement age**.

Arrangement fees

1.4   Arrangement fees are more likely to be charged for **fixed interest mortgages**. The adviser will need to find out the following:

(a)   the amount of the fee;

(b)   whether it is refundable if the mortgage does not go ahead;

(c)   whether it can be transferred to another property;

(d)   whether it can be added to the loan.

Overall APR

1.5   (a)   APR stands for **Annual Percentage Rate**.

(b)   If an adviser is trying to find out the **true cost of the client's borrowing,** he must look beyond the interest rate which is to be paid on the loan. It is the APR which gives a better indication of the total cost. The APR will be higher than the lending rate because it will take into account:

(i)   costs and fees incurred in arranging the mortgage;

(ii)   actual payment of interest, whether it is charged annually, quarterly, monthly or daily.

2   COMPARING DIFFERENT PROVIDERS OF A PARTICULAR MORTGAGE

2.1   The **factors** to be taken into account are as follows:

(a)   Annual payment review;

(b)   Portability;

(c)   Availability of further advances;

(d)   Compulsory ancillary products;

(e)   Quality of service.

Annual payment review

2.2   (a)   Most lenders review mortgage payments, whether capital and interest or interest, only **once a year**. This is excellent if interest rates have risen but not if they have fallen.

(b)   It is however a useful budgeting tool if clients know that their payments will remain **constant for 12 months**.

(c)   Some lenders will give the borrower the option to switch to **monthly variable interest payments**.

Portability

2.3 If a client is considering a fixed interest mortgage, he will need confirmation that if he **moves during the period** of the fixed rate, he has the ability to carry this with him to his next property and mortgage so long as he remains with the existing lender.

Availability of further advances

2.4 When clients are considering buying a new house, they often have plans to improve the property in a few years' time; perhaps build an extension, a granny annex or more bedrooms. They therefore need reassurance that, should they require **more finance in future**, the building society will be sympathetic to their needs.

They may wish the adviser to ascertain whether any further loan:

(a) could be added to the existing loan;

(b) could be repaid within the same term;

(c) could be available at the same rate of interest, if the original loan was on a fixed rate basis.

Compulsory ancillary products

2.5 (a) Many banks and building societies are 'tied' to their own or other insurance companies and are keen to sell **ancillary protection products**. Sometimes this is voluntary and sometimes compulsory.

(b) In return for a fixed rate mortgage or a capped mortgage the lender may **require compulsory buildings and contents insurance**, at least for the first year.

Quality of service

2.6 (a) The client wishes to buy the 'house of his dreams' and does not want to be thwarted by the red tape of the lender, so the **speed and efficiency of the service** is vital.

(b) The first important step is to get the **survey** arranged as quickly as possible so that both the lender and the borrower can feel secure that the purchase is viable.

(c) An **interview** with the client is often essential and this needs to be undertaken by a member of the bank or building society staff who has good powers of communication and can explain the complexities of the mortgage and house moving in simple terms.

(d) Some building societies are still willing to **interview borrowers in their own homes** and this can be very helpful particularly if the client works, say, shifts.

(e) The **speed of a decision** is vital once the survey has been completed. Many lenders are now centralised and there is very little scope for discretion from a local building society manager.

(f) Finally, the ability of the building society to **deal promptly** with the borrower and their solicitor is of paramount importance.

Chapter roundup

- In this chapter we have looked, at perhaps the most important aspect of the mortgage process, selecting the lender. Flexibility, penalties and above all service are of paramount importance in making this selection.

Quick quiz

In the following questions, mark each option as TRUE or FALSE.

1   Which of the following products may a building society attempt to sell to a new borrower as a condition of the loan?

   A   Endowment policies
   B   Buildings insurance
   C   Motor insurance
   D   Contents insurance for one year

2   APR is higher than the normal lending rate because:

   A   It is a special rate for first time borrowers
   B   It takes into account the costs and fees of borrowing
   C   It takes into account the frequency that interest is charged
   D   The building society charge it to those borrowers who are in arrears

3   Arrangement fees

   A   Help to avoid timewasters
   B   Are always refunded
   C   Can be added to the amount of the loan
   D   Are usually charged for fixed interest loans

The solutions to the questions in the quiz can be found at the end of this Study Text. Before checking your answers against those solutions, you should look back at this chapter and use the information in it to correct your answers.

Updates for this Study Text are available on the BPP website:
www.bpp.com
See page (v) of this Study Text for further details.

Appendix:
Tax tables

INCOME TAX

TAX RATES	2000/2001	1999/2000
Lower rate	10%	10%
Basic rate	22%	23%
Higher rate	40%	40%
Lower rate payable on income up to	£1,520	£1,500
Higher rate payable on income over	£28,400	£28,000

(Dividends are taxable at 10% and 32.5% of the gross
dividend, for basic rate and higher rate taxpayers respectively)

MAIN PERSONAL RELIEFS

	£	£
Personal allowance	4,385	4,335
Married couple's allowance★	Abolished	1,970
Additional personal allowance★	Abolished	1,970
Widow's bereavement allowance★	Abolished	1,970
Mortgage interest loan limit (MIRAS★★ relief)	Abolished	30,000

AGE ALLOWANCE

Aged 65-74:		
Personal allowance	5,790	5,720
Married couple's allowance★	5,185	5,125
Aged 75 and over:		
Personal allowance	6,050	5,980
Married couple's allowance★	5,255	5,195

★ *Relief at 10%.* Widow's bereavement allowance abolished for 2000/2001 for those widowed after 5 April 2000. An allowance of £2,000 applies for 2000/2001 for those widowed during 1999/2000 and who have not remarried before 6 April 2000.

★★ Relief for 1999/2000 is restricted to interest on 10% of loan, with loan limit set at £30,000.

INHERITANCE TAX

RATES OF TAX APPLICABLE ON DEATH

Estate value	Rate
Up to £234,000	Nil
Excess over £234,000	40% of excess

MAIN EXEMPTIONS

	£
Inter spouse transfers (UK domiciled spouse)	No limit
Gifts to UK registered charities	No limit
Lifetime transfers:	
- annual exemption per donor	3,000
- small gifts, annual amount per donee	250
(note that this cannot be used to cover part of a larger gift)	
Normal expenditure	Depends on circumstances

CAPITAL GAINS TAX

RATES OF TAX

For individuals, chargeable gains, after deduction of allowable losses are taxable at the income tax rates which would apply if the gains were treated as extra income. From 1999/2000, the rates of tax are those which would apply to savings income, ie 20% and 40%. From 2000/2001, however, the starting rate of 10% also applies.

In the case of trustees, the rate is 34%.

INDEXATION

In calculating the chargeable gain, the purchase price can be adjusted to allow for inflation as measured by the RPI for periods up to 5 April 1998. In the case of assets purchased on or before 31 March 1982, the value of the asset on 31 March 1982 is normally used, and is adjusted by the increase in RPI since that date.

In general it follows that only gains made since 31 March 1982 are chargeable, although a number of exceptions apply.

For disposals on or after 6 April 1995, it is not possible to utilise indexation relief to create or increase a loss for CGT purposes

TAPER RELIEF

For disposals on or after 6 April 1998, indexation relief will apply only for the period up to April 1998, and taper relief applies thereafter. The relief operates to reduce the amount of any gain which is liable to CGT, and reflects the period of ownership after 5 April 1998. For non-business assets acquired before 17 March 1998, 1 year is added to years of ownership after 5 April 1998 in determining the taper relief percentage. For business assets, this 'bonus year' does not apply for disposal in 2000/2001 onwards (but did apply for disposal in 1999/2000).

The taper relief scale, showing the percentage of any gain which is subject to CGT, is as follows:

Years of ownership	Business assets	Other assets
0	100%	100%
1	87.5%	100%
2	75%	100%
3	50%	95%
4	25%	90%
5	25%	85%
6	25%	80%
7	25%	75%
8	25%	70%
9	25%	65%
10 or more	25%	60%

From 2000/2001, the definition of what constitutes a business asset has been relaxed, so that the following qualifies as business assets

- All shares in unquoted trading companies, including AIM-listed companies.
- Share hold by employees in quoted trading companies.
- Shares held by outside investors in quoted trading companies above a 5% minimum threshold.

ANNUAL EXEMPTION

For individuals, the annual exemption for 2000/2001 is £7,200, which applies individually to husband and wife.

For trusts, the exemption in most cases is £3,600.

CGT CHATTELS EXEMPTION

Gains on chattels (ie items sold where the proceeds are no more than £6,000 per item) are wholly exempt.

PENSION CONTRIBUTIONS

The table below shows the maximum allowable contribution to Personal Pension Schemes or Retirement Annuity Contracts, expressed as a percentage of Net Relevant Earnings (NRE)

Age on 6 April	Personal Pension Schemes	Retirement Annuity Contracts
Up to 35	17.5 %	17.5 %
36-45	20.0 %	17.5 %
46-50	25.0 %	17.5 %
51-55	30.0 %	20.0 %
56-60	35.0 %	22.5 %
61-74	40.0 %	27.5 %

The earnings cap for 2000/2001 is £91,800 (£90,600 in 1999/2000), and restricts NRE for the purposes of Personal Pension Schemes.

BPP PUBLISHING

Practice examination 1

Time allowed: 2 hours

MULTIPLE CHOICE QUESTIONS

1   Which of the following do you think is the most important protection cover for a single man with no outstanding loans?

A   Term assurance
B   Permanent health insurance
C   Whole of life assurance
D   Family income

2   How should you protect a capital and interest mortgage?

A   Family income benefit policy
B   Level term assurance
C   Decreasing term assurance
D   Renewable term assurance

3   Under which of the following contracts does the sum assured *not* reduce?

A   Decreasing term assurance
B   A mortgage protection policy
C   Convertible term assurance
D   Family income benefit policy

4   Why is it important that a policy should be 'qualifying'?

A   So as not to pay tax on the premiums
B   So as not to pay tax on the proceeds on death or maturity
C   So that the proceeds roll up in a tax free fund
D   So that the policy can be surrendered early with no payment of tax

5   If tax has to be paid on the proceeds of a policy owned by the life assured which tax is paid?

A   Capital gains tax
B   Inheritance tax
C   Corporation tax
D   Income tax

6   Which of the following illnesses would not be covered by a critical illness policy?

A   Heart attack
B   A stroke
C   A slipped disc
D   Cancer

7   Which of the following medical conditions is of more concern to the permanent health underwriter than to the life assurance underwriter?

A   History of high blood pressure
B   History of asthma
C   History of chronic back pain
D   Diabetes

8   In what circumstances can directors claim tax relief on contributions paid to a permanent health policy?

   A   If they inform the Revenue they have taken out such a policy.

   B   If they effect individual policies.

   C   If they become part of a group arrangement which is open to a large number of their employees.

   D   If there is a group arrangement restricted to directors only.

9   In which of the following circumstances may tax relief be available on payment of a premium?

   A   Life assurance policy taken out in 1989
   B   Individual permanent health policy
   C   Personal pension life cover
   D   Personal accident and sickness policy

10   The offer price of a unit is

   A   The price at which the investor buys the unit
   B   The price at which the investor sells the unit
   C   The price at which the manager cancels the unit
   D   The price at which the investor surrenders the unit

11   Which of the following people would pay most for permanent health insurance cover? Assume that the cover, the term and the deferred period is the same.

   A   A postman
   B   A postwoman
   C   A male insurance clerk
   D   A female accountant

12   Under which of the following agreements can 100% business relief for inheritance tax be claimed?

   A   A buy and sell agreement
   B   A cross option agreement
   C   Automatic accrual agreement
   D   An option to sell a 1% holding of quoted shares

13   How would a married man write a mortgage protection policy to ensure that he achieved the benefits in the right hands on the death of either himself or his wife?

   A   On a single life basis in trust for the children
   B   On a joint life first death basis
   C   On a joint life second death basis
   D   On a single life basis with no trust

14   Which of the following cannot be protected by an insurance policy?

   A   Loss of income through sickness
   B   Loss of income through redundancy
   C   Loss of capital through a fall in the stock market
   D   Loss of income through death of a partner

15   Which of the following charges would you find on a level term assurance?

A   Annual management charges
B   Initial units
C   Policy charge
D   Bid/offer spread

16   A savings plan with index-linked premiums is most suitable for which of the following?

A   A client who does short term contract work
B   A single client who is considering emigrating in four years' time
C   A client who has a steady job with promotion prospects
D   A client who may need access to money

17   Which of the following investments always gives a guaranteed income?

A   A cash ISA
B   National Savings Pensioners Bond
C   National Savings Income Bond
D   Building society postal account

18   Which of the following investments pays an income or dividend on a monthly basis?

A   A Marks and Spencer ordinary share
B   An index-linked gilt
C   National savings income bond
D   A local authority bond

19   Which of the following National Savings products pays interest net of 20% tax?

A   Pensioners income bond
B   Fixed rate savings bond
C   National savings ordinary account
D   National savings investment account

20   What is the running yield on a gilt priced at £104 with a coupon of 8.5%?

A   8.84%
B   8.5%
C   8.17%
D   8%

21   Which of the following taxes is not paid on a gilt investment?

A   22% tax on income
B   40% tax on income for a higher rate taxpayer
C   Capital gains tax on gain
D   Inheritance tax on a legacy

22   Calculate the price/earnings ratio of a share where the earnings are 20p per share and the current price 200p.

A   p/e = 40
B   p/e = 100
C   p/e = 10
D   p/e = 5

23   If an investment trust is 'highly geared', which of the following is correct?

A   It means that the shares are being sold at a premium.

B   It means that the company's borrowings are high compared to the capital value of the trust.

C   It means that the shares are being sold at a discount.

D   It means that the company is investing in high risk shares.

24   Which is the least tax efficient investment for a higher rate taxpayer wanting some income?

A   A preference share
B   A low coupon gilt
C   An existing TESSA
D   A high income unit trust ISA

25   On which of the following investments may there be a tax charge on the proceeds on the death of the owner?

A   A share
B   A unit trust
C   A single premium bond
D   A gilt

26   Which of the following statements about a single premium bond is false?

A   There is a facility to switch between funds at a modest cost
B   There is a small element of life cover
C   The scheme runs for a fixed term
D   There are facilities to take an 'income'

27   Which of the following policies is most likely to be used in conjunction with a mortgage?

A   A low cost endowment policy.
B   A flexidowment.
C   A maximum investment policy.
D   A friendly society savings plan.

28   Which is the most tax-efficient endowment policy?

A   A low start endowment
B   A low cost endowment
C   A unit linked endowment
D   A friendly society savings plan

29   Which type of annuity is required by a person who wants the safeguard that in the event of his death at least the balance of the original investment will be returned to his estate?

A   Immediate annuity guaranteed for 5 years
B   Immediate annuity guaranteed for 10 years
C   Increasing annuity
D   Capital protected annuity

30   The income from a purchased life annuity is taxed in which of the following ways?

A   As earned income
B   As unearned income
C   Subject to capital gains tax
D   Only the interest portion of each payment is taxed as unearned income

31   Which of the following investments does not normally have an early surrender penalty?

    A   A notice account
    B   An equity ISA
    C   National Savings certificates
    D   A guaranteed income bond

32   Which of the following investments cannot be moved to another 'provider' during the term of the scheme without suffering a considerable penalty?

    A   An existing TESSA
    B   A cash ISA
    C   Unit trust savings plan
    D   A friendly society savings plan

33   What is a 'tracker fund'?

    A   A fund of funds
    B   A fund which tracks an index
    C   A high risk fund
    D   A very specialist fund

34   OPRA:

    A   is part of the Inland Revenue
    B   approves pension schemes
    C   will regulate all occupational pension schemes
    D   is regulated by the FSA

35   A divorced woman who has only worked for a short time will:

    A   receive no basic state pension.
    B   receive a very small state pension based on her own contributions.
    C   receive a state pension based on her ex-husband's contribution history.
    D   receive a full state pension regardless of contributions.

36   Which of the following offer the most immediate tax benefit to a self-employed person?

    A   A contribution to an ISA
    B   A contribution to an existing TESSA
    C   A contribution to a retirement annuity
    D   A contribution to a friendly society savings plan

37   Which of the following retirement age ranges is set down in the Inland Revenue Practice Notes for an Occupational Pension Scheme?

    A   50 - 75
    B   60 - 75
    C   60 - 70
    D   65 - 75

38   An employee has a basic salary of £20,000 plus benefits in kind of £2,000. He contributes 5% of his basic salary to a company pension scheme. He now wants to pay a maximum AVC contribution. What gross payment can he make?

    A   £3,300
    B   £2,300
    C   £3,000
    D   £2,000

39   An employee retires on a full pension of £5,000 from an occupational pension scheme. However he takes a tax free cash sum of £8,000 and as a result his pension reduces to £4,280. He subsequently dies leaving a widow who is entitled to a 50% spouse's pension. How much will she get?

   A   £2,500
   B   £2,140
   C   £4,280
   D   £3,333

40   Which definition of 'pensionable salary' is most suitable for a salesperson?

   A   Previous year's P60 earnings
   B   Basic pay
   C   Basic pay plus 50% of previous year's bonus
   D   Anticipated pay and bonus for next year

41   Which of the following benefits would you not find included in a company pension scheme?

   A   Group life assurance
   B   Group sickness cover
   C   Travel insurance
   D   Personal accident and sickness

42   What is the maximum pension allowed from an occupational pension scheme on retirement on grounds of ill health?

   A   Pension based on years of service to date of leaving.
   B   Pension based on years of service to date of leaving, less an early retirement penalty.
   C   Pension based on potential service to normal retirement date.
   D   Pension based on potential service to normal retirement date less a penalty.

43   A person leaving an occupational pension scheme after 18 months membership of the scheme under Inland Revenue rules will receive

   A   A return of the employer and employee's contributions
   B   A return of the employee's contributions
   C   A return of the employee's contributions less 22% tax
   D   A return of the employee's contributions less 20% tax

44   A high earner can have his tax-free lump sum based on maximum earnings of £100,000 if he joined an occupational pension scheme

   A   Before 17 March 1987
   B   In the period from 17 March 1987 to 31 May 1989
   C   After 1 June 1989
   D   After 5 April 1988

45   Which of the following is a disadvantage of a FSAVC?

   A   Freedom of choice of investment

   B   Higher charges than an inhouse AVC

   C   Confidentiality

   D   The FSAVC can stay with the same insurance company even if the employee changes jobs and schemes

46   How much can a male aged 47 pay into a personal pension?

 A 17.5% of net relevant earnings
 B 25% of net relevant earnings
 C 20% of net relevant earnings
 D 15% of net relevant earning

47   If a male aged 38 is currently paying 5% of net relevant earnings into a personal pension, how much can his employer pay?

 A 15% of net relevant earnings
 B 10% of net relevant earnings
 C 12.5% of net relevant earnings
 D Nothing

48   If a married policyholder with a personal pension was in ill health at retirement date, which of the following pensions would be a sensible choice?

 A Single life pension level throughout life no guarantee
 B Single life pension escalating
 C Joint life with pension reducing by 50% on pensioner's death
 D Joint life with no reduction in pension on pensioner's death

49   Which of the following features is *not* common to both a personal pension and a retirement annuity?

 A Open to anyone in non pensionable employment.
 B There is no need for the policyholder to retire to take the benefits.
 C 5% of the net relevant earnings can be used to purchase a life assurance benefit.
 D The policy can be used to contract out of SERPS.

50   A pensioneer trustee is needed to run which of the following?

 A A SIPP
 B A retirement annuity
 C A SSAS
 D A FURB

51   If a doctor's wife worked part time as her husband's assistant, which of the following schemes would be the best method to pension her earnings?

 A An executive pension
 B A personal pension
 C Group personal pension
 D FSAVC

52   What is the stamp duty on the purchase of a house valued at £260,000?

 A £7,800
 B £2,600
 C Nil
 D £1,040

53   If a client is concerned about the structure of a property he is buying, which type of survey does he need?

 A A basic building society valuation
 B Report and valuation
 C Structural survey
 D Drains test

54   Which type of endowment has a guaranteed sum assured sufficient to repay the loan on death or maturity?

    A   Low cost endowment
    B   Low start endowment
    C   Non profit endowment
    D   Unit-linked endowment

55   Which of the following mortgage repayment methods has the lowest risk?

    A   Interest only and equity ISA
    B   Capital and interest and mortgage protection policy
    C   Interest only and unit-linked low cost endowment policy
    D   Interest only and low start endowment policy

56   Which of the following statements is incorrect?

    A   A whole of life policy can be assigned to a trust
    B   An endowment policy can be assigned to a building society
    C   A personal pension can be assigned to a building society
    D   An endowment policy can be assigned to a new owner.

57   From a tax point of view which of the following type of repayment is most suitable for a self-employed higher rate taxpayer?

    A   Capital and interest
    B   Interest and endowment
    C   Interest and an ISA
    D   Interest and a personal pension

58   In which of the following types of mortgage is a redemption payment most likely to occur?

    A   Capital and interest, fixed rate
    B   Capital and interest, variable rate
    C   Interest only, variable rate
    D   Low start variable rate

59   Which of the following does not yield an income?

    A   A gilt
    B   National savings certificates
    C   National savings deposit account
    D   Building society postal account

60   If a basic rate tax-paying client wants to take a low risk and tie his capital up for five years for capital appreciation which of the following investments would be most suitable?

    A   An individual savings account
    B   UK equity unit trust
    C   National savings certificate
    D   Fund of funds unit trust

ANSWER EACH PART OF THE FOLLOWING QUESTIONS AS TRUE OR FALSE

61 In deciding on the level of sickness cover required a client should take into account:

101 Possible state benefits
102 Other sources of income
103 Outgoings
104 Benefits insured under a family income benefit policy
105 Spouses' income

62 Consider the following statements concerning providers of life assurance.

106 Mutual companies are owned by the shareholders
107 Industrial life offices traditionally collect premium weekly door to door
108 Friendly societies deal in small sums assured in their tax-exempt fund
109 Only certain brokers can place life business on the Lloyds market
110 Composite insurance companies only write life assurance
111 All life offices must be authorised by the Department of Trade

63 Consider the comments on the features of a traditional level term assurance.

112 The policy has a fixed term
113 There is a surrender value after year two
114 There is a guaranteed sum assured
115 Premiums during the term are known at the outset

64 A convertible term assurance can be converted to:

116 Critical illness cover
117 A whole of life policy
118 A permanent health policy
119 An endowment assurance
120 Further term assurance
121 Personal accident and sickness cover

65 The disadvantages of a fixed term level temporary assurance are:

122 Inability to increase the sum assured
123 Inability to extend the term of the cover
124 Inability to obtain a return on maturity
125 Inability to obtain a return on death

66 A man has been out of work for five years. He has investment income. Which of the following policies can he keep in force?

126 An endowment policy
127 Personal pension
128 Permanent health insurance
129 Medical sickness insurance
130 Mortgage protection
131 A whole of life policy

67 Some life policies still retain life assurance premium relief, consider the following statements.

132 LAPR will be given to premiums paid on policies effected prior to 13 March 1986
133 If LAPR is in force, the relief may cease if the policy is altered
134 Premium relief is given at source
135 LAPR is given on premiums no greater than £1,600 per annum or one-sixth of income

68   In this question we look at some features of terminal bonuses.

    136 A terminal bonus reflects the fund performance close to the maturity of the policy or a death claim

    137 All policyholders are guaranteed a right to participate in a terminal bonus

    138 Lenders do not normally allow insurance companies to take the terminal bonus into account when estimating the proceeds available to repay a mortgage

    139 Terminal bonuses have been increasing during the last 5 years

69   A unit-linked whole of life policy has the following attractions.

    140 No medical underwriting is required

    141 High death cover and high investment content

    142 The choice of level of death cover

    143 The ability to write the death cover in trust

    144 Non-reviewable premiums

    145 The investment content can be altered

70   In this question we will look at the risk levels of various unitised funds.

    146 There is a currency risk in an international fund

    147 A Japan smaller companies fund is a high risk fund

    148 A unit trust gilt fund has no risk because it is backed by the Government

    149 A managed fund has a medium risk

    150 Property funds can be a medium risk because of the illiquidity of the underlying asset

    151 A UK smaller companies fund has a lower risk level than a tracker fund

71   Consider the following statements regarding individual permanent health insurance.

    152 The minimum deferred period offered is 26 weeks

    153 The deferred period can be changed when a claim arises

    154 Normally premiums do not have to be paid during a period of claim

    155 A policyholder can claim any number of times for the same medical condition

    156 Pre-existing conditions are excluded for the first two years by use of a moratorium

    157 Pre-existing conditions are dealt with by exclusions to the cover

72   If an individual claims under a permanent health insurance policy, which of the following statements will be true?

    158 Income will be paid via the PAYE system

    159 Payments made to the individual under the policy will be tax free

    160 The income can be treated as net relevant earnings for pension purposes

    161 The income could be paid to the partner's wife to avoid tax

73   Which of the following are ways of reducing the cost of medical expenses cover?

    162 Accepting an excess

    163 Only having cover for in-patient care

    164 Asking for a medical exclusion to be imposed on the policy

    165 Restricting the number of members of your family covered by the scheme

74   Which of the following policies would be needed by a partnership to provide business cover?

    166 Family Income Benefit

    167 Permanent health insurance

    168 PA and sickness

    169 Long term care

    170 Critical illness

    171 Immediate annuity

75   Which of the following factors would you take into account when comparing different providers offering permanent health insurance?

    172 Ability to handle claims promptly
    173 Periods of deferment offered
    174 Definition of incapacity
    175 Hospital bands available
    176 Premium level
    177 Attitude to change of occupation

76   In what circumstances may an insurance company be asked by the Treasury to make more regular returns of its financial affairs?

    178 If it was recently authorised
    179 If it was launching a new product
    180 If it was being investigated for mis-selling
    181 If the Treasury was concerned about the insurance company's trading position

77   In recommending a savings vehicle for a client, which of the following factors should you take into account?

    182 Existing savings schemes
    183 Available spare income
    184 The client's tax situation
    185 Available capital
    186 Risk profile
    187 Reason for saving

78   If a client has a building society notice account:

    188 Interest will be variable
    189 If the client is a non-taxpayer the income can be paid gross after completion of a form R87
    190 All the interest will be lost if the capital is withdrawn without notice
    191 The amount of notice is communicated to the client at the outset.

79   Consider the following features of National Savings products.

    192 The first £70 of interest earned on an ordinary account is paid tax-free
    193 There is no fixed term for an income bond
    194 3 months notice is required when withdrawing from an income bond
    195 8 working days notice is needed to withdraw from a pensioners bond

80   A client makes the following remarks about a gilt. Which are true, which false?

    196 A gilt is 'no good' because the capital invested can never keep pace with inflation
    197 A medium term gilt will be redeemed at a date in excess of 15 years
    198 The client thinks interest rates will rise soon so short gilt prices should rise
    199 The client says he will buy the gilts from the Post Office because it will be cheaper

81   A client is confused about types of share. He says:

    200 An unpaid share is a free share
    201 An unquoted share is a share in a private company and is virtually unmarketable
    202 A preference share usually carries a guaranteed dividend
    203 A convertible preference share allows the owner to convert to an ordinary share in the future
    204 A warrant gives a right to buy free shares
    205 A 'blue chip' share is guaranteed not to fall in value

82   An investment trust is:

206 A pooled investment
207 A closed end fund
208 A company
209 An open ended fund

83   The following features would prevent an ISA from receiving the CAT mark standard.

210 Inclusion of an OEIC in the equity component
211 Issuing a cash card from the cash component
212 Using single pricing for the equity component
213 Having no minimum surrender value for the life assurance component

84   A guaranteed income bond written as a single premium endowment:

214 Can roll up the income to provide a growth bond
215 Is a non-qualifying policy
216 Can give rise to a charge to higher rate tax on encashment
217 Can produce a gross income for a non-taxpayer

85   If a client takes a 5% withdrawal from a bond

218 The value of the original investment may reduce
219 This is tax free
220 The client is deferring tax
221 The withdrawal could be subject to tax at 22%
222 The withdrawal could be subject to tax at 18%
223 The value of the withdrawals will be taken into account in the final tax calculation

86   The Government allows contracting out of SERPS. Let us look at its features.

224 It is advantageous for all
225 If the client is contracting out via a personal pension it is only advantageous below a 'pivotal' age
226 It makes no difference what age you are, if you are contracting out via a final salary pension scheme
227 Rebates are age related only if you contract out using a personal pension

87   In order for an occupational pension scheme to be exempt approved:

228 It must be set up under a revocable trust
229 There must be a trust deed and rules
230 There must be a pensioneer trustee
231 There must be a definitive deed

88   A member of a public sector pension scheme would be ill advised to opt out because:

232 The schemes are often non-contributory
233 The pensions increase in payment
234 They are defined contribution schemes
235 They offer excellent pension benefit if an employee retires early on grounds of ill health.

89   What are the advantages of a money purchase scheme for the employer?

236 A known cost
237 He can offer his staff guaranteed levels of pension
238 He can pay a lower contribution rate than for a final salary scheme
239 He can pay different levels of contribution for different employees

90   If an employee dies in the service of his employer, which of the following benefits may his family receive from the company pension scheme?

    240 A tax free lump sum
    241 A disability benefit
    242 A spouse's pension
    243 A dependant's pension

91   Which of the following statements is true, which false?

    244 You can take a tax-free lump sum from the state pension scheme
    245 The state pension is pay-as-you-go
    246 All women will receive the basic state pension at age 65 in 2010
    247 If you defer taking the state pension it increases
    248 The state pension is paid tax-free
    249 The basic state pension is means tested

92   Which of the following are correct statements?

    250 Protected rights confer no guarantees

    251 A guaranteed minimum pension gives a guarantee

    252 A guaranteed minimum pension will be equivalent to the SERPS benefit for the period of contracted out service

    253 A protected rights pension will always give a better return than SERPS

93   If a client uses 'carry back' to make a contribution to a personal pension:

    254 The contributions will be based on the net relevant earnings for the previous tax year

    255 Tax relief will be given on the premium paid based on the client's tax rate for the current year

    256 Tax relief will be given on the premium paid based on the client's tax rate for the previous tax year

94   The advantage of moving funds from a retirement annuity to a personal pension may be:

    257 The ability to obtain a return of fund on death
    258 Benefits can be taken from age 50
    259 You can always take a larger tax free lump sum
    260 You can have the pension paid tax free
    261 To obtain wider investment choice

95   Who can use an appropriate personal pension to contract out?

    262 An employed person who is not in a company pension scheme.
    263 An employed person who is in a contracted in occupational pension scheme.
    264 A self employed person.
    265 A married woman who is not working.

96   What is a 'headroom check'?

    266 A check on the financial strength of an insurance company

    267 A check on the maximum benefits which can be provided for any employee from the main occupational pension scheme to ensure that there is scope to make a free standing additional voluntary contribution (FSAVC)

    268 A calculation to ascertain the maximum contribution which can be paid to a FSAVC

97   A client who has had a number of different employment statuses during his life is trying to consolidate his pension payments. Consider the advice given to him.

269   The personal pension which he took out when self employed can now be transferred to his Section 32 policy

270   The benefits from a previous employers contracted out pension scheme an be transferred to a personal pension without the loss of the guaranteed minimum pension.

271   The benefits of a poor performing personal pension can be transferred to another personal pension.

98   For which of the following people would a FURB be an advantage?

272   A married woman working part-time for her husband

273   A high earner who has already accrued the maximum pension up to the earnings cap

274   An employee for whom his company has already funded maximum benefits

275   A self-employed person wishing to buy a property

276   A Company Director with no approved pension benefits

277   A computer expert who changes jobs frequently

99   Premiums under a unit-linked endowment policy used for mortgage purposes may have to rise on review:

278   To ensure better performance
279   To ensure that there are sufficient funds to pay off the mortgage
280   To ensure that the level of life assurance cover can be maintained
281   To allow a fund switch

100   Let us look at the tax relief relating to premiums and mortgages.

282   There are no circumstances in which tax relief is available on interest and on endowment premiums

283   It is possible to obtain tax relief on mortgage interest on a repayment mortgage and on the associated life cover

284   It is possible to obtain tax relief on the mortgage interest and a personal pension scheme contribution

285   It is possible to obtain tax relief on the mortgage interest and an ISA contribution.

Practice
examination 2

Time allowed: 2 hours

MULTIPLE CHOICE QUESTIONS

1   Which of the following people most requires protection?

    A   A company director
    B   A student
    C   A retired widow
    D   A single person with no debts

2   Which of the following policies cannot be paid for by a single premium?

    A   A one year term assurance
    B   A non qualifying whole of life policy
    C   A qualifying endowment policy
    D   A gift intervivos policy

3   A client takes out a fifteen year family income benefit policy and dies in year 13, what benefit will his family receive?

    A   An income for life
    B   Income for 2 years
    C   Income for 15 years
    D   Income for 13 years

4   In which of the following circumstances would a person pay capital gains tax on the proceeds of a qualifying life policy?

    A   If the policy was assigned for no money
    B   If the policy was purchased at auction
    C   If a policyholder surrendered the policy after 3 years
    D   If the policyholder was a higher rate taxpayer at maturity

5   Which of the following statements is true?

    A   A chargeable event always gives rise to a chargeable gain

    B   A chargeable event never gives rise to a chargeable gain

    C   If a chargeable gain occurs it always gives rise to the payment of income tax on the gain

    D   If a chargeable gain occurs it may give rise to the payment of income tax on the gain.

6   A whole of life policy for a sum assured of £200,000 which is not written in trust becomes a claim. Which of the following taxes may be paid on the proceeds?

    A   Income tax
    B   Inheritance tax
    C   Capital gains tax
    D   VAT

7   Which of the following funds would you use to give a geographical spread to a portfolio?

    A   A property fund
    B   An international equity fund
    C   A building society fund
    D   UK equity fund

8   Which may be the cheapest method of selling a small holding of shares?

    A   Via a stockbroker
    B   Via the post office
    C   Via a bank
    D   Via a share exchange scheme

9   Which of the following is not an asset-backed investment?

    A   A property fund
    B   A building society instant access account
    C   A share
    D   A unit trust

10   Which of the following types of investment is *not* likely to be found in a managed fund?

    A   Commodities
    B   Property
    C   Equities
    D   Fixed interest securities

11   Under which of the following policies may the premium be increased at renewal because of the individual policyholder's claims experience?

    A   Medical expenses insurance
    B   Personal accident and sickness insurance
    C   Permanent health insurance
    D   Redundancy insurance

12   If the owner of a business took a low remuneration from the firm, how would it be best to calculate the sum assured if you wished to insure him as a keyperson?

    A   Multiple of salary
    B   Loss of profit
    C   Contribution to profitability
    D   Annual dividend paid

13   How would you write a whole of life policy which was to be used to provide a sum on death to pay any inheritance tax which was due? The clients, a married couple, have written their wills leaving all assets to the survivor.

    A   Single life in trust for the children
    B   Joint life first death
    C   Joint life second death
    D   Joint life second death in trust for the children

14   Which of the following policies is of no use to a retired person aged 72 with no earnings?

    A   Critical illness
    B   Long term care
    C   Medical expenses insurance
    D   Permanent health

15   Which of the following policies has a guaranteed premium payable throughout the term of the contract?

    A   Unit-linked whole of life
    B   Family income benefit
    C   Unit-linked permanent health insurance
    D   Renewable term

16   Which of the following is not a long term savings need?

    A   School fees
    B   Retirement
    C   Savings for university costs
    D   Savings for summer holiday

17   Pound cost averaging allows you to:

A   Buy more units when the bid price is high
B   Buy more units when the offer price is high
C   Buy more units when the bid price is low
D   Buy more units when the offer price is low

18   If a client invested £60,000 in a bank which went into liquidation, how much compensation could she hope to receive?

A   None
B   £18,000
C   £48,000
D   £20,000

19   Which of the following National Savings products does not give a tax-free return?

A   A premium bond
B   A pensioner's bond
C   Fixed rate National Savings certificate
D   Index-linked National Savings certificate

20   If a client has £1,000 to purchase a gilt currently priced at 94p, how much stock will he buy?

A   £1,000 of stock
B   £940 of stock
C   £1,064 of stock
D   £1,128 of stock

21   Calculate the dividend yield on a share if the dividend is 25p and the price of the share 500p. Is it:

A   2%?
B   5%?
C   10%?
D   20%?

22   On which of the following sources of income can a non-taxpayer *not* reclaim tax?

A   Building society interest
B   A withdrawal from a single premium bond
C   The interest content of an annuity
D   The income from a National Savings Income Bond

23   Lily starts contributing to an ISA from 6 April 2000 and she contributes the maximum possible every year. How much will she have contributed by 5 April 2005?

A   £25,000
B   £27,000
C   £35,000
D   £37,000

24   Which of the following is *not* a feature of a unit trust?

A   It is a pooled investment
B   It is a means of spreading risk
C   A unit trust has a finite number of units
D   It can be used for a monthly savings plan

25 Which of the following is the only correct definition of a single premium bond?

    A   It is a single premium non-qualifying whole of life policy

    B   It is an insurance company regular savings plan

    C   It is a type of unit trust investment

    D   It is a type of investment trust investment

26 The type of endowment most likely to be used for a safe savings plan for school fees is:

    A   A flexidowment

    B   A non-profit endowment

    C   A friendly society savings plan

    D   A low cost endowment

27 A client with £100 per month to save for a short period asks which of the following investments is the most tax-efficient and flexible.

    A   An ISA savings plan

    B   A unit trust savings plan

    C   A friendly society savings plan

    D   Investment trust savings plan

28 If a client takes out a deferred annuity certain which of the following is the correct description of the contract?

    A   The annuity will be paid for a selected period

    B   The annuity will not commence for a selected time and will then continue to be paid for an agreed term

    C   The annuity will not commence for a selected time and will then continue to be paid for an agreed term irrespective of the survival of the annuitant

    D   The annuity will be paid at the end of each year

29 A client effects an annuity paying £200 per half year in June and December and asks for payment without proportion. When she subsequently dies in September 2000, how much is returned to her estate?

    A   £100

    B   nothing

    C   £200

    D   £50

30 A client effects a capital protected annuity for a purchase price of £50,000. The annuity is £8,000 per annum and the client dies after receiving 5 years payments. How much, if anything, is returned to the estate?

    A   £18,000

    B   nothing

    C   £10,000

    D   £25,000

31 Which of the following investments does not have easy access?

    A   Unit trusts

    B   Investment trusts

    C   ISAs

    D   Building society fixed term bond

32   In purchasing a new unit trust, which of the following features is the most important?

A   A discount on the offer price
B   Potential for excellent fund management in a growth sector
C   Excellent literature
D   A high bid/offer spread

33   In selecting an annuity which is the most important feature?

A   Payment method
B   Availability of a choice of annuities
C   Competitive rates
D   Good underwriting facilities

34   Which of the following investments would offer the least *immediate* tax benefits to an employed higher rate taxpayer, if he was eligible to make such an investment?

A   Equity ISA
B   FSAVC
C   Existing TESSA
D   Gilt

35   Which of the following options is available to a member leaving an exempt approved occupational pension scheme to effect a personal pension?

A   A transfer of the cash equivalent of accrued benefits from the occupational scheme to the personal pension
B   A transfer of the cash equivalent of accrued benefits from the occupational scheme to a free standing additional voluntary contribution scheme
C   Take a tax free refund to the value of accrued employee and employer contributions in the occupational scheme
D   A transfer of the cash equivalent of accrued benefits to a buy-out plan ('section 32') and continue to contribute to the buy-out plan

36   Which retirement age group is applicable to a retirement annuity?

A   50 - 75
B   65 - 75
C   60 - 75
D   60 - 70

37   An employee has decided to pay FSAVCs. He currently earns £25,000 per annum and pays £1,500 pension scheme contributions. What is the net AVC payment he can make in the 2000/01 tax year?

A   £2,250
B   £1,755
C   £3,750
D   £2,925

38   If an employee takes a pension of £5,000 per annum with a five year guarantee and dies after 3 years payments have been made, how much will be returned to the estate?

A   nothing
B   £10,000
C   £5,000
D   £2,500

39   If an employee joined an occupational pension scheme before 17 March 1987, he can take maximum tax free cash of 1.5 × final remuneration after:

    A   10 years

    B   40 years

    C   20 years

    D   30 years

40   What is the maximum death in service benefit which can be paid according to the Inland Revenue rules?

    A   A lump sum of four times salary

    B   A lump sum of four times salary plus return of contributions with interest

    C   A lump sum of four times salary plus return of contributions with interest (or £5,000 if greater) plus a spouse's 2/3rd pension

    D   Lump sum of four times salary plus return of contributions with interest plus a spouse's 2/3rd pension plus a dependant's pension

41   If a FSAVC is over-funded and the surplus has to be returned to the member, what rate of tax is paid by a basic rate taxpayer?

    A   20%

    B   22%

    C   32%

    D   40%

42   An employee who joined a pension scheme in June 1990 and retires on a salary of £150,000 can, under current rules, have a maximum tax free lump sum of which of the following?

    A   £100,000

    B   £150,000

    C   £131,400

    D   £137,700

43   Which of the following people are *not* eligible to make contributions to a FSAVC?

    A   A self employed person

    B   A person in a company pension scheme using a personal pension to contract out

    C   An employed person in a company pension scheme

    D   An employed person with two jobs, one of which is not pensionable

44   How much can a female aged 54 in the year of assessment pay to a personal pension?

    A   35%

    B   30%

    C   20%

    D   15%

45   The proceeds from a retirement annuity can be moved to an alternative insurance company to buy:

    A   A purchased life annuity

    B   An open market option annuity

    C   A compulsory purchase annuity

    D   An immediate annuity

46   An employed person aged 54 has a personal pension and a retirement annuity. In 2000/01, he earns £95,000 and pays £4,000 to his retirement annuity. How much can he pay to his personal pension?

   A   £14,360
   B   £18,950
   C   £27,540
   D   £27,180

47   Which of the following is a disadvantage of joining a company pension scheme?

   A   The employer contributes
   B   The pension increases in payment
   C   Benefits are fixed and are not necessarily attractive to the unmarried
   D   Often provides substantial life assurance

48   What is a pivotal age?

   A   The age at which a person can start drawing a pension
   B   An age at which clients should consider effecting AVCs
   C   An age above which clients should contract back into SERPS
   D   An age at which a client's life style changes

49   Which type of survey will cost the buyer the least?

   A   Basic building society valuation
   B   Structural survey
   C   Report and valuation
   D   Structural survey with damp and timber report

50   Which of the following contracts cannot be used to repay an interest only mortgage?

   A   An ISA
   B   A convertible term assurance
   C   An endowment
   D   A pension

51   Which of the following interest methods gives the borrower stability of repayment?

   A   Fixed rate
   B   Variable rate
   C   Low start
   D   Capital and interest

52   Why would a self-employed person want to effect a SIPP?

   A   Because the Revenue allow larger contributions
   B   In order for the fund to buy a commercial property
   C   To retire before age 50
   D   To avoid inheritance tax

53   Which of the following guarantees to repay a mortgage on maturity

   A   Low cost start endowment
   B   Unit linked endowment
   C   Personal pension
   D   Full with profit endowment

54 Which is the highest risk method of repaying a mortgage?

A Capital and interest
B Interest only and an ISA
C Interest only and a personal pension with profits
D Interest only and a with profits low cost endowment

55 Which of the following policies are likely to give the greatest additional tax free lump sum after repayment of the mortgage?

A Non-profit endowment
B With-profits endowment
C Personal pension
D Low cost endowment

56 Which of the following investments is not for a fixed term?

A National savings index linked certificates
B Guaranteed income bond
C Pensioners bond
D National savings income bond

57 A client wants to take a transfer from a contracted out occupational pension scheme. He wishes to retain his guaranteed minimum pension. To which of the following policies should he transfer his benefits?

A A s 32 buy out policy
B A personal pension
C A retirement annuity
D A Hancock annuity

58 Which of the following would not be taken into account when calculating an annuity rate?

A Expenses
B Mortality
C Interest
D Annual management charge

59 An investor is selling his portfolio. On which of the sales will he receive an immediate dealing price?

A Sale of a share through a stockbroker
B Sale of a gilt through the post office
C Sale of a unit trust direct with the dealers on forward pricing
D Advertisement to sell shares in a newspaper

60 A client who suffers from asthma takes out four policies. Three have exclusions for asthma and one does not. Which of the following is the policy with no exclusion?

A Permanent health insurance
B Medical expenses
C Endowment policy for 10 years
D Disability insurance

ANSWER EACH PART OF THE FOLLOWING QUESTIONS AS TRUE OR FALSE

61   A client takes out a whole of life with profits policy.

   101   In the event of his death, the insurance company will pay out the guaranteed sum assured plus bonuses accrued to the date of death.

   102   Each year a terminal bonus is added to his sum assured and once added it cannot be removed.

   103   The life office declares a compound rate of bonus.

   104   Only 90% of the surplus of the life fund is distributed to the with profits policyholders because the policy was effected with a proprietary company

62   A whole of life policy has certain advantages not found in a term assurance.

   105   Cover throughout life
   106   An investment element
   107   The premium is always cheaper than a term assurance for the same sum assured
   108   The policy can be on a unit-linked or with profits basis

63   If a client has a unit-linked policy of any kind, in the event of early surrender which of the following units may have their value delayed or adjusted (True) and which may not (False)?

   109   Japanese
   110   Property
   111   UK equity
   112   With profits
   113   Fixed interest
   114   International

64   A minimum cost whole of life policy is:

   115   A combination of a with-profits endowment and a reducing term assurance
   116   Often used in inheritance tax planning
   117   Likely to attract a terminal bonus on a claim
   118   Is an excellent way of providing a high level of life cover at low cost

65   The attractions for a client joining a group permanent health scheme are:

   119   The level of benefit is decided by the employer

   120   The benefit is paid for by the employer

   121   There is unlikely to be a need for evidence of the member's state of health

   122   The member can join the scheme on the first renewal date after joining the company even if he has been away sick for six months

66   The attractions of a PA and sickness policy to a self-employed person are:

   123   A guarantee that claims will be paid
   124   Short deferred periods
   125   Cheap premiums
   126   Lump sum payments can be made as well as a weekly benefit
   127   Benefits can always be paid until retirement age
   128   Cover can be arranged quickly

67   Consider the following statements with regard to the tax treatment of medical expenses schemes.

129 Benefits when paid are taxed as unearned income.

130 Tax relief on premiums is available to a policyholder aged 70.

131 If an employer takes out a scheme for his employees, his contributions paid to the scheme on their behalf are treated as a benefit in kind.

132 Tax relief, if available, is only at a rate of 15% of the premiums paid.

68   Which of the following features would you take into account ('True') when comparing different providers offering a convertible term assurance policy and which would you not ('False')?

133 The insurance company's likely attitude to underwriting at the time of the conversion.

134 The insurance company's range of policies offered at conversion.

135 The insurance company's investment performance history.

136 Premium rates.

69   Which of the following features would you take into account (True) when recommending a particular insurance company's permanent health insurance contract and which would you not (False)?

137 Exclusions
138 Situation in the event of the client changing occupation
139 Likelihood of the insurance company increasing the premiums after a claim
140 The company's attitude to periods of unemployment

70   A deposit type investment would be particularly suitable for:

141 An investor who wished to take no risk
142 An emergency fund
143 A 26 year old saving for retirement
144 Saving money to pay a tax bill
145 A 15 year savings plan
146 A client who wanted his investment to be protected against the risks of inflation

71   If a client has only £20,000 to invest which of the following risk rated investments should he choose?

147 High
148 Medium to high
149 Low
150 Low to medium

72   A client interested in buying a gilt has some of the terms explained to him by a stockbroker. Is the information correct?

151 All gilts have a redemption date
152 The redemption date is when the Government promises to repay the loan
153 Gilts are a loan to the Government
154 The interest paid on a gilt is known as the coupon

73   A new issue of an investment trust can be dealt with in a number of ways.

155 Offer for sale
156 The Bank of England will pass them on to the market, known as a tap
157 A placing

74 A client is considering the income which may arise from certain investment.

 158 A unit trust will produce a dividend
 159 A share produces dividends which may increase over the years.
 160 A building society account produces an income and the capital is secure.
 161 A National savings income bond produces an income at a guaranteed level.
 162 A gilt produces a guaranteed income.
 163 A compulsory purchase annuity will produce a payment taxed as earned income.

75 In order for a CAT-marked ISA to be approved it must:

 164 Only be open to UK residents over the age of 21

 165 Allow a maximum investment of £5,000 in a unit trust or investment trust with more than 50% of its assets inside the EU from 2000/01 onwards

 166 Be run by an authorised manager

 167 Allow £1,000 per annum per eligible person into the insurance element from 2000/01 onwards

76 Taking the 5% withdrawal from a bond:

 168 Defers tax.
 169 May give rise to a loss of age allowance whilst the withdrawal is being received.
 170 Can reduce the underlying value of the capital invested.

77 If a tax-paying client has an existing TESSA:

 171 It is possible to deposit £9,000 in a feeder account and automatically obtain gross interest on the whole investment.

 172 It is possible to withdraw the entire gross 'income' each year and retain the tax free status.

 173 It will now be possible to roll over the whole account into a TESSA-only ISA at maturity

 174 The maximum investment in year three is £1,800.

78 If a client wishes to secure an increasing income from an annuity he may:

 175 Have a fixed increase.
 176 Link the increase to the RPI.
 177 Link the increase to some underlying fund performance.
 178 Link the increase to the FTSE100.

79 Consider the following statements concerning the State Pension.

 179 A person who has always been self-employed will receive some SERPS benefits.

 180 Anyone retiring after 1998 who has been contracted in since 1978 will receive a full SERPS benefit.

 181 SERPS pensions all earnings above the lower earnings level.

 182 Women who have always paid the lower married women's national insurance contribution will receive SERPS.

80   A client tells you that he is considering retiring early. He has a number of different policies, so you explain:

183   He can withdraw his AVC benefits before his main occupational scheme benefits

184   Under his retirement annuity contract he cannot take benefits until age 65 unless he is retiring on grounds of ill health.

185   Under his company pension scheme he can retire early with a reduction factor.

186   If he is retiring through ill health the company pension scheme may pay out without the early retirement factor.

187   He can retire at any time from age 50 under his personal pension.

188   He may need to transfer his benefits from a retirement annuity to a personal pension in order to take benefits at age 50

81   A self-administered pension scheme:

189   Cannot be an exempt approved scheme.
190   Is run by independent administrators or in-house.
191   Has to hire fund managers.
192   Cannot provide defined benefits.

82   What are the advantages of a final salary scheme for the employee?

193   Pensions accrued after April 1997 must increase by LPI in payment

194   Known employee contribution.

195   Pension based on salary close to retirement.

196   He can receive a maximum approvable pension irrespective of his number of years in the scheme.

197   He can take 25% of his fund as a tax free lump sum.

198   The employer normally pays the majority of the cost of the scheme.

83   Consider the following statements related to offering occupational pension scheme membership.

199   The scheme must be offered to both men and women.
200   Part timers cannot be excluded from the scheme on the basis of sex.
201   The scheme must be offered to all grades of employee.
202   Membership of the scheme must be a condition of employment.

84   In order for tax relief to be given to a company on pension contributions and for it to be allowed in one year and not spread:

203   A special contribution can be made of £30,000.
204   A special contribution can be made of £1,000,000.
205   A special contribution can be made of £60,000 and a regular contribution of £30,000
206   The contributions can be equal regular and special.

85   Consider the following statements.

207   The trustees of an occupational scheme must allow a transfer of benefits to another scheme

208   A person leaving an occupational scheme is always allowed a return of his contributions

209   A preserved pension must be revalued

210   On leaving service the benefit can be transferred to a s 32 policy

211   Death in service benefits usually cease on leaving an occupational scheme

86   Consider the following comments on AVC contributions.

212   If a member took out an AVC prior to 1987 the benefits can be taken as a tax-free lump sum.

213   AVCs can be used to buy additional spouse's pensions.

214   A member can pay 17.5% contribution to an AVC.

215   Employees cannot pay more than £2,400 per annum as an AVC contribution.

87   If a client wishes to make use of the 'carry forward' provisions:

216   He must first use up his maximum contribution for the current year of assessment.

217   Tax relief is given based on the rates applicable to the 'carry forward' year.

218   The total pension contribution made in the current year must not exceed the total net relevant earnings for that year.

219   The unused relief for the earliest year must be used first.

88   Consider the tax situation of a personal pension.

220   The employed person pays premiums gross.

221   The self-employed pay premiums net.

222   A higher rate taxpayer who is employed collects 40% tax relief from the Revenue through his tax coding.

223   The self-employed use a form PPCC to claim the tax relief from the Revenue.

89   Which of the following people are eligible to pay contributions to a FSAVC ?

224   A self-employed person
225   An employed person in an occupational pension scheme
226   An employed person in a statutory pension scheme
227   A company controlling director
228   A member of a simplified final salary arrangement
229   A member of a money purchase scheme

90   Consider the following statements concerning FSAVC.

230   A FSAVC is taken out by someone wanting to fund for early retirement.

231   A FSAVC does not have to have the same retirement age as the main scheme so long as there is provision in the main scheme for early retirement.

232   A larger contribution can be made to a FSAVC than an AVC.

233   Tax free cash can be taken from a FSAVC.

91   There are twin brothers, one employed and a member of a company pension scheme, the other self-employed. Both brothers are considering making a pension contribution prior to the financial year end.

234   The employed brother says he will make use of 'carry forward' to pay a larger AVC contribution.

235   The self-employed brother says that as he had no relevant earnings in the previous year of assessment, he will be able to carry back pension contributions for two tax years.

236   The employed brother says he will pay his FSAVC contributions net of basic rate tax.

237   The self-employed brother says he has a retirement annuity policy and as he made a great deal of profit in his current year of assessment, he will make contributions into this as the earnings cap will not apply.

92   The managing director of a small family company says he does not believe in pensions, his business is his pension scheme. Consider the following points.

238 He is wrong because the business may go into liquidation.

239 A company pension scheme is a method of keeping assets separate from the company assets.

240 On the sale of his business, CGT could be payable.

241 A SSAS could be set up and 80% of the company shares could become an asset of the pension scheme.

93   Can an employed person be a member of a company pension scheme and a personal pension?

242 Yes, if the company pension scheme is contracted in and the personal pension is just used for contracting out.

243 Yes, if the employed person has earnings from two sources, one of which is not pensioned.

244 Yes, if he wants to provide additional pension benefits.

94   After a full fact find and comparison, which of the following transfers could normally be a viable proposition?

245 From money purchase occupational scheme to final salary scheme with 1/60th accrual rate.

246 From final salary scheme with 1/60th accrual rate to a personal pension.

247 From a statutory scheme to a personal pension.

248 From a money purchase arrangement with poor investment performance to another money purchase with a choice of funds with consistent performance and low charges.

95   A client says he understands that he cannot have more than one pension scheme at a time. Consider the following statements.

249 He could be a member of a company pension scheme and a s 32 buy out policy
250 He could contribute to any number of personal pension arrangements
251 He could contribute to a retirement annuity and a personal pension
252 A controlling director could be a member of a SSAS and a FSAVC

96   An indemnity guarantee premium may be needed for a mortgage:

253 If the deposit is less than 25%
254 If the lender advances more than 75%
255 If the lender advances less than 75%

97   If the client has a capital and interest mortgage:

256 The outstanding capital reduces over the term
257 The term of the loan can easily be extended
258 Interest rates are higher than for an endowment mortgage
259 A low cost endowment policy is required

98   Which of the following payments can an employed non-taxpayer make, having deducted 22%?

   260 A life assurance premium
   261 A personal pension contribution
   262 A retirement annuity
   263 A critical illness policy premium
   264 A medical insurance premium

99   Which of the following are features of a pension mortgage (True) and which are not (False)?

   265 The pension can be cashed in before age 50 to repay the mortgage

   266 The pension benefits must be taken at the same time as the tax-free cash used to repay the mortgage.

   267 Tax relief is available on the pension premiums and part of the mortgage interest payment.

   268 It limits the level of contributions which can be paid to secure pure pension.

100   Home income plans were sold to elderly clients as a means of increasing income. Consider the following statements.

   269 The clients have to be in their late 70s or early 80s for the annuity rate to be high enough to make the scheme viable.

   270 It is in the client's best interest if interest is allowed to roll up with the outstanding capital.

   271 Rather than investing the amount raised in an annuity, it is in the client's best interest to re-invest in an equity-linked single premium bond.

Answers

ANSWERS TO QUICK QUIZ QUESTIONS

Chapter 1

1   C, D

2   B

3   F, F, T, T

4   B

5   C

Chapter 2

1   D

2   B

3   C

4   C

5   D

6   C

7   A

8   A   F
     B   T
     C   T
     D   T

9   A   F
     B   F
     C   T
     D   T

10   A   T
     B   F
     C   F
     D   T

11   A   T
     B   F
     C   T
     D   T

12   A   T
     B   T
     C   T
     D   T

13   A   F
     B   T
     C   T
     D   F

14   A   T
     B   T
     C   F
     D   T

Chapter 3

1   B

2   D

3   B

4   A   F
     B   T
     C   T
     D   F

5   A   T
     B   T
     C   T
     D   T

6   A   F
     B   T
     C   T
     D   T

7   A   T
     B   F
     C   F
     D   T

Chapter 4

1   A

2   B

3   B

4   B

5   A   T
     B   T
     C   F
     D   T

6   A   T
     B   T
     C   F
     D   T

BPP PUBLISHING

7	A	F
	B	F
	C	F
	D	T

8	A	F
	B	T
	C	F
	D	T

9	A	T
	B	F
	C	F
	D	T

Chapter 5

1   B

2   A

3	A	F
	B	T
	C	T
	D	F

4	A	T
	B	F
	C	T
	D	T

Chapter 6

1   C

2   C

3   B

4   A

5   A

6   C

7   B

8   D

9   C

10	A	T
	B	T
	C	F
	D	F

11	A	T
	B	T
	C	F
	D	T

12	A	T
	B	T
	C	F
	D	T

13	A	T
	B	F
	C	T
	D	T

14	A	F
	B	F
	C	T
	D	F

15	A	F
	B	T
	C	T
	D	F

16	A	T
	B	T
	C	F
	D	T

17	A	F
	B	T
	C	F
	D	F

18	A	F
	B	T
	C	F
	D	F

19	A	F
	B	T
	C	F
	D	F

Chapter 7

1   D

2   D

3	A	T
	B	T
	C	T
	D	F
4	A	T
	B	F
	C	F
	D	F

Chapter 8

1	B	
2	A	T
	B	T
	C	F
	D	T
3	C	

Chapter 9

1	C	
2	C	
3	A	T
	B	F
	C	F
	D	T
4	C	

Chapter 10

1	B	
2	D	
3	C	
4	C	
5	C	
6	C	
7	A	T
	B	T
	C	F
	D	T
8	A	T
	B	F

	C	T
	D	F
9	A	F
	B	T
	C	T
	D	T
10	A	F
	B	T
	C	T
	D	F
11	A	T
	B	T
	C	T
	D	F
12	A	T
	B	F
	C	F
	D	T
13	A	F
	B	T
	C	T
	D	T
14	A	F
	B	T
	C	T
	D	F

Chapter 11

1	A	F
	B	F
	C	F
	D	F
2	A	F
	B	T
	C	T
	D	F
3	C	

Chapter 12

1	A	F
	B	F
	C	F
	D	T

2	A	T
	B	T
	C	F
	D	T

3	A	T
	B	F
	C	T
	D	T

8	A	F
	B	F
	C	T
	D	F

Chapter 13

1	D

2	B

3	B

4	A	F
	B	T
	C	F
	D	F

5	A	T
	B	F
	C	F
	D	T

Chapter 14

1	B

2	C

3	B

4	D

5	A	T
	B	F
	C	F
	D	T

6	A	T
	B	F
	C	F
	D	F

7	A	F
	B	F
	C	T
	D	T

Chapter 15

1	A

2	A	T
	B	T
	C	F
	D	F

3	A	T
	B	F
	C	T
	D	F

Chapter 16

1	A	T
	B	T
	C	F
	D	T

2	A	F
	B	T
	C	T
	D	F

3	A	T
	B	F
	C	T
	D	T

ANSWERS TO PRACTICE EXAMINATION 1

1	B		31	B
2	C		32	D
3	C		33	B
4	B		34	C
5	D		35	C
6	C		36	C
7	C		37	B
8	C		38	B
9	C		39	A
10	A		40	A
11	B		41	C
12	B		42	C
13	B		43	D
14	C		44	B
15	C		45	B
16	C		46	B
17	B		47	A
18	C		48	D
19	B		49	D
20	C		50	C
21	C		51	A
22	C		52	A
23	B		53	C
24	A		54	C
25	C		55	B
26	C		56	C
27	A		57	D
28	D		58	A
29	D		59	B
30	D		60	C

61	101	T	70	146	T
	102	T		147	T
	103	T		148	F
	104	F		149	T
	105	T		150	T
				151	F
62	106	F			
	107	T	71	152	F
	108	T		153	F
	109	T		154	T
	110	F		155	T
	111	T		156	F
				157	T
63	112	T			
	113	F	72	158	F
	114	T		159	T
	115	T		160	F
				161	F
64	116	F			
	117	T	73	162	T
	118	F		163	T
	119	T		164	F
	120	T		165	T
	121	F			
			74	166	F
65	122	T		167	T
	123	T		168	T
	124	T		169	F
	125	F		170	T
				171	F
66	126	T			
	127	F	75	172	T
	128	F		173	T
	129	T		174	T
	130	T		175	F
	131	T		176	T
				177	T
67	132	F			
	133	T	76	178	T
	134	T		179	F
	135	F		180	F
				181	T
68	136	T			
	137	F	77	182	T
	138	T		183	T
	139	F		184	T
				185	F
69	140	F		186	T
	141	F		187	T
	142	T			
	143	T			
	144	F			
	145	T			

78	188	T
	189	F
	190	F
	191	T
79	192	T
	193	T
	194	T
	195	F
80	196	F
	197	F
	198	F
	199	T
81	200	F
	201	T
	202	T
	203	T
	204	F
	205	F
82	206	T
	207	T
	208	T
	209	F
83	210	F
	211	F
	212	F
	213	T
84	214	T
	215	T
	216	T
	217	F
85	218	T
	219	F
	220	T
	221	F
	222	T
	223	T
86	224	F
	225	T
	226	T
	227	F
87	228	F
	229	T
	230	F
	231	T

88	232	T
	233	T
	234	F
	235	T
89	236	T
	237	F
	238	T
	239	T
90	240	T
	241	F
	242	T
	243	T
91	244	F
	245	T
	246	F
	247	T
	248	F
	249	F
92	250	T
	251	T
	252	T
	253	F
93	254	T
	255	F
	256	T
94	257	T
	258	T
	259	F
	260	F
	261	T
95	262	T
	263	T
	264	F
	265	F
96	266	F
	267	T
	268	F
97	269	F
	270	F
	271	T

98	272	F
	273	T
	274	T
	275	F
	276	F
	277	F
99	278	F
	279	T
	280	T
	281	F
100	282	F
	283	T
	284	T
	285	F

ANSWERS TO PRACTICE EXAMINATION 2

1	A		31	D
2	C		32	B
3	B		33	C
4	B		34	B
5	D		35	A
6	B		36	C
7	B		37	B
8	D		38	B
9	B		39	C
10	A		40	D
11	B		41	C
12	B		42	D
13	D		43	A
14	D		44	B
15	B		45	B
16	D		46	C
17	D		47	C
18	B		48	C
19	B		49	A
20	C		50	B
21	B		51	A
22	B		52	B
23	B		53	D
24	C		54	B
25	A		55	B
26	A		56	D
27	A		57	A
28	C		58	D
29	B		59	A
30	C		60	C

BPP PUBLISHING

61	101 T		70	141 T
	102 F			142 T
	103 T			143 F
	104 T			144 T
				145 F
62	105 T			146 F
	106 T			
	107 F		71	147 F
	108 T			148 F
				149 T
63	109 F			150 T
	110 T			
	111 F		72	151 F
	112 T			152 T
	113 F			153 T
	114 F			154 T
64	115 F		73	155 T
	116 T			156 F
	117 T			157 T
	118 T			
			74	158 T
65	119 F			159 T
	120 T			160 T
	121 T			161 F
	122 F			162 T
				163 T
66	123 F		75	164 F
	124 T			165 T
	125 T			166 T
	126 T			167 T
	127 F			
	128 T		76	168 T
				169 F
67	129 F			170 T
	130 F			
	131 T		77	171 F
	132 F			172 F
				173 F
68	133 F			174 T
	134 T			
	135 T		78	175 T
	136 T			176 T
				177 T
69	137 T			178 F
	138 T			
	139 F		79	179 F
	140 T			180 T
				181 F
				182 F

80	183	F	89	224	F
	184	F		225	T
	185	T		226	T
	186	T		227	F
	187	T		228	F
	188	T		229	T
81	189	F	90	230	T
	190	T		231	T
	191	T		232	F
	192	F		233	F
82	193	T	91	234	F
	194	T		235	T
	195	T		236	T
	196	F		237	T
	197	F			
	198	T	92	238	T
				239	T
83	199	T		240	T
	200	T		241	F
	201	F			
	202	F	93	242	T
				243	T
84	203	T		244	F
	204	F			
	205	F	94	245	T
	206	T		246	F
				247	F
85	207	T		248	T
	208	F			
	209	T	95	249	T
	210	T		250	T
	211	T		251	T
				252	F
86	212	T			
	213	T	96	253	T
	214	F		254	T
	215	F		255	F
87	216	T	97	256	T
	217	F		257	T
	218	T		258	F
	219	T		259	F
88	220	F	98	260	F
	221	F		261	T
	222	F		262	F
	223	T		263	F
				264	F

BPP PUBLISHING

99	265	F
	266	T
	267	T
	268	T
100	269	T
	270	F
	271	F

List of key terms
and Index

BPP PUBLISHING

BPP
PUBLISHING

ORDER FORM

BPP publish Study Texts and Practice & Revision Kits for papers of the Financial Planning Certificate, the Advanced Financial Planning Certificate and SOFA Associateship/Fellowship. Each Study Text is, like this one, tailored precisely to the syllabus. Practice and Revision Kits contain banks of questions and answers, plus full Mock Exams.

To order Study Texts and Kits, telephone us on 020 8740 2211. Alternatively, complete the order details below and send your order to us at the address shown or by fax on 020 8740 1184.

We aim to deliver to all UK addresses inside 5 working days; a signature will be required. Orders to all EU addresses should be delivered within 6 working days. all other orders to overseas addresses should be delivered within 8 working days.

To: BPP Publishing Ltd, Aldine House, Aldine Place, London W12 8AW
Tel: 020 8740 2211   **Fax: 020 8740 1184**   **Email: publishing@bpp.com**

Full name (Mr/Ms): _____

Daytime delivery address: _____

_____ Postcode: _____

Please send me the following books:

		Quantity	Total (£)
Financial Planning Certificate			
Study Texts (5/00)			
FP1: Financial Services and their Regulation	£25.95		
FP2: Protection, Savings and Investment Products	£25.95		
FP3: Identifying and Satisfying Client Needs	£25.95		
Practice and Revision Kits			
FP1: Financial Services and their Regulation	£15.95		
FP2: Protection, Savings and Investment Products	£15.95		
FP3: Identifying and Satisfying Client Needs	£15.95		
Advanced Financial Planning Certificate			
Study Texts (7/00)			
G10: Taxation and Trusts	£32.95		
G20: Personal Investment Planning	£32.95		
G30: Business Financial Planning	£32.95		
G60: Pensions	£32.95		
G70: Investment Portfolio Management	£35.95		
G80: Long-term Care, Life and Health Protection	£35.95		
H15: Supervision and Sales Management	£35.95		
H25: Holistic Financial Planning	£35.95		
Practice and Revision Kits			
G10: Taxation and Trusts	£19.95		
G60: Pensions	£19.95		
		Subtotal	

Postage and packaging
UK: £3 for first book, £2 for each extra   p & p
Europe (inc ROI & CI): £5 for first book, £4 for each extra
Rest of the world: £20 for first books, £10 for each extra
                                                               Total

I enclose a cheque for £_____(Cheques to BPP Publishing Ltd) or charge to my Access/Visa/Switch

Card number ☐☐☐☐ ☐☐☐☐ ☐☐☐☐ ☐☐☐☐ ☐☐☐☐

Start date (Switch only) _____ Expiry date _____ Issue no. (Switch only)_____

Signature _____ Daytime Tel. (for queries only) _____

REVIEW FORM & FREE PRIZE DRAW

All original review forms from the entire BPP range, completed with genuine comments, will be entered into one of two draws on 31 January 2001 and 31 July 2001. The names on the first four forms picked out on each occasion will be sent a cheque for £50.

Name: _____   Address: _____

_____

Date: _____   _____

How have you used this Text?
(Tick one box only)

☐ home study (book only)

☐ on a course: at _____

☐ with 'correspondence' package

☐ other _____

Why did you decide to purchase this Text?
(Tick one box only)

☐ recommended by training department

☐ recommendation by friend/colleague

☐ recommendation by a lecturer at college

☐ saw advertising

☐ have used BPP Texts in the past

☐ Other _____

During the past six months do you recall *(Tick as many boxes as are relevant)*

☐ seeing our advertisement in *Financial Adviser*

☐ seeing our advertisement in *Money Management*

☐ seeing our advertisement in *IFA Contact*

Which (if any) aspects of our advertising do you find useful?
(Tick as many boxes as are relevant)

☐ prices and publication dates of new editions

☐ checklist of contents

☐ facility to order books off-the-page

☐ none of the above

Your ratings, comments and suggestions would be appreciated on the following areas.

	Very useful	*Useful*	*Not useful*
Introductory section	☐	☐	☐
Main text	☐	☐	☐
Questions in chapters	☐	☐	☐
Chapter roundups	☐	☐	☐
Quizzes at ends of chapters	☐	☐	☐
Practice examination	☐	☐	☐
Structure and presentation	☐	☐	☐
Availability of Updates on website	☐	☐	☐

	Excellent	*Good*	*Adequate*	*Poor*
Overall opinion of this Study Text	☐	☐	☐	☐

Do you intend to continue using BPP Study Texts?   ☐ Yes   ☐ No

Please note any further comments, suggestions and apparent errors on the reverse of this page, or write by e-mail to rogerpeskett@bpp.com

Please return this form to: Roger Peskett, BPP Publishing Ltd, FREEPOST, London, W12 8BR

REVIEW FORM & FREE PRIZE DRAW (continued)

Please note any further comments, suggestions and apparent errors below.

FREE PRIZE DRAW RULES

1 Closing date for 31 January 2001 draw is 31 December 2000. Closing date for 31 July 2001 draw is 30 June 2001.

2 Restricted to entries with UK and Eire addresses only. BPP employees, their families and business associates are excluded.

3 No purchase necessary. Entry forms are available upon request from BPP Publishing. No more than one entry per title, per person. Draw restricted to persons aged 16 and over.

4 Winners will be notified by post and receive their cheques not later than 6 weeks after the relevant draw date.

5 The decision of the promoter in all matters is final and binding. No correspondence will be entered into.